The Prayer Life of Jesus

Shout of Agony, Revelation of Love, a Commentary

William David Spencer
Aída Besançon Spencer

UNIVERSITY PRESS OF AMERICA

Lanham • New York • London

University Press of America®, Inc.
4720 Boston Way
Lanham, Maryland 20706

3 Henrietta Street
London WC2E 8LU England

Printed in the United States of America
British Cataloging in Publication Information Available

Library of Congress Cataloging-in-Publication Data

Spencer, William David, 1947–
The prayer life of Jesus : shout of agony, revelation of love : a commentary / William David Spencer and Aída Besançon Spencer.
p. cm.
Includes bibliographical references and indexes.
1. Jesus Christ—Prayers. 2. Bible. N.T. Gospels—Criticism, interpretation, etc. I. Spencer, Aída Besançon. II. Title.
BV229.S64 1990 248.3'2—dc20 90–46108 CIP

ISBN 0–8191–7779–2 pbk.

To Helen Catherine Collis Spencer

and Stephen William Besançon Spencer

grandmother and grandson in faith

and warriors in prayer

GOD OF THE TRINITY
(a hymn)

Some praise banners waving bravely in the wind,
And some the sun when its ride cross the universe begins.
But I with my might on bended knee,
I praise the sovereign majestic God of the Trinity.

In word and in deed in love I will now proclaim
The One who gives to us all the gift of the summer rain,
Who holds in a hand all history,
I praise the sovereign majestic God of the Trinity.

In faith and in hope both now and forevermore,
I will extol the Creator, Conqueror, Comforter,
The Lion, the Lamb, the One While Three,
I praise the sovereign majestic God of the Trinity.

I praise the sovereign majestic God of the Trinity.

William David Spencer

To Annette Jones, her
delightful staff and the
People of South Hamilton,
North Hamilton and all
Hamilton,

William David Spencer
3/25/91

WIND AND BRANCH

Peaceful I stay
until you come,

And then I am thrilled
but also frightened.

I reach to the heavens
and fall to the earth

Trembling from your call.

Aída Besançon Spencer

TABLE OF CONTENTS

PART II

THE LORD PRAYS

Indices

PREFACE

When the God-head set about the task of creation, dialogue was continual.

God broods upon the face of the silent dark formless water that had been created, and then God speaks. "Let there be light."

God views the light, approves it, and calls it "Day." And God names the corresponding darkness "Night."

God speaks again, "Let there be an expanse in the midst of the waters, and let it separate the waters from the waters."

God goes on speaking forth commands and all is brought into existence until all that earth is has been created.

Then the triune God-head dialogues its considered intention, "Let us make humanity in our image, according to our likeness." When the created human looks around in bewilderment, God orients him. God points out acceptable and nonacceptable behavior to the creature. Then God speaks again. God observes the necessity of companionship for the human. Each of God's acts is accompanied by God's spoken observations. When the man sees the companion God has created for him, man exclaims happily to God, "This at last is bone of my bones and flesh of my flesh! She shall be called woman, because she was taken out of man!" (Gen. 2:23).

That is Prayer. Humans speaking with God.

The Old Testament continues to record the history of humanity's communication with its Creator. As in the days of our first parents we see again and again an easy flow of conversation rolling back and forth between the Creator and the created. Adam is not disrespectful, not familiar in that sense. His exclamation is warm, and appreciative, and supportive, and open, and loving. And that vital channel, that open flow he knew, had become blocked up in the days of the disciples, just as it often seems as equally choked shut today some two thousand years later.

Our book attempts to look again from the perspective point of our time at communication with God. Of all who have been successful over the ages one supreme voice articulates the fullest expression of what communication with God can be. Jesus, God Incarnate, prays in the center of history, Jesus communicates with God and teaches people to do the same. For eight years we have carefully studied every aspect of Jesus' own teaching and practice of prayer. As the sections of our study emerged, we employed them in seminary class lectures, presented them as papers at scholarly meetings, taught them in adult Sunday School and Lenton classes, practiced them in our ministries. Dialoguing and praying together and with others, we translated and discussed the material together, editing each other's sections carefully. Aída wrote the first drafts of chapters 3, 5, 6, and Appendixes A and B. For chapter 4 we studied each New Testament passage together and William wrote up our notes. For chapter 10 Aída isolated the crucial material in each chapter which William wrote down. William wrote the first drafts of chapters 1, 2, 7, 8, 9, and Appendix C.

Aída wrote a complete study guide which may be ordered from Gordon-Conwell Bookcentre, South Hamilton, MA 01982.

We especially want to thank all the typists who so carefully worked on the different chapters of this book: Pamela McDonald, Mark Dubis, Pamela Kohring, Janet G. Eldridge, and, the final copy, Heidi Hudson. Gordon-Conwell Theological Seminary graciously gave us for 1987-88 a Lilly Foundation Faculty Scholarship Grant which was used to pay for half of the typing and to test the manuscript at a local church. The Rev. Linda J. Foody of the United Methodist Church in East Greenwich, Rhode Island did test the manuscript with an adult study group led by Greg Hudson in the fall of 1987.

1
Introduction

"Lord, teach us to pray, as also John taught his disciples," begged one of Jesus' followers when he perceived that Jesus had ceased praying. What a curious question for an adult Jew of the first century to ask. As a mature heir of the great Levitical and rabbinic traditions, this Israelite inherited thousands of years of rich heritage of communication with God his Father. For this Jew, God was knowable as the God of Israel, Isaac, and Jacob. What a designation for the God of the whole universe! To know the Master Creator of everything so intimately that you could call God by the names of your parents!

Rich Heritage

While all the rest of the earth groped in ignorance, one people knew God, and their calling by God was to be a nation of prophets, revealing God's nature and commands to the rest of the earth. They were called to be a nation of teachers, a nation of priests to whom others would turn and ask, "Please teach us to communicate with God as you do." The Jews were the proprietors of God's house of worship. And that house, God's temple, was still standing in Jerusalem. Year in and year out it sponsored unfailing daily prayer and rich religious ritual. Proudly it stood in the land where Moses had brought God's people after daily consultation with the God of Heaven and Earth in its predecessor, the traveling tent, called the tabernacle. It boasted a complex temple organization of the best minds in Israel, the ruling Sanhedrin, and a high priest who stood in the succession of Aaron himself, chosen by God. It ruled over a network of synagogues far flung across the Jewish world where daily prayer was offered to God. And above all, the Temple kept open a steady channel of communication through sacrifice and daily ritual.

In addition to all these services, the temple and the synagogues served as a repository, a living archive of the records of the great leaders of the past. The Temple and its synagogues were above all else schools wherein the lives of the great leaders of the past were recorded and studied assiduously by all Jewish boys. At every religious service the accounts of their lives, their wisdom, psalms, or prophecies were read and expounded, and as each document was studied it revealed that every one of these great historic leaders was a great warrior of prayer. Moses, the liberator who led the Israelites out of bondage, had stood in the Presence of God. So close was his contact the Shekinah glory transferred itself to Moses' own face and the people were blinded at his advent. Moses' prayer life was so vital to him and so intimate with God that Exodus 33:11 tells us: "And the Lord spoke to Moses face to face, just as a man speaks to his friend." There stood indeed a great prince of prayer. David's prayers were so poignant that many of them have endured for centuries in the sacred writings themselves, chronicled in his Book of Psalms, whose power edified and comforted the people a thousand years later as it still does for that matter four thousand years later today. Pleading for his child, the great King had flung himself face down all night before God in intercessory prayer. He who had been magnified by God as king had fiercely humbled himself by choice in God's supra-kingly presence. Abraham, so much an intimate with God, bargained with God, wheedling like a merchant for the sparing of Sodom and Gomorrah. With Enoch, the Scriptures tell us, God walked, perhaps as intimately as God did with Adam. Joshua's prayer made even the sun stand still. Elijah's brought rain.

What did these disciples then mean, "Lord, teach us to pray"? All of this rich heritage at their fingertips, in their minds, in their hearts, on their lips, and they could not pray? With the temple the repository of all their great heritage still alive and active, could they not go and ask the Sanhedrin, the cream of their religious leaders? Could they not ask their priests? How could they approach Jesus like some unlearned Gentiles, some pagan barbarians, lost and frustrated by the silence of the divine? What does this question tell us? It tells us that something they had had before was lost.

Lost Heritage

The days of Abraham, Moses, Joshua were past. Somewhere in the daily compromise that was life under the fist of Rome the vital communication-link with the great dread warrior God of Israel was broken. As the temple authorities sought to placate Rome and quiet the seditious people of Israel, contact had been lost with the Great Warrior who rules Heaven and Earth. What the Temple had become was the mirror of a North American shopping mall at Christmas.

From a vantage point of 2,000 years in the future in self-determining lands conducive to the free expression of religious worship, we might easily scoff at the priests of the Temple and condemn their hypocrisy. But looking at them as priests ourselves, trying to project our minds into their lot, we can readily see that their position was one fraught with extreme difficulties. These priests sub-ruled a nation of people painfully conscious of their glorious past. They were descended from that nation of conquerors who had burned across the Near East in triumph after triumph until they cut out a country for themselves. Their list of heroes and heroines read like a Who's Who of ancient warriors, from warrior women like Deborah, judge and conqueror of the Canaanites, to that superman Samson, killer of hordes with his bare hands. In more recent days the Israelites had enjoyed a *déjà vu* glimpse of the past through guerilla raids of the Maccabaeus family. And that spirit of insurrection was not yet dead. In a few short years they would ignite their last great uprising with battles that were death struggles at the sieges of Jerusalem and Masada. And then they would crash and disperse. Too wild to be tamed long by Rome, Israel was only able to be destroyed and disbanded. And now in anticipatory uprisings guerilla resistance smoldered everywhere.

On this powder keg the Sanhedrin sat. Their task was to keep the people quiet, staving off Pontius Pilate from executing any more heavy-handed policing tactics. Popular sympathy accordingly ran against the temple administration and favored apparent insurgents like John the Baptist who heralded a new Messiah with a new kingdom. The zealots wanted Rome out. The people wanted the Messiah in. And the temple authorities wanted the situation quieted down and above all no more ugly reprisals from the Roman legions. Thus compromise followed compromise. They gave a little here and wheedled a little there. Merchants took advantage of the temple's attempts to placate the people and set up shops in the courtyard of the temple. Rituals were kept alive, but in the mercenary sense of easy compromise. So far removed was all this from the barren sober rite of Moses and Aaron and the first fierce warrior priests. The temple went on day by day trying to keep national identity, without national insurrection, alive. And in this give and take atmosphere of daily compromise something was definitely lost: satisfying communication with the God-head who controlled the entire earth.

Found Heritage

Small wonder then when John, bold and wild and free, came storming through the desert calling on the God of justice, the people thrilled and flocked to him. John was everything that the suave, astute, politically-oriented, priestly-diplomats were not. John the Baptist lived in the desert, dressed up like some kind of brigand. He ate like a caveman, devouring the locust and wild honey of the land. His reputation was that of a folk prophet. His fierce, unequivocal message of repentance had great appeal to that conquered, compromised people, and his anti-temple establishment tirades no doubt titillated them. But John was not joking and his apparent antics were serious gestures aimed at the complacency of the status quo. His disciples took him extremely seriously, as did his enemy Herodias, and his disciples had apparently discovered in John's example a new kind of "speaking with God" that filled some kind of need in a way forgotten by the well-intentioned, hard-pressed leaders of the temple.

When John the great cast down his staff before Jesus, all turned in wonder to the newcomer. Who was this before whom the great John himself bowed, unworthy to untie even his shoe?

The complete question the disciples asked is interesting, and its full import is worth considering. Often when these verses are expounded, commentators, like the great Andrew Murray in his classic *With Christ in the School of Prayer*, for example, break off the first half of the disciples' request, preferring to deal directly with the words "Lord, teach us to pray." But the disciples added "just as also John taught his disciples to pray."

As we have seen, John and his disciples had made a great impact on all of Israel. Was it John's example, rather than Jesus', that then so impressed the followers of other rabbis that they would want their rabbi to instruct them as well as John did his followers? Obviously, John had made a great impact on Jesus' disciples' view of prayer. Yet, we do not find them deserting Jesus to return to John to learn prayer. Luke has already recorded John's death, of course, two chapters earlier in chapter 9, so perhaps this account is chronologically placed, and John was already imprisoned and beheaded. Still, Jesus' disciples could have sought out John's former disciples and learned from them. Instead, when John abdicated his power to Jesus, we are told disciples of John abandoned him to cling to Jesus (John 1:35-37). Therefore, the import of the disciples' request seems to be a hopeful, suggestive one: "John taught his disciples to pray, will you teach us to pray, Master?" In Jesus they had seen prayer perfected. What the disciples may not have realized is that they were being afforded a glimpse of what prayer is really all about in the context of eternity. They were glimpsing the pure prayer extant in the God-head, the communicating of one person of the Trinity with the others. In a sense what was happening before their ears was that ages of sin-cursed history were rolling away, and they were hearing the pristine communication that had flowed so freely at creation.

Our Heritage

As the disciples we have all that rich religious history, too. We have those precious records extant and printed and disseminated and available that they had, and ours contain the same incredible glimpses of the pre-fall state of communion with God, too. The recorded prayers and detailed results in the lives of the great Jewish prayer warriors of the Old Testament are at our finger-tips, as well, and in a multitude of languages, not just in the Greek and Hebrew of the educated of that day. In addition we have the New Testament records which preserve accounts of both the presence of Jesus and his teaching and also the example of his disciples. We have further the writings and records of the fathers and mothers of the early church, faithfully recorded by their contemporaries and disciples, Papias, Clement, Eusebius, and many others. And finally we have two thousand years more of Christian history passing on through the Reformation, the great awakenings, the historic revivals, our modern revivals and awakenings into contemporary times. Our religious heritage is still alive and pulsing, embedded in the cores of our societies. All this we have, and yet today we find ourselves still asking, "Lord, teach us to pray." Why is that?

In our state of contemporary confusion, close analysis shows us that our plight is not all that different from that of the disciples. In addition to facing swift annihilation as they were, we are surrounded by contrasting religious rituals, and, what is more, by competing religions springing up right and left. And this confusion of ours, like the sellers that crept into their temple, has penetrated to the very core of our churches and our institutions of theological learning.

In this book we are looking at the prayer life of Jesus Christ. We want to learn more about the nature of prayer by studying comprehensively Jesus' teachings on prayer and Jesus' practice of prayer. Every New Testament prayer text of Jesus is discussed.

In Part I, The Lord Teaches Us to Pray, we look at Jesus' teachings on prayer in the form of model prayers (ch. 2), stories about prayers (ch. 3), and teachings on prayer in the midst of action (ch. 4). In Part II, The Lord Prays, we study Jesus' own examples of praying in the light of his teachings. What words for prayer are used by and about Jesus (ch. 5)? What postures does Jesus take in prayer (ch. 6)? What can we learn from Jesus' own extensive prayers at and after Passover (chs. 7-9)? After a summary of our findings (ch. 10), we offer a number of useful appendices and a bibliography.

What we hope to offer to the reader who desires to learn more about prayer or about God is a commentary on prayer. For six years we have studied the New Testament in its original Greek. We hope to give an in-depth look at the New Testament in an engaging style. All readers have a smooth English translation available to them, but all readers will not have facility with the Greek language to look that little bit deeper into the meaning of the Bible text. So we have attempted to take all readers deeper by translating as literally as possible and particularly setting word order in the original manner to show emphasis. In this way all readers can see what is happening in the Greek and understand what the writers are emphasizing.

What did we discover? We learned about God. And, we learned about communication with God. Prayer is not divorced from a life of action, but it is married to it. And the prayers that humans give should reflect Jesus' own shouts of agony and revelation of love.

PART I

The Lord Teaches Us To Pray

2

The Lord's Prayers in Matthew 6 and Luke 11

The disciples begged their master teacher, "Lord, teach us to pray, as also John taught his disciples." So that is exactly what Jesus did. Gathering his followers around him on at least two recorded occasions, Jesus opened up before them a simple verbal pathway to communication with their God.

From the poignant setting sketched for us by Matthew in 5-7, we can easily imagine Jesus seated at the commanding vantage point of the base of a mountain, his disciples gathered about his feet in true rabbinic fashion, and a crowd of others seated in respectful silence listening to his words on farther up the slope or at the top of the hill. Such a setting on a sufficient incline would have made a natural theater complete with a backing slope that might echo his words out to the crowd. There is no reason to suppose he would have had to shout to reach them. Scripture in Luke 8:8 specifies when he did shout for emphasis. After all, he had drawn his disciples out of the crowd and he was teaching them. The crowds, we might then suppose, were listening in. On the other hand, there is no reason to suppose Jesus' voice would not have been loud enough to address all of the great crowd. We recall that when Benjamin Franklin measured out the amount of people George Whitefield could address in the half mile his voice carried, he concluded that that figure was 30,000. If an average large crowd of Jesus' day could be measured by the feeding of that "great throng" (Matt. 14:14), the five thousand, which, if we triple the number to account for the women and children Matthew 14:21 mentions, was 15,000, there is no difficulty in assuming Jesus, the master speaker, could address half Whitefield's number comfortably and clearly. Further, Jeremias in his *Jerusalem in the Time of Jesus* estimates about 25,000 people lived in all of Jerusalem at that time (though others do estimate higher).[1] Even if we concede 5,000 inhabitants more, Whitefield's 30,000 would have emptied the city! And he still would have addressed them with his own unaided voice. Therefore, Jesus, who we are told could astonish audiences (Matt. 7:28), would have commanded the crowds of his day. And so graphically does Matthew draw this scene in the text that St. Augustine equates it with the giving of the ten commandments on Sinai, seeing God through Jesus now giving even greater precepts (*The Lord's Sermon on the Mount* 1.1:2).

In Luke 11:1 we have but the barest particulars of the setting. Luke records simply that Jesus was praying in a place when his disciples, respectfully waiting until he had finished, summoned up the courage to approach him and make an unusual request. With that he plunges us into a lesson on how to approach our Creator, the Ruler of the Universe. Luke's technique here is as effective as Plato's. The setting is like a parable itself. It is stripped of all particulars. We have no idea what place it was. Was it crowded with people? Perhaps it was a part of the wilderness since Jesus was so mobbed wherever he went that he had to escape from the usual haunts of people to snatch any time for quiet reflection. Perhaps it was in the early morning or late in the evening when he habitually stole away. But it could just as well have been in the middle of the afternoon. We are not told. Luke is determined instead to detonate portions of the many spectacular things he did and said in a series of active and verbal explosions that overpower the hearer/reader with the conviction that Jesus is the Messiah, the Presence of the Mighty God on earth. Therefore, we do not know exactly where or when in the three years of Jesus' ministry among us this incident took place. But this event's complete anonymity gives it its universal applicability. Jesus had picked out some nameless place and there he had pitched his sanctuary while at least more than one faithful disciple stood humbly by. And what these disciples saw obviously impressed them. When their Master was done, they crept up and asked humbly, "Lord, will

---

[1] Joachim Jeremias, *Jerusalem in the Time of Jesus* (Philadelphia: Fortress, 1975), p. 27.

you teach us to pray just as John taught those disciples of his to pray?"

In Matthew (6:9-13) Jesus teaches about prayer to his disciples, but he allows others to listen in and thus apply the prayer to the revitalization of their own prayer lives. In Luke 11 Jesus, after praying himself, imparts his teaching to a small group of intimates. In each case he amplifies the taught prayer with a helpful series of explanatory teachings. Possibly when Matthew tells us that Jesus, seeing the crowds, sat down, and his disciples came to him to be taught, Matthew means all of Jesus' disciples who separated themselves from the mere curious among the crowd and not just the called few. After all, according to Matthew 9:9, Matthew himself had not yet been called, so Jesus was still in the process of recruiting his intimates. This would be quite a number of disciples, from whom later on would be recruited the seventy-two missionaries Jesus sent forth (Luke 10:1). Possibly, then, the teaching of the prayer in Matthew was given to all manner of Jesus' disciples, the faithful women, those who would become the seventy-two, the healed who may have followed him, the newly attracted who had not yet experienced opposition and slunk silently away. Origen, in his classic *On Prayer* (XVIII, 3), suggests one might surmise that Jesus taught Matthew's version of the prayer and then at a later time was approached by a single intimate disciple who either was absent on that occasion (like Matthew, who had not yet been called) or failed to comprehend the message the first time around and needed a refresher course. The simplicity of the prayer makes the latter suggestion difficult to credit, the former is, of course, possible. Perhaps the disciple (though Luke's version suggests although one spoke he was speaking for several since he said, "Teach *us* to pray . . .") had just joined Jesus since the Sermon on the Mount. On the other hand, if, as some argue, Luke's is earlier, perhaps Jesus first taught the lesson to his intimate disciples as recorded in Luke 11 and then repeated it to them (a good teaching technique, repetition cementing memory) and to the larger crowd in a formal address on the mount. However, we can speculate another even more contextual and therefore compelling reason that may have prompted Jesus' teaching of the shortened prayer at a later time in Luke, and this reason is intimately entwined in the intriguing puzzle of why he dropped that most essential petition "Deliver us from evil" in Luke's version. We will propose it when we examine that petition. The important aspect to note at this point is that Jesus' teaching was not just restricted to his inner circle but was apparently generalized to be shared with all his disciples. Therefore, as did the people who gathered just beyond the inner circle of disciples, we as the heirs of the disciples can appropriate these model prayers of Jesus for our own fledgling communication with God.

We call the two prayers recorded in Matthew and Luke, "the Lord's Prayer." Repeatedly, commentators have pointed out that they should more accurately be called the Disciples' Prayer since Jesus' intention is to give his disciples a sample of what correct human prayer should look like. Jesus' own prayers are recorded later in the gospels and we will compare his own communication with the Father with his suggestions for us.

Still, the Lord's Prayers or Disciple's Prayers are imparted to us by Jesus himself and therefore we must study them closely. Readers should note that when citing these prayers we have written the Lord's or Disciple's Prayers rather than Prayer, for a first glance at Matthew 6:9-13 and Luke 11:2-4 reveals that the wording for each is different, suggesting we are actually dealing with two prayers rather than a single model prayer.

Jesus Taught Us Two Model Prayers

Many new inquirers into Biblical scholarship often find recent discussions on why we find two similar prayers disquieting. Expecting to discover some insights into Jesus' method of teaching, an unsuspecting student will find instead in many commentaries an essay on the early church's use of the Lord's Prayer as a tool for teaching and a subsequent suggestion that there are not two prayers but one, each variant a result of a different tradition. In pursuing our study a critic using form criticism may feel the Lord's Prayer is a creation for the liturgy of the early church and will therefore ask, "How exactly was the Lord's Prayer used by the second century church?" This line of attack would supposedly be tracing the prayer to its source. Whether it is the *ipssima verba* of Jesus, his true words, may never even be thought to be asked, for if the church is the source, the question is moot.

However, such an argument is more apparent than real. Eusebius, bishop of Caesaria, a church historian from the early 300's, in his *The History of the Church from Christ to Constantine*, quotes Papias (c. 60-135) (who may have known the Apostle John personally), who writes that Matthew the disciple recorded the various sayings of

Jesus in Aramaic, and everyone who wished to repeat them translated them as best he could (3.39). Further, Eusebius notes that Matthew began by preaching to the Hebrews, and when he decided to travel on a missionary journey to preach to others, he wrote down his gospel to continue his proclamation among his own people in his absence. Eusebius concludes that the first three gospels were already extant in the lifetime of John the disciple, who reviewed them and affirmed their accuracy. John wrote his fourth gospel, remarking that the others though accurate lacked sufficient details of Christ's work at the beginning of his mission (3.24). Therefore, we do hold historical attestation that the actual words of Jesus were recorded by his disciples and therefore available to the disciples' heirs in the early church. If Jesus' words were available, there then would be no need to create them. One would conclude, then, that the burden of accepting Matthew's authorship for the Book of Matthew, or Luke's, the fellow missionary of Paul, for Luke's gospel for that matter, does not lie on one to prove. Their authorship is cogently attested by these disciples' own disciples. In the same way, one would need to prove in the face of the historical attestations cited that these words credited to Jesus are later concoctions by the early church. A truly careful scholar who feels the necessity to take into account the contemporary a-historical tendency to late-date the two prayers to the early church would do well to heed the sensible words of Jeremias: "Of course, we must be cautious with our conclusions. The possibility remains that Jesus himself spoke the 'Our Father' on different occasions in a slightly differing form, a shorter one and a longer one."[2] Jeremias recognizes that a true scholar will neither damage nor ignore the attestations of history and will allow for the rabbinic technique of repetitious teaching to be Jesus' method of schooling his disciples in a model prayer on these two and perhaps upon further unrecorded occasions.

Therefore, there is no need to make the material more complex than it is. The two settings are different, the two prayers are differently worded, the occasions are differently depicted. Matthew's is given in Jesus' Galilean days, Luke's during his long roundabout wandering toward Jerusalem. So, perhaps the prayer in Matthew is the earlier and the one in Luke is a condensation. Of course, the prayer may have been repeated many times in between. Whatever is true, the two prayers contain striking similarities and differences and a careful parallel study will yield many riches for us as it

---

[2] Joachim Jeremias, *The Prayers of Jesus* (Philadelphia:Fortress, 1978), p. 91.

indubitably did for the early disciples. Since we can see no cogent reason scholarly or otherwise not to believe that both of these prayers were taught to disciples directly by Jesus himself, as contemporary disciples, let us now take our place at the feet of the Lord and study these parallel prayers together.

The Lord's (or Disciples') Prayers

Jesus begins both the sample prayer recorded by Matthew and the sample prayer recorded by Luke with the word "Father" used as an address for the God of the Universe. The designation of God as parent did not originate with Jesus. As with many concepts which are true, its influence was exerted on many ancient faiths. Ancient Indian religious texts such as the Sanskrit Rigveda were already speaking generally of *Dyaus pita*, father heaven, a concept invoked as well by the Babylonians, Assyrians, Aramaeans. The Greeks localized the concept and designated Zeus as father, while the Romans designated Jupiter. In the Old Testament God is called father, though this is done sparingly. Joachim Jeremias cites a mere fifteen instances of "Father" as a referent for God in the Old Testament and but four more in the Apocrypha (two of which he considers disputable).[3] Philo, the great Jewish philosopher who was a contemporary of Jesus, calls God "Father" on a number of occasions in his *Embassy to Gaius* (3, 115, 293). We see by these instances a precedent for understanding God as parent already extant in the Jewish faith as in other faiths. What Jesus did was to select this image and emphasize it as appropriate for us to use in approaching God. Paul explains in his letter to the Ephesians (1:5) that God had decided through Jesus to make us believers God's children, therefore Jesus used his identity as "Child of God" among us to be an example for us in the proper deportment of heirs. Paul develops this imagery not only in his letter to the Ephesians but also throughout his entire correspondence, particularly emphasizing it in Galatians 4 where he carefully draws a picture of the benefits and responsibilities of heirdom as a program for the Galatians to adopt for their lives. Therefore, when Jesus sets a model prayer for his followers to employ, appropriately he begins it by encouraging them to adopt his example and consider themselves children of God.

---

[3] Jeremias, *Prayers*, pp. 11-15. See also "Pater" in *Theological Dictionary of the New Testament* (1967), V, 945-1014.

"Father of Ours, the One in the Heavens,
Let It Be Hallowed the Name of Yours" (Matthew 6:9)

We see immediately that the conception of divine Parenthood Jesus orders for his disciples to understand is collective not individual. Jesus may speak uniquely of God as "My Father in Heaven" (e.g. "My Father's business" Luke 2:49, "My Father's kingdom" Matt. 26:29, "My Father's house" John 2:16, etc.), but we are to understand God as "*our* Father." The New Testament scriptures carefully foster the understanding that our relationship to God is as part of God's community on earth, Christ's body. We who are North Americans seem continually to misunderstand this truth. In the Transcendental Meditation-maddened sixties it was in vogue to rip out the scripture that claims "the kingdom of God is within you" (Luke 17:21) and suggest that that means that it can be reached by meditation, tapping our inner resources, as we discover God within each of us. Luke 17:21, however, actually says that the kingdom of God is among you plural. In other words, it exists where Christ is present, among the disciples who make up the body of Christ. Since Jesus was bodily present as the Holy Spirit is present among us, a decision to enroll as a citizen is to be made at once, today. Even if as war-protestor Daniel Berrigan (and as Moses) we see the rest of the family at times as "a stalking horror,"[4] the Holy Spirit dwells in its midst, just as God dwelt in the tabernacle in the center of the wandering covenant people. When as individuals we approach our Creator, we do so as part of God's body on earth. Our position is never "Me and God." It is always "We and God." Therefore in-built in our prayer is our own responsibility for other members of the body as well as our assurance that we are part of a collective mutually supportive family that will one day gather in celebration at the Marriage Supper of the Lamb. That Greek word used for father, *pater,* by the way, is still with us in English words like "paternity" and is affectionately reduced to that term that melts father's hearts when we hear it from our little children, "Papa." God is not remote when we use it but very personal.

The particular parent Jesus teaches us to address herein is "the One in the Heavens." Lest there be any misunderstanding, we are addressing the Chief Deity, the One God, maker of heaven and earth. *Ouranos* is a Greek term which is usually said to be adopted

---

[4] Daniel Berrigan, *The Words Our Savior Gave Us* (Springfield: Templegate, 1978), p. 12.

from mythology. Elizabeth Wordsworth, late principal of Lady Margaret Hall, Oxford, however, traces its origin to an ancient Sanskrit root meaning to "clothe" or "invest" the firmament.[5] In mythology *ouranos* was the husband of Gaea the earth, from whom we get "geo" for geology and geography. He was also the father of the Titans, those great monsters like the Furies and the Cyclops who warred with the gods. Naturally, the Jews did not share this mythology, so an attempt would be absurd to adopt from this employment of the Greek term the view that the first century Jews pictured God as a sort of Zeus or Jupiter sitting in the heavens as if upon Mount Olympus. We still employ the term today in our words uranology, the study of the heavens, and in our names Uranus for the planet and uranium for the mineral, and we do not have such a picture of God. In fact, despite the prevalent common contemporary mythology that the superstitious ancients believed in some sort of three story universe, we find such early church writers as Augustine and Tertullian singularly modern in their attempts to understand the seemingly locative quality of the word "heavens." Augustine points out that God is not tied down to a space or place. The heavens, he argues, are mere physical bodies similar in that respect to ours. He conjectures, they cannot mean that God is located somewhere in the sky or else the birds would be closer to God's presence than we would be and count for more since their lives would be lived out nearer to God! Instead, since God cannot be said to be more in one place than another, the heavens must mean the people. God dwelling in the heavens must mean dwelling among the saints (*The Lord's Sermon on the Mount* 5:17). Tertullian agrees, speculating "we are 'heaven' and 'earth'" (*On Prayer* 4). We doubt if we modern Christians are prepared to take that naturalistic a view of the meaning of heaven. But the ancients thought surprisingly concretely. Therefore, rather than superimposing our snobbish "age-ism" on what Jesus meant when he spoke about "our Father in heaven," we more correctly see the significance of the term for Jesus is to point out to his disciples that the God they are addressing as Parent is no mere golden calf but is the actual Central Power of the universe, the One we identify as on the throne, as it were, over us. And addressing God we are immediately cautioned to announce, let the name of Yours be hallowed.

Hagiastheto is the imperative form for the word "bless." "Bless the Lord, O my soul," cries the Psalmist David (Psalm 103:1, 2). We

---

[5] Elizabeth Wordsworth, *Thoughts on the Lord's Prayer* (New York: Longmans, Green, 1898), p. 20.

still use the word in hagiology, the study of the blessed ones, the saints. In approaching God, the first duty disciples are commanded to do is to bless or praise God, for God is our eternal Parent and worthy of our praise.

Our Lord Jesus points out this is definitely the manner by which we are to begin to embolden ourselves to approach our Parent - with reverence, humility, and respect. Thus we must pray at the outset, "Father of ours, the one in the heavens, let it be hallowed the name of Yours."

"Father, Let It Be Praised the Name of Yours" (Luke 11:2)

In contrast Luke's version of the Lord's or Disciples' Prayer immediately begins by omitting both the collective nature of our relationship with God and the identification of the God we are addressing as the one who is in the heavens. Instead, after the initial mandatory addressing of God as Father that immediately puts us in the position of God's children, it moves to glorifying God's name. In that sense it follows closely the command given in another collective statement to rule the conduct of God's chosen people, the ten commandments as recorded in Exodus 20. Immediately upon announcing who it is that gives such commandments, "I am the Lord your God, who brought you out of the land of Egypt" (Exodus 20:2), God commands, "You will not worship other gods over against me" (20:3). Jesus moves this second model of the prayer immediately from identifying the Recipient to giving God the acknowledgement which is God's due, immediate verbal worship. This is certainly a sound practice to follow when addressing our Creator, before whom we are naught but animated dust. Protocol demands we give immediate respect to the heads of state with whom we come in contact. Tragically, we rarely seem to recall the necessity to do this when we approach *their* great Head. Instead, when dire circumstances, the usual impetus for the neglected practice of prayer, finally drive us to our knees, the first thing we usually do is begin to pour out our requests as if we have just arrived at the counter of a clerk at a supermarket. We should cringe when we consider this usually thoughtless practice we all fall into so readily and so boorishly.

Perhaps we are inclined to forget ourselves so blatantly because prayer, and particularly the Lord's Prayer, has become so familiar to us through our repetitions in worship that it has nearly bred our contempt. The great evangelist Charles Finney in the book *Prevailing Prayer* warns against this tendency by pointing out that Jesus himself as evidenced in our two passages intentionally varied the words of his model prayer.[6] Jacques Ellul in his *Prayer and Modern Man* goes even further, loathing the mechanical insistence that we need the "official prayer" at the opening of the business meetings of the church, such as presbytery and regional councils. He finds these mere mouthings "fictitious prayers . . . an affront to the honor of God" and a source to Ellul of humiliation.[7]

"Let It Come the Rule (or Reign or Kingdom) of Yours" (Matt. 6:10)

Next we are advised to ask for the advent of the reign or rule or kingdom of God. Interesting to note is that the central message of Jesus' teaching was, "Repent, for the rule of Heaven is at hand" (Matt. 3:2; 4:17, etc.). The Greek word employed, *basileia*, is a fascinating one. We have come to think of a Basilica as a grand and noble building indicating power, riches, and splendor. The basil leaf, the spice we use so blithely in making pizza, spaghetti sauce, and basil carrots, was considered royal in Greek times. And in India the spice basil is considered sacred to Vishnu.

When Jesus came proclaiming the reign of God, he was announcing the advent of something royal, something sacred. Paradoxically, he could say that his kingdom was "not of this world" (John 18:36), at the same time proclaiming "the kingdom of God is among you" (Luke 17:21). Soren Kierkegaard, the Danish Christian thinker, has done more than any other Christian writer to emphasize the paradox that lies at the core of all understandings of the nature and truths of God. Because God's wisdom is so far above our thinking, each pursuit of understanding leads us inevitably to paradox where we simply fall on our faces acknowledging God is God. Yet these seemingly contradictory statements of Jesus may not be as paradoxical for us to understand as the true relation of God's determination and our free action, or the exact manner in which the Trinity can be both distinct in personhood and unified in essence and nature so that there is one God not three. When Jesus proclaimed the reign of God, he proclaimed his own advent. The rule of Heaven (God)

---

[6] Charles Finney, *Prevailing Prayer: Sermons on Prayer* (Grand Rapids: Kregel, 1965), pp. 5-6.

[7] Jacques Ellul, *Prayer and Modern Man*, trans. C. Edward Hopkin (New York: Seabury, 1970), pp. 19-20.

is at hand means "I am standing here before you. I am the Ruler. Where I am is my reign." "The heavenly kingdom of God is not of this world" also means "I am born of a divine Father. I am not Joseph's son. And I reign where that divine Parent is."

Jesus teaches us to pray for God's reign to come. What we are asking for when we do is that the rule of God through the rulership of Jesus be extended over our lives and over the whole earth. We are asking for the state of heaven, God's complete rule, to become the state of this rebellious world, beginning with our lives, our community, the reign of God on earth.

"Let It Come the Rule (or Reign or Kingdom) of Yours" (Luke 11:2)

If Jesus varied the first phrase freely in the various versions he provided of the Lord's Prayer, he certainly did not choose to vary the second. Luke notes that Jesus employed the precise words he did in Matthew's account even to the case of the verb and number of the words in the phrase which commands his disciples to pray for the advent of God's rule. This proclamation was apparently a constant in Jesus' teaching, one to which he rigidly adhered. And in the varieties of the prayer he taught, it is one phrase that does not mutate. It is an imperative constant. This same author Luke, who recorded the events in the Gospel of Luke, notes in the second scroll or volume of his work, the Book of Acts, an interesting fact about Jesus' teaching on the advent of the kingdom. Luke notes in Acts 1:3 that Jesus employed the forty days after his resurrection, when he was orienting his disciples to their responsibilities as newly recruited citizens in the new era he was ushering in, in "speaking the things concerning the rule of God."

When we note that this was also the message he gave both the twelve and the seventy-two disciples he sent out to preach (Luke 9, 10), that John the Baptist preached it in preparation for Jesus' advent, and that the word *basileia* occurs some 148 or so times in Jesus' teaching, particularly as a point in many of his parables, we are given pause for thought. When we then take into account the renewal of the proclamation of the reign of God as the post-resurrection message to be imparted by the disciples to the world and the fact that Paul, the greatest of these apostles (or ones sent), proclaimed it continually, as recorded in such passages as Acts 19:8, 20:25, and 28:23, we have to re-evaluate the accuracy of our own understanding of the central point of Jesus' message. Normally, we North American

Christians automatically identify the phrase Jesus said to Nicodemus "You must be born again" as the central core of the gospel message. In point of fact this "core" only appears in the writings of John and Peter. Besides the Nicodemus passage, the First Epistle of John employs the concept "born" of God in 2:29, 4:7, 5:4, etc. John lists a variation of the new birth motif some 11 times. Peter employs it most poignantly in I Peter 1:3, 23, but against the 116 times Jesus proclaimed the advent of the reign, being "born again" pales as the central message of his proclamation. Individualists simply find it appealing: "I must be born again into the kingdom." But Jesus as the new Adam saving our race thinks of our role collectively. We have to enroll as new citizens under God's reign. Of course, personal change and regeneration, "being born again," is called for just as poignantly and completely in our lives. But brother and sisterhood, not individualism, is now as integral a part.

This is by no means to deprecate an individual's personal regeneration. By no means! One must be born in the first place to be eligible for citizenship. But it does reveal that simply being born into the kingdom of Heaven was not the end-all of Jesus' message and was not the final focal point. Jesus' central message was given to the body of citizens, the whole new nation, the new Israel, the Church collectively, to become together the fully mature Nation of Heaven. The message is just the same: repent and be renewed, but the emphasis and responsibility are expanded. We are not just responsible for ourselves. We *are* our brothers'/sisters' keepers. We are not seen by God as alone.

"Let It Become the Will of Yours, as in Heaven also upon Earth" (Matthew 6:10)

Matthew now records a phrase missing in Luke's rendition. One might speculate why the phrase is included in the fuller amplification of Matthew and missing in the shorter succinct summary of Luke. It may be that the thought "Your will be done" is already included in the previous petition "Your kingdom come" and therefore is a repetition for emphasis and not strictly needed as a new thought. Tertullian, the famous North African lawyer who so ably defended the faith before he fell prey to the Montanist heresy, felt both petitions had the same referent - that is, to take place in us. Therefore, he surmised, the working out in us of the will of God is the manifestation of God's kingdom on earth or the consummation of the age, in other words, *the end* (*On Prayer* 5). Charles M. Laymon, noted

Methodist educator, following C. F. Burney, takes their relationship even further, suggesting the two petitions are a matched pair set in Hebrew poetic parallelism. The second phrase "Your will be done" would then simply restate the first "Your kingdom come," a common characteristic of Semitic poetry.[8] He also believes the same poetic restatement would be true of the later petitions "deliver us from evil" and "lead us not into temptation," the former petition being also deleted in Luke. This could be argued, as he does, to show a liturgical quality to Matthew's version. What produces its catechetical quality for the early church, we would observe, is that the version Matthew records, being presented to a multitude, is consciously structured by Jesus to be easily taught and remembered by these balanced couplets, while Luke's version, simply given to a few intimate associates in private, is stripped to its barest propositions.

One thing the petition does not suggest. In asking for God's will to be done on earth and for God's kingdom to come, we are implying that the advent of God's kingdom depends upon our willingness to perform God's will. True, for a time God deferred to human unbelief enough to restrict the performance of Jesus' miracles within his unaccepting home country (Matt. 13:58). But this near thaumaturgical bracketing by God was totally temporal, restricted to Jesus' earthly sojourn. When the fullness of time comes, the kingdom of God will not be held back. Even in Jesus' case, as events mounted toward his passion, Jesus pointed out that if the people were silenced at his triumphant entry into Jerusalem, the stones would have cried out (Luke 19:40). Our performance of God's will and enrollment into God's kingdom are privileges not good works done for the benefit of helping God carry out an otherwise impossible plan. Paul's Roman citizenship was a treasured prize that many purchased for a price. When necessary he would troop out his credential for the clout it possessed and the consternation it caused. Do not molest me, I am a Roman citizen. What a stir its revelation caused to the jailers of Philippi who imprisoned him and allowed him to be beaten. One does not touch the potent elect behind whose rights stands the might of the empire. Similarly, the doing of God's will, like the protection of citizenship in God's kingdom, is our privilege beyond the fact that it is the duty of all creation.

When we pray for God's kingdom to come and will to be done, we are actually praying proleptically. We are looking forward to the

---

[8] Charles M. Layman, *The Lord's Prayer in Its Biblical Setting* (Nashville: Abingdon, 1968), pp. 13, 99.

time when heaven, the reign of God, will descend to earth, and the conflict, the distinctions, will be no more (see Eph. 1:10; Rev. 21). We are all to be invited to the wedding supper when this great event takes place. But to be admitted we have to don our wedding garments. What are these? John in Revelation 19:8 tells us: "the fine linen is the righteous deeds of the saints." Admission to God's kingdom is by the doing of God's will - righteous deeds. What we are praying for here essentially is the fulfillment of the Old Testament picture of God ruling a chosen people directly, the answer to the disciples at Jesus' ascension: "Lord, will you at this time restore the kingdom to Israel?" (Acts 1:6). No, God will restore the kingdom to a renewed Israel in God's own time. And for the beginning of this we pray, so that our earth will reflect God's heaven in a mirror image - world without end, amen.

"The Bread of Ours, the Daily One, Give to Us Today" (Matthew 6:11); *"the One according to Today"* (Luke 11:3)

Striking, how many studies of the Lord's Prayer have been done in the wars of this century. In Germany while Friedrich Heiler nursed the wounded by day he contemplated the nature of prayer by night, producing the master work *Prayer: A Study in the History and Psychology of Religion*. Ernst Lohmeyer assiduously studied the *"Our Father"* too, before he disappeared forever behind the Russian lines. During the bombing of Stuttgart Helmut Thielicke preached his sermons on *The Prayer that Spans the World* until the very church building he preached in was blown up and he bravely finished the series in the parish house. Meanwhile in Great Britain Edward Vernon in *The Lord's Prayer in War Time*, Canon Leonard Hogdson in his sermon series and many others chronicled the great turning away from what Hogdson called "science" back to "God" that marked the advent of the world wars. When the illusion of security is shattered and the face of evil stares malevolently into our own, the simple words of the great prayer become bedrock foundations beneath our feet. And no more firmly does the prayer strike at the heart of our security than in this petition for "our daily bread." Vernon points out that bread is the thing we most might imagine we could get by our own efforts and this is the one thing we are taught to ask God to "give" us. Where we might think ourselves most independent, Jesus teaches us about our dependence. In wartime this truth is brought home. As Harry Rimmer has put it, "We truly live a hand-to-mouth existence, but it is 'from His hand to our mouths . . .'"[9] As Vernon explains, what we are asking for in this petition in wartime is: "Protection to the great mercantile fleets that bring our food; alertness, courage, and skill to those who keep ceaseless vigil in stormy seas against the lurking submarine; favorable conditions and seasons for those who dig for victory and produce our home-grown commodities; protection of our stored supplies against destruction by air-raid. For all these, and how much more, we are asking God when we pray in wartime, 'Give us our bread.'"[10] Such a perspective certainly brings the basic quality of what we are saying home to us when we examine it.

In the text there are but two minor variations by Matthew and Luke for this petition. The first concerns the imperative form for the word "give." In Luke this has a progressive flavor "be giving" us our daily bread. In Matthew it is punctiliar - "give us." The only other variation in this petition is the very last phrase. Matthew has recorded simply a word for "today," while Luke has included with it a preposition "according to today." However, an unsolved enigma exists with the word we, and most other translators, have rendered "daily." This word *epiousios* exists to our knowledge nowhere outside the Bible in extant manuscripts of any sort. Therefore, some scholars have tried to break it into its parts and render it "necessary for existence," relying on its etymology and hoping the original meanings remain. Others have noticed a feminine form *epiouse* in Acts 16:11 and hope it is merely the masculine equivalent. In this case the word could be rendered "following" as in "give us today the bread for the following day." But, really, who knows? For a while excitement existed concerning an alleged occurrence of the word unearthed in a papyrus fragment of a Greek householder's account book listing a purchase of provisions. The entry allegedly ran "1/2 obol for *epiousios*." An obol was both a small coin worth about a couple pennies and a measure. The word was also used in different dialect forms for "nail," a handful of nails being used in early times for money. Six were an equivalent of a drachma.[11] From this some commentators have guessed it meant "1/2 obol per day or daily," hence our reading. However, renowned textual critic Bruce M. Metzger has shaken this interpretation in his article "How Many

---

[9] Harry Rimmer, *The Prayer Perfect* (New York: Revell, 1940), p. 18.

[10] Edward Vernon, *The Lord's Prayer in Wartime* (London: James Clarke, 1941), pp. 56, 58.

[11] Henry George Liddell and Robert Scott, *A Greek-English Lexicon*, ed. Sir Henry Stuart Jones and Roderick McKenzie (9th ed.; Oxford: Clarendon, 1968), p. 1196.

Times Does 'Epiousios' Occur Outside the Lord's Prayer?"[12] Perhaps none, he writes. Professor Metzger points out that its editor was given to misreading inscriptions. Of course, we would have only to check the papyrus to see, except that apparently the owner lent the document to a friend who either proceeded to lose it or never bothered to return it. And this unfortunate event took place sometime around 1889. It has never been recovered. In its absence scholars are still puzzled.

Perhaps the word is in reality a neologism - a bit of Semitic/Greek *patois* created regionally as a business term and either not usually written down or, if so, not usually kept long. After all, how many sales slips have we lost? Perhaps Jesus suddenly dipped into common regional commercial language to ground the prayer down into earthly needs, dropping it from any heavenly plane it might have appeared to be reaching to the common workaday concerns it now addresses. Since his audience was regional and mixed their own Aramaic dialect with Hebrew and Greek in their pluralistic culture, perhaps a neologism brought the petition for daily sustenance forcefully into their common existence. After all, in the next petition he employs the Aramaic image "debts" for sins, adapting his message, as he so often did with his parables, to common experiences to teach a basic theological point. This daily bread for which we pray is earthly, common, and workaday. If the term was of regional commercial slang it would not necessarily be widespread outside that region, and the poor, the fishermen, the small shop keepers, the farmers with whom he communicated would not necessarily write it on lasting materials. If there is any validity to "1/2 obol for *epiousios*," the word would make little sense to mean "tomorrow." Is this a sale that is always becoming? A sort of process theology of weights and measures? It makes more sense to mean "per day" or "daily."

Cambridge scholar Frederic Henry Chase has dealt with one argument against this meaning. Considering whether it would add tautology, that is meaningless repetition, to an otherwise tightly worded prayer, he concludes, it would not if liturgical use was intended, especially for a morning prayer.[13] We would add further if the prayer is based on Semitic thought patterns, the force of such an

---

[12] Bruce M. Metzger, "How Many Times Does 'Epiousios' Occur Outside the Lord's Prayer?", *The Expository Times*, LXIX/2 (November, 1957), 52-4.

[13] Frederic Henry Chase, *The Lord's Prayer in the Early Church*, Texts and Studies, Vol. 1, No. 3 (Cambridge: University, 1891), pp. 44-6.

argument pales. Hebrews used repetition regularly for emphasis. So if Jesus said, "Give us today today's bread" he would be making a point. Further, theologically, "give us today the bread for tomorrow" would seem to weaken some of the effect of immediate dependence on God that appeared to be Jesus' message. After all, he was the one who said not to worry about the morrow (Matt. 6:34). He did not seem even to carry money, producing his tax from a fish's mouth (Matt. 17:27)! (Matthew, the former tax collector, was the one interested enough to record this in his gospel, by the way.) He extolled the flowers who do not toil or spin (Matt. 6:28-29; Luke 12:27), and he had no place to lay his head. This is extreme, of course, but it does totally emphasize the fact that God wants us to look for our security in heaven and not in barns where we store up provisions as did the wise fool (Luke 12:16-21), except when God specifically recommends such hoarding as God did with Joseph (Gen. 41:25-36). In the 1950's security-mindedness especially among North Americans became something of a nearly pathological mania. One can easily recall the fall-out shelters that were dug all over the country and the hoards of food stocked within them. Of course, God in his mercy did not let an atomic disaster strick us and now decades later one wonders how palatable that stock-piled food still is.

This is not to say that the mania is not with us still, lying dormant just below the surface of our national consiousness. We recall in recent years in a number of prominent Christian magazines an advertisement appearing summoning up visions of an impending Armageddon and calling for the faithful to buy that company's conveniently available survival food. Stockpiling in that clever advertisement was now equated with an act of Christian faith! But the petition tells us to ask for today just what we need for today. The Psalmist has already told us that security lies in the strong arm of the Lord, not in the war horse or the engines of battle (Ps. 20:6-8). The God who feeds the birds and clothes the grass is going to look out for our daily needs. That lesson is repeated over and over again in Scripture and here it is embodied in the prayer we are directed to pray. Security resides in the Lord.

Origen and other mystical interpreters felt disposed to spiritualize the term "bread," deprecating the supposition that it could apply merely to that ground and baked flour we all eat. Surely, they felt, it must have a higher spiritual meaning, and so they wrote long explanations of how this term must be referring to spiritual communion with Jesus, who called himself the "bread of life" (John 6:22-40). Certainly, theirs is a noble aim, to wish to look beyond the mere gifts of the Lord to the Giver. And yet God has so constructed our bodies that we *do* need the humble ground and baked flour, and mystics throughout history who have tried to forget that fact have suffered many resultant physical infirmities because of their deprivation. Scripture itself pays much attention to satisfying the hunger needs of the body, and bread, as a synecdoche for all food, has constant play throughout the Bible. Adam's curse in Genesis 3:19 was to eat his bread in the sweat of his face. The punishment of males at the fall was cataclysmic in dimensions. Men were promised death, the loss of earthly paradise, the disruption of family relations, and in the same league as all these catastrophes a hard time getting bread to eat. If food was unimportant to God, God would not have rated difficulty in obtaining it in the same level as those other disasters meted out in the fall. Isaiah and the prophets paid a serious attention to the way people who claim they are followers of God use their food. Isaiah 58:7 orders hearers to "share your bread with the hungry." Ecclesiastes 9:7, that panegyric of the simple life, observes nothing is better than to eat your bread with enjoyment (see also Eccles. 2:24). So significant is bread in God's scheme that Jesus uses the remark in Luke 14:15 "Blessed is he that shall eat bread in the kingdom of God" to teach about the great banquet that is heaven, the great eternal breaking of bread, the Marriage Supper of the Lamb.

Further, sharing bread with others is stewardship of God's resources in a way that satisfies the prophets because it pleases God. The rich fool died for just this reason: he hoarded. He was a thief in God's sight. Thus, a restriction to one's daily needs as one's primary security-oriented concern leads to greater dependence on God and less opportunity to steal from others through hoarding. Ernst Lohmeyer reminds us of the Near Eastern custom only to bake the unleavened bread needed for the very day of consumption.[14] Such was also true in the case of the manna God provided in the wilderness. Except in provision for the Sabbath, manna was only gathered each day and would spoil if one disobeyed and attempted to hoard it overnight. The lesson is continually taught by God and reiterated on earth by Jesus when he charged the twelve missionaries to take nothing for their journey, not even bread or bag or money (Mark 6:8), and it is repeated in these prayers. God will provide for our daily needs.

---

[14] Ernst Lohmeyer, *"Our Father": An Introduction to the Lord's Prayer*, trans. John Bowen (New York: Harper & Row, 1965), p. 140.

In this simple truth is where those who would seek a higher meaning for the Biblical symbolism for bread ought to look. Hebrews 9:1 and following reminds us of what worship was like under the Old Covenant. A tent was put up in which stood a lampstand and a table on which bread was offered to God. Behind a curtain was the most holy place where the high priest went only once a year, taking blood which he offered to God for his own and the people's unwitting sins. Behind that curtain stood the Covenant Box, filled with the holy memorabilia: manna, Aaron's sprouted stick, and the two stone tablets with the commandments written on them. When Jesus died, that curtain tore in two forever, and humanity stood suddenly face to face with God. No longer would a series of priests be needed to intercede. Now part of what this system had symbolically imaged, the heavenly original, had come to earth in the presence of Jesus. From that day until the end of earth's age Jesus would himself directly represent us to the Father by his sacrifice. Instead of bread ever again being offered on the holy table of God, now the heavenly original of manna descends again to us. Jesus came calling himself "the bread of life" (John 6:48). In his hard saying he ruled that only those who ate his flesh and drank his blood would have life in them (John 6:53).

As God did when God first called Israel into the wilderness, God again provides bread for the people. Eternal bread like living water through the sacrifice of Christ assures us that we will never hunger and thirst eternally, just as temporal daily bread from the land all owned by God shows us that we need not hunger on earth. Earthly manna and heavenly manna both proceed from the generous Giver, satisfying our bodies, satisfying our spirits. Jesus fed the five thousand plus on bread and fish while he nourished their spirits. God has proved again and again through human history that our Parent will not abandon us children to physical or spiritual starvation. God provided for us through the garden in Eden, through the manna in the wilderness, and today through the Church, the *body* of Christ, where we are required to feed the hungry among us. For our eternal spirits God provided for us Jesus, the Bread of Life. So the petition for daily bread takes into account our humanity. It is the reassurance that God daily acknowledges concern for people's well-being. The God who created children with bodily and spiritual needs will hear the prayer of those children to have their needs fulfilled.

"And Forgive to Us That Which Is Owed by Us, as Also We Have Forgiven (Already) the Things Owed to Us" (Matthew 6:12); *"And*

Forgive to Us Our Sins, for Also We Are Forgiving All Owing to Us" (Luke 11:4).

Hobha, the Aramaic word used for sin, literally means "debt." Romans 6:23 tells us sin's wage is death. Sin causes a debt that needs to be paid in God's sight, and no more poignant proof of this fact exists than in the differences in wording of the Disciples' Prayers in Matthew's and Luke's renditions. That Jesus paid the debt owed to God by all sinners is a basic proclamation of the Church as old as the recognition of the substitutionary death of Jesus on our behalf. That there were debts owed to God that had to be paid was understood thoroughly by the disciples and was used by Jesus to explain the way that God wants us to deal with each other's sins. In Matthew's prayer, given formally, this metaphor is spelled out by Jesus for his hearers. In the prayer we are allowed to use the imperative command toward God "forgive us these debts of ours," if while praying we can give God the assurance implied in the perfect tense of the verb, which is that our past action affects our present state. If I have already cooked my dinner, I can now sit down and eat it. If I have already worked my shift, I can demand my wages. Or, more applicable to this very example, if I have bought an item or gone on a trip on the "enjoy now, pay later plan," when the bill comes, I pay. Karl Barth in his *Prayer*, emphasizing God's grace, disagrees there can be any previous condition to have God's forgiveness,[15] but in Matthew 18:23-35 Jesus tells a serious parable about a servant who was forgiven by his master of a large debt. When that servant refused to extend a similar mercy to another for a smaller debt, the enraged boss threw him into prison, exacting every last measure of justice. Grace is withdrawn in the parable. Jesus was serious about humans forgiving one another.

In the same sermon in which he gave us the formal version of the model prayer, he tells us in 5:23-24 that if you have something against your brother, do not approach God's altar with a gift, but throw down that gift, go and be reconciled with your brother and then approach God. This is the teaching present in the Disciples' Prayer. We have to assure God we *have already forgiven* our brother or sister before we can expect God to forgive us. No wonder we are told not to let the sun go down on our wrath! If we do, we stand unforgiven by God for our own sins! Small wonder we need to throw ourselves on the mercy of Christ. And how dare we not extend our miniscule

---

[15] Karl Barth, *Prayer According to the Catechisms of the Reformation*, trans. Sarah F. Terrien (Philadelphia: Westminster, 1952), p. 66.

mercy to the sins of others against us? As the more informal Luke passage shows us, we must make no mistake about it, when we talk about the metaphor "debts," we mean literally "sins."

Luke's version, we recall, was given to a small group of disciples who asked Jesus privately for information. Jesus was accustomed to explain parables to his disciples privately after the mobs had left, and this is what he does in this private version. He drops the metaphorical language and says plainly, you can ask God to forgive your sins, if you are already forgiving others their debts to you. In the second part of the sentence the metaphor is renewed. The first part makes it plain what the referent is. Another interesting variation in the version in Luke is that the present tense is used. We have to have as our present way of life a continual state of forgiving others. In the formal version in Matthew Jesus teaches we must assure God we have already forgiven others in the past before we pray the prayer. In Luke he explains this attitude and practice have to be our present way of life, if we want to be forgiven. The truth of these two versions taken together is a sobering one. Holding a grudge is a luxury that we disciples cannot afford, if we want God's mercy to take our repentance seriously and apply the gracious blood of Jesus, his holy gift of salvation, to us.

We all recall in the famous title of his best-selling book Presbyterian doctor Karl Menninger asked, *Whatever Became of Sin*? True, in our self-styled enlightened age we prefer to talk about crimes, debts, mistakes, lapses, anything but sin. We think it is an outmoded word. The Greek for sin is *harmatia*, hamartiology is the doctrine of sin. In Middle English the verb we call today "to harm" was spelled "harmen" and it appears to be derived etymologically from the Greek word for sin. Sin is harm, harm done to others and to ourselves. When we talk of sin, we talk of doing harm. A nice aspect of our age emphasizes love, but when harm is done to us, we want retribution. We call the police, we go to court. Harm is sin. The concept is not outmoded in anybody's vocabulary, even if the word is changed.

A wider application of the principles implied in this petition might be made to prison reform. An increasing number of judges have gotten into trouble for ordering lawbreakers to return the cost of their crimes to their victims by working instead of merely vegetating in jail. Romans 4:4 points out that to one who works, his wages are not seen as a gift, but as his due. James the Righteous One, the brother of Jesus, explodes against the rich who try to cheat the poor of their justly earned wages (James 5:4). By the same token, one who hurts another physically or financially in God's sight owes that person for his sin. In God's sight, both good and evil need to be paid back. No wonder God says retribution and vengeance are God's province. In Revelation 6:9-11 even the dead martyrs are aware of God's implacable interest in debts being paid up, and they want to know when the bill will be delivered to those prospering wicked.

The authors, who have worked with inmates for several years at Trenton State Prison, New Jersey's maximum security prison, realize firsthand the foolishness of simply incarcerating prisoners to vegetate and fester and grow more and more warped in the artificial hothouse of an over-crowded, out-of-date, dilapidated prison. Inmates talk about "paying their debt to society" and "paying for their crimes," but deep inside, each responsible inmate really wonders if he or she has really paid by simply wasting years in the suspended animation of prison life. The guards by and large say no. Their attitude is that prison is not a "pay-off," it is merely an attempt to keep these "animals" off the streets as long as possible in the hopes that the sheer waste of time will deter them from further crime. So the inmate is made to realize over and over that despite his angry assertions, the debt is *not* paid, can never be paid. No wonder inmates go half crazy with frustration and anger. We want to pay our debts. They want to pay their debts. God has decreed that we must write *canceled* on the debts owed to us before God will write *canceled* on ours. If this is Heaven's decree, why cannot our legal systems see the wisdom and allow inmates to work hard for the time it takes and pay back every bit of the debt they have incurred until the law and the victims say to them, "Canceled in full"? The next step above that, of course, is mercy. God's way is to extend to us unmerited grace, to let Christ pay in our stead. But the first step is justice, to be willing to pay, and whatever it takes - an actual act of retribution on the former victimizer's part, or a gracious act of mercy on the victim's part to write canceled on a human bill, God demands that payment be done before God will forgive any of us, victims and victimizers, for those are roles we sinful humans continually interchange.

"And Do Not Bear Us into Temptation (Matthew 6:13 and Luke 11:4), *but Rescue Us from Evil"* or perhaps, *"the Evil One"* (Matthew 6:13).

We have seen how Jesus increasingly yields the prayer to an accounting of our needs and frailties before God, and the movement culminates in the final petition of the prayer. If the plea for daily bread takes into account our humanity, the cry for salvation underscores our mortality, for this is indeed how the prayer ends - with a desperate cry to God. As we mentioned earlier, in conservative Christianity we often talk of "being saved." Here is one of the well-springs of that expression, its presence in the Scriptures.

St. Christopher has fallen into disgrace in contemporary Roman Catholicism ever since his poignant tale of bearing the Christchild to safety was relegated to legend, but the image of that erstwhile saint is a good one and reflective of our understanding of God's relationship to us. Any good image in literature or legend points to an aspect of truth, and the truth the Christopher legend points to in God illuminates one aspect of God's character and activity. In a contemporary popular Christian narrative and song a Christian complains to God that life is like footprints in the sand, and when he looks back over his life, so much like a walk through the thick sands of the seashore, he sees in the most troubled times but one set of footprints. Yes, the Lord replies, that is when I carried you. "Christopher," a compilation of the two words "Christ" and *phero*, the Greek word for "bear," means "Christ-bearer," and it is an inverted image of what the prayer tells us God does for us. We have come regularly to translate this petition, "And *lead* us not into temptation," as if the Greek word employed were *"ago"* - "lead." But the image both versions of the prayer actually present is that of God "bringing" or "bearing" us. When we speak of God sustaining the world, lifting us in the everlasting arms, teaching us to bear one another's burdens (even as God bears and Christ has borne all of ours), we reflect the truth that God carries us in those brawny arms as we carry our small children. In the prayer we beg God not to bear us into temptation.

Before we begin puzzling over how a good God could bear us into temptation, we ought to note what the great Southern Baptist grammarian A. T. Robertson writes about the negative particles: "If *ou* denies the fact, *me* denies the idea," giving us a perspective why the negative particle *me,* rather than the usual simple *ou,* may have been employed here.[16] Of course, when the imperative is used, *me* is the appropriate negative to employ, yet the use of this construction may still suggest to us, even if only hesitatingly, that the very idea that God may bear us, God's children, into a temptation that would destroy us is an idea to be negated. Perhaps the force of this *me*

---

[16] A. T. Robertson, *A Grammar of the Greek New Testament in the Light of Historical Research* (Nashville: Broadman, 1934), p. 1167.

negative with the imperative here might be phrased, "God forbid that you the good God who cares for us should bear us into a destroying temptation!" Certainly James, the Lord's brother, in his epistle has adjured us not to say that "by God I am tempted" (for "God cannot be tempted with evil and the same God tempts no one" James 1:13). The idea of God tempting anyone into evil is negated, giving more strength to the reason for the use of the imperative in the Lord's Prayer and its entailed *me* negative as a negation of the suggestion that the good God would bear us into temptation. True, God permits temptation to exist. The writer of Ecclesiastes in 7:14 tells us that God has made both the days that contain prosperity and adversity, corroborating the idea of God's allowing temptation to test us, though that being limited to what we can endure (1 Cor. 10:13), Job's tolerance obviously being vastly superior to most of the rest of ours. Most commentators, ancient and modern, prefer to see the petition as asking not that God not lead us into temptation but that God preserve us during it. Further, we find the Scriptures speak of God hardening the heart of Pharoah (e.g. Exod. 10:1) or giving evil people over to their own desires, but neither of these - the allowing of testing or the giving up of the chronically willful to their own wills - is the same as a malicious act of the perfect Parent of Lights in whom is no shadow to carry us, God's beloved dependent children, into evil temptation.

Thus, the attempts by theologians like John Hick in his *Evil and the God of Love* to update the ancient Roman missal's theory of the "happy fall" to suggest that God ordained Adam and Eve to fall so that they might leave childhood and reach maturity or further that God continually allows us to fall into evil that we might be cleansed are not what Jesus has in mind. "Should we continue in sin that grace might abound?" asks Paul. "God forbid!" (Rom. 6:1-2). God forbid, suggests the Disciples' Prayer, that we should be brought into evil, but, as Matthew adds, *rusai*, rescue us from evil. Save us. Deliver us. Our last cry in the prayer is to be delivered from the evil which stalks and curses and destroys us and our world.

If what we are arguing is the case, then one might ask why even pray, "Lord, bring us not into temptation"? What is the point if by the very construction of our prayer we are inherently saying, "God will not bear us into temptation"? To this we might ask a further question. Why should we pray "Your kingdom come"? We know it will come inevitably whether we request it to, or want it to, or not. It will even come if we attempt to block it. Inexorably. For that matter, why should we pray "Thy will be done"? It *will* be done. The reason why we pray these prayers, of course beside the fact that our Saviour has commanded us to do so, is that in praying them we are affirming who God is and saying, "Yes, I also want your kingdom to come and your will to be done." We are adding our voice of affirmation to God's desire, aligning ourselves with God's forces, declaring ourselves on God's side. In the present petition we are in effect saying, "Yes, I affirm you as the God who will not bear us into temptation, so *please* deliver us from evil." Jesus' shorter version in Luke, we will notice, does not even contain the second part, the request to be delivered from evil, perhaps implying that it is already contained in the first petition. We have affirmed that God is the good God who will not have us carried into the jaws of evil. And God will not disappoint us.

Another possible reason for the absence of the petition, however, might be suggested by the context. Luke 9:51 tells us that when the days drew near for Jesus to be received up, he set his face to go towards Jerusalem. At this point Jesus makes up his mind to go to Jerusalem to suffer and die. Scholars often call Luke's next section "the travel narrative." But it is not just a travelogue. What Jesus does is circle around Jerusalem, homing in on it - to be delivered up to evil. Thus, the prayer he now gives is a terse one - a sufferer's prayer. In the more halcyon days of his ministry centered around Galilee, the time of the Sermon on the Mount, he could give a full measured prayer to be prayed in comfort and reflection. But in Luke 11 on the threshold of his passion in Jerusalem the prayer is stripped down to its barest essentials. It reflects the terseness of Jesus' own last prayers. And it omits the last petition that is given in Matthew. Jesus still asks for his followers not to be brought into temptation. But he does not ask for them or himself to be delivered from evil - for his hour has come.

If This Ends the Prayer, Where Did We Get the Doxological Ending?

Today liturgically when we repeat the Lord's Prayer in worship, we tack on to the end of it that benediction first noticed in a shortened version in *the Didache* (8) and in translations in the second to third centuries appearing in the Syriac and Coptic: "For Thine is the kingdom and the power and the glory forever, Amen." This doxology became particularly popular in Africa about A.D. 400 and was copied into the widely used Italic (old Latin) and brought to the Irish monastery at Bobbio in Northern Italy. However popular in early Christianity it was, it does not appear in either the earliest papyri nor in Vaticanus or Sinaiticus, the best of the codex manuscripts, so it is not attested as being part of the prayers that originated with Jesus. Rather, many feel that it is an adaption of David's prayer in 1 Chronicles 29:11, reworked for a liturgical ending. Most probably, if the early church has made any contribution to the prayers of Jesus, this benediction is it. In contrast, the prayers Jesus gave to his disciples simply break off with the plea for deliverance from evil or the request for not even being brought into temptation in the first place, and with those endings our model conversations with God conclude.

What Strikes Us About the Prayers Jesus Has Given Us to Pray?

Simplicity is the overriding feature that first impresses us. The God who can stir up new languages at Babel is not impressed with eloquence. As Simon, the son of Rabban Gamaliel, wisely observed: "Whoever indulges in too many words brings about sin" (m. Aboth 1:17). God wants prayer short and sincere.

The Disciples' Prayer begins with an acknowledgment of God's loving and parental relationship with us and then poetically parallels the first three phrases after the address. In English we do not usually translate them as parallel, but in Greek they stand in a poetic line, the verb of command preceding the noun: "Let it be hallowed . . . Let it come . . . Let it become . . . ." By this construction the word "Your" is then made to stand out, for each phrase ends with it. "*Your* name . . . *Your* kingdom . . . *Your* will . . . ." The emphasis is on God and on God's interests. This is a God-centered prayer. The first three things we ask beg that God's name be hallowed, God's kingdom come, God's will come about. As Andrew Murray points out in his classic devotional book *With Christ in the School of Prayer*, we often come to God burdened down with our own problems and concerns, but this prayer makes us readjust our focus upon God and puts our own problems into perspective.[17]

Thus, having been oriented in the correct fashion and having our minds centered on the eternal God and God's eternal wishes and decrees, we now turn to our own behavior, being made to recognize that when we ask for God's will to be done, the behavior we are about to assure God is ours and ought to be ours is already the norm in the heavens, and it ought to be the norm on earth. By this means we

---

[17] Andrew Murray, *With Christ in the School of Prayer* (New York: Revell, 1885), pp. 25-6.

assure God that our colony earth will reflect the ruling seat of empire, God's heaven, that our outpost earth will serve its heavenly headquarters.

At this point we finally are permitted to submit our requisitions. And these requests we are directed to make are simple. We merely ask for temporal sustenance and eternal protection! When we ask for God's forgiveness in Matthew's version, we assure God we have already forgiven our fellows, and in Luke's we assure God we are in the continual process of forgiving them at the same time we are seeking to be forgiven. We understand that we do not deserve to be forgiven first before we choose to act, though God's grace may do it initially. As far as destructive temptation is concerned, we ask God not to bring us into it, implying that the very idea of God bearing us to our eternal destruction is negated. Instead, we call out to God for rescuing.

At that point, the essentials being over, the prayer concludes. The church has tagged the doxology onto the end of the prayer for liturgical purposes. God does not prescribe it, though, of course, God still may enjoy it.

How Does Jesus' Example Relate to the Rest of the Sermon on the Mount's Points on Prayer?

Jesus' prayer in Matthew is set within a sermon. And in the context of that sermon, woven around the simple prayer Jesus recommends to his friends, is a tapestry of teachings about prayer. Jesus has created a setting in which to display the prayer and the contrasts heighten its effect. When introducing the prayer, which directly follows his commands on how to give alms, Jesus warns against the practice of hypocrites. Do not be like those falsely pious who want everyone to see them bowing "piously and humbly" in prayer. Jesus' own example, as we shall see, was simple and humble, so, of course, it is diametrically opposed to those who would strut proudly about to draw praise. How can one be humble before God if one's mind is occupied busily with drawing praise to one's self? No wonder Jesus expended so much affection on children. Children want others to notice them as much as adults do. But in serious moments, children abandon all pretense and cling to a parent for love and protection. Even in difficulty, adults seldom drop all concern for the opinions of others. No wonder the Lord's Prayer has been called a simple, child-like prayer. It is a prayer without pose or pretense.

Jesus next warns against verbosity. In the prayer which he gives, one example (Luke) is briefer than the last (Matthew). God is no simpleton, and God cannot be bullied or bribed (Matt. 6:7-8). God already knows what we need before we ask it. Only the pagans repeat, because, as Elijah so dramatically points out, their gods cannot hear them anyway! The great Walter Rauschenbusch in his *Prayers of the Social Awakening* decries the paganizing that has been done to the Lord's Prayer in otherwise Christian worship. "The general tragedy of misunderstanding which has followed Jesus throughout the centuries," he writes, "has frustrated the purpose of his model prayer also. He gave it to stop vain repetitions, and it has been turned into a contrivance for incessant repetition."[18] Rauschenbusch's criticism may be a bit harsh, but it does point up an irony.

How did the Lord's Prayer come to be repeated as it is today, perhaps even in direct though unconscious defiance of Jesus' own wishes? Actually, it has rankled Christians throughout the ages. Isaac Watts, the great hymnist, was so set against set prayers that he viewed the Lord's Prayer as an indulgence by Jesus to his weak disciples. Watts preferred spontaneous prayers, beefed up with repeated acknowledgments of God's exalted holiness against our sinfulness, unworthiness, and general "worm-hood" in God's sight. He only allowed an occasional reliance on excellent set prayers as when one could firmly establish that the prayer was so fine an expression it superceded one's own spontaneity, when one suffered from dryness, or in the extreme case of "melancholy, cold palsies, or the like distempers."[19] With this much prejudice against repetition and the added weight of Jesus' teaching against it in Scripture, how then did the practice come about? This, alongside the appended liturgical ending, is also the contribution of the early church. *The Didache*, that early Christian manual for instruction and liturgy which dates from the early second century, sets down the Lord's Prayer (and includes a form of the doxological ending) and at the conclusion, possibly in imitation of the Jewish practice, orders the reader to "Pray thus three times a day" (VIII.3). Readers obviously heeded that command as they did the rest of *the Didache's* teaching

---

[18] Walter Rauschenbusch, *Prayers of the Social Awakening* (Boston: Rilgrim, 1910), p. 16.

[19] Isaac Watts, *A Guide to Prayer*, ed. Harry Escott (London: Epworth, 1948), p. 40.

and therein the practice of repeating the Lord's Prayer in the liturgy of the church probably came about. The practice is nearly as early as formal Christian worship itself.

After Matthew presents Christ's simple prayer, the sermon moves on to other topics, fasting, money, trust and security in God, and then in 7:7-12 returns briefly to display prayer once more in a final didactic setting. Echoing his words found in Luke 11:9-10 to "ask, seek, knock," Jesus points out an ironic teaching that he will use at another time by another illustration when teaching again on prayer through the parable of the widow and the unjust judge recorded in Luke 18:1-8. Jesus argues that if we evil humans know enough to give good gifts to our children, will not the eternally good God of the universe give good things to God's children? The point is embarrassingly irrefutable. Jesus then caps it with the symbiotic teaching that has come to be called the Golden Rule. Do what you ask be done to you. And, of course, inversely, do not expect either from humans or from God what you will not do for others. If the term cheap grace means anything, it means trying to swindle God's mercy while withholding your mercy from your brothers and sisters. No wonder Jesus ends the sermon sternly with three sets of warnings. He tells us in 7:13-14 to watch our step when choosing our path to God (apparently to Jesus Christ all paths of faith *do not* lead to God). In 7:15-20 he admonishes us to watch out for false prophets. In conclusion in 7:21-27 he warns us to treasure his words and keep his rules lest we be destroyed. No wonder the crowds were astonished at his sermon. They had heard the authoritative voice of God.

What Does the Setting of Luke 11 Tell Us about Prayer?

In the more private conversation recorded in Luke, Jesus follows his presentation of the prayer with illustrations. They are more comic examples, echoing his end of the Sermon on the Mount, highlighting the final, essential, irrefutable point. In telling of a bedded-down neighbor who is hassled into getting up to provide the pest next door with some food for an equally inconsiderate guest who has arrived in the middle of the night, and by concluding that tale with the same admonition to "ask, seek, knock" since even we total losers do good to the children we love, Jesus' exasperation with the frailties of human behavior makes a lasting point about our immutably loving Father (Luke 11:5-13). Look, he is saying, if you uncooperative, unhelpful, stiff-necked people will even help, what do you think your perfect loving Parent will do? You just have to ask God once. God *will* help.

Conclusion

We often wonder if we can teach others to pray, or more closely to home, if we ourselves can be taught to pray. Jesus himself did it by modeling, showing how to pray by his own example. In Matthew's sermon he gave a prayer, illustrating it on both sides of his presentation. In Luke, he prayed himself and then explained what he was doing. That is the way we can teach prayer to our children and those the Holy Spirit brings to Christ through our words and actions, by kneeling humbly in holy prayer ourselves and then explaining carefully, illustrating when necessary, what we are doing.

In two different settings, formally and informally, Jesus taught his disciples how to pray and teaches us how to pray. In Matthew he has given a formalized presentation complete with easily remembered couplets to be taught to a large crowd in a helpful didactic style. In Luke the prayer is stripped down to its bare essentials. The core of the prayer is displayed to a few intimates. Both prayers give the same information. Paul picked up this flexible technique of Jesus' teaching when he declared himself to be all things to all people, urging them in and out of season.

If we want to summarize the answer to the plea, "Lord teach us to pray . . .," we would observe that the following is how and what the Lord teaches us to pray. Humbly pray a simple prayer, focused on God, assuring God the behavior God expects of us is being done. Bring God two simple requests: sustenance in this temporal life; deliverance from evil. At that point stop. The prayer we have prayed is simple, strong and secure. It matches the revealed personality and wishes of the eternally good God, our loving Parent.

3

Jesus' Parables on Prayer (Luke 18:1-14)

The parables of the widow and the judge and the Pharisee and the tax-collector are teachings concerning prayer given by Jesus to the disciples but probably in the hearing of Pharisees who were antagonistic. Luke's overall goal in his gospel is to challenge Theophilus (who as some kind of governmental official may be more like the Pharisees than the disciples) to follow the God who has come in the person of Jesus, empowered by the Spirit and with authority to liberate all oppressed people. Luke shows how Jesus' true nature as God come to liberate all oppressed persons is attested to before he begins his formal ministry (1:15-4:13) and during his ministry which centers around Galilee (4:14-9:50). Jesus attracts large crowds. However, these crowds begin to be less receptive to Jesus when he "set his face to go into Jerusalem" (9:51). Jesus' resolve to go to Jerusalem, a meandering circular approach to the city, is a macrocosm of Jesus' prayer in Gethsemane - he knew his cup of suffering must be accepted. Jesus knows that in Jerusalem, he, like all other prophets, will be shamefully treated and killed but he on the third day will rise (18:31-34; 11:47-54). The crowds become less receptive to Jesus as they begin to understand Jesus' message of suffering. Jesus not only liberates all oppressed people, he also, ultimately in the crucifixion, identifies with the oppressed by becoming oppressed himself.

The Parable of the Widow and the Judge

The parable of the widow and the judge fits well in the context of Chapter 17. Jesus tells his disciples about their duty as servants which is to forgive repentant believers and to have faith (17:1-10). The importance of faith is then illustrated by the Samaritan leper who remembers to thank God for the healing. Jesus tells him: "Your faith has saved you" (17:19). In contrast to this believing Samaritan leper are the religious leaders who were studying the signs of God's reign, observing and watching, while blinded from seeing God standing and talking and acting in their very midst (17:20-21). Jesus then directs his teachings to his disciples (probably hundreds of others), explaining how his return will not be a matter of observing signs, but rather it will be clear and sudden. The day of "the Son of Man" (or "the Heir of Humanity")[1] will be as clear and evident as "lightening lighting shines up the heavens from one side to another side of the heavens" (17:24). This day will also come suddenly. It can happen any time. "They were eating, they were drinking, they were marrying, they were being given in marriage" when the flood came or fire and sulphur came (17:27-30).

Since the day of Christ will come suddenly it will not leave any opportunities for mixed priorities (17:31-32). Jesus exhorts his readers to "remember Lot's wife" who wanted one more look at her home. Judgement is coming: loss of life to those who seek to gain life, gain of life to those who seek to lose life. Those who are judged will be taken up to the vultures for destruction (17:33-37).[2]

---

[1] "The Son of Man" is a traditional rendering for the Greek *ho huios tou anthropou*. *Anthropos* is the generic term for "person" or "human." *Huios* refers to a "son or child." The significance of being a "son" was that now one was an "heir" or "inheritor." For example, Paul uses "sons" and "heirs" (*kleronomos*) as synonyms in Galatians 3:26-29. An heir was as much an owner of the possessions as the "father." See Aída Besançon Spencer, *Beyond the Curse: Women Called to Ministry* (Peabody: Hendrickson, 1985), pp. 68-71. Christ is called the "Heir of all things" in Heb. 1:2. Francis Lyall has a fine discussion of inheritance in *Slaves, Citizens, Sons: Legal Metaphors in the Epistles* (Grand Rapids: Zondervan, 1984), chs. 4-5. Consequently, "the Son of Man" can be rendered as "the Heir of Humanity" in order to communicate that Jesus identifies with all humans, not only males. Jesus is a literal son of humans because Mary was his mother. In that sense Jesus is "the Human One" (*An Inclusive Language Lectionary*: *Readings for Year One* [Philadelphia: Westminster, 1983], appendix.)

[2] The idea of birds being vehicles of *destruction* is repeated in Rev. 19:17-18. In the parable of the wheat and the tares the weeds or "tares" are gathered for destruction before the wheat in Matt. 13:30. According to 1 Thess. 4:17 the

Thus, Christ's return will be a day of judgement which can happen anytime and will be evident to all, leaving no opportunity for other priorities. These three themes which Jesus discusses with the day of Christ in 17:22-37 should come as no surprise to Luke's reader since they are mentioned throughout Jesus' travels "to Jerusalem." That the day of judgement can happen anytime is described metaphorically also as a master returning from a marriage feast (12:35-48) or as a householder shutting a door (13:22-30). Being a follower of Jesus who has God's reign in priority is another continuing theme. Like the people who seek to get their goods from their houses (17:31), the people along the road want to bury their father[3] or say farewell to their family (9:59-62); Martha is distracted with much serving (10:38-42); and the builder cannot finish the building, or the king his war (14:25-33). As Jesus says, "Whoever among you does not renounce everything cannot be my disciple" (14:33).[4] Those who do not set obedience to God as a priority always have waiting for them a devastating judgement. Salt without taste is thrown away (14:35). No one who rejects the king's banquet will taste it (14:24). The large crowds only receive the sign of Jonah, a sign which calls for a change of life to avert condemnation (11:29-32).

In the parable of the widow and the judge, Jesus continues the topic of his second return. Although the day of judgement will be sudden and clear, yet the intervening time until the day of judgement may appear to those who are being oppressed to be a wearisome wait. Jesus in 17:22-27 calls people to repentance, calling his disciples to give up their lives' priorities in order to gain their lives. Jesus in 18:1-8 exhorts these committed disciples to be patient. Both chapter 17 and 18:1-8 speak of the return of the "Heir of Humanity" beginning and concluding with almost the same issue: Will Jesus find faith on earth when he returns (18:8)? Will the disciples have done their duty (17:10)?

---

believers afterwards will be taken up to the clouds to meet the Lord, as the old heaven and the old earth are destroyed (Rev. 21:1).

[3] Incidentally, Josephus proudly tells the pagan Apion that the Jews' concern for others is shown, among other reasons, by their never leaving "a corpse unburied" (*Against Apion II* (29) 211).

[4] Many early Christians practiced renouncing everything for the sake of Jesus so well that even the Greek philosopher Epictetus who lived around A.D. 50-120 uses the Christians or "Galileans" as an exemplary group which for non-stoical reasons could "be in such a frame of mind . . . that he cares not one whit about having, or not having" material things, property, children, or spouse (*Arrian's Discourses of Epictetus* IV. 7, 5-6).

And [Jesus] was saying a parable to them about their need at all times to pray and not become weary (18:1),

Luke records a number of parables not found in the other gospels including several parables which clearly teach about prayer.[5] A parable is a story drawn from nature or common life with one main point illustrating a principle or moral. It is usually an extended simile[6] as in Luke 13:18-19. The parables on prayer are all extended metaphors. One or more properties of the parable (the image) are attributed to the literal concept, thing, or person being explained. In this sense a parable as any metaphor is in essence a type of analogy. Luke tells us that Jesus "was saying"[7] this parable (thereby grammatically connecting chapters 18 and 17 or implying that the parable occurred more than once) to "them." The audience seems to be the disciples mentioned earlier, possibly in the presence of the Pharisees (17:20, 22). The disciples would identify with the "elect" (18:7). The call to faith would be a call to disciple and skeptic.

Luke gives us the main point of the parable: "the need of the disciples always to pray and not become weary." Often readers conclude that the point of the parable, which Luke explains in 18:1, is illustrated by the widow who persists in bothering the unjust judge. Luke does say we must "always" pray. *Pantote* which means "at all times, always, ever" is an adverb of time. Usually adverbs in Greek follow the verb, but Luke places *pantote* before the verb to emphasize it. We must not only "pray," but we must "*always*" pray. Therefore, we might conclude that we too like the widow must persist in asking God again and again if we hope to get a positive response. Such persistence is not optional, according to Luke it would be "necessary" (18:1). Possibly, we might say, that such persistence illustrates our "faith" (18:8). However, the danger with such an interpretation is that Jesus would contradict the teaching of the Sermon on the Mount that his disciples should not pray like the Gentiles who think they will be heard because of their "many words" (Matt. 6:7). Moreover, Jesus in

---

[5] Luke 11:5-10; 18:1-4. Other parables unique to Luke are in 10:29-37; 12:16-21, 35-48; 14:7-14, 25-33; 15:8-32; 16:1-9, 19-31; 17:7-10; and 19:11-27.

[6] The most commonly employed figures of speech in the New Testament are all defined in Appendix II of Aída Besançon Spencer, *Paul's Literary Style: A Stylistic and Historical Comparison of II Corinthians 11:16-12:13, Romans 8:9-39, and Philippians 3:2-4:13*, Evangelical Theological Society Monograph Series (Winona Lake: Eisenbrauns, 1984), pp. 280-313.

[7] In 18:1 Luke uses the imperfect tense as opposed to the aorist tense in 18:9, "he said."

the parable accentuates the contrast rather than the similarity between the human judge and the divine Judge. The context and the parable itself signify that as Christians may innocently suffer in this world they should not lose faith in God's promise to remove their oppressors. Disciples should "at all times pray" or continue in devout communication to God (*proseuchomai*) through time, in other words, until the day of judgement. The continuing prayer would be one way the disciples show that they have faith in God. Jesus' point in this parable, in different words, would be similar to his point in Luke 21:36. We need to pray for the strength to endure in 21:36 because we can so easily be ensnared by the less important cares of this world. In 18:1 we need to continue to believe that God will vindicate the righteous even though God may appear to favor the unrighteous.

The contrast to prayer is "becoming weary." *Egkakeo* is used in an unusual sense in the New Testament. Etymologically, *egkakeo* is made up of *eg* or "in" and *kakeo* or "bad." Properly *egkakeo* means "to behave badly or remissly in," as "they culpably neglected to send aid."[8] Usually *egkakeo* is used to signify "to be faint-hearted, lose heart, grow weary." However, the New Testament does seem to use *egkakeo* with a sense of weariness as in, "But you, brothers, do not *become weary* in doing good" (2 Thess. 3:13). In Galatians Paul adds that we should not *become weary* or "give up" because "in due time we will reap" (6:9). 2 Clement explains that "in saying 'Cry thou that travailest not,' he means this, that we should offer our prayers in sincerity to God, and not *grow weary* (*egkakeo*) as women that give birth" (2 Clement II.2). Possibly Paul might have intended that *egkakeo* include a sense of "behaving badly" in Ephesians and 2 Corinthians. Paul asks the Ephesians not to *lose heart* over his troubles in light of the fact that believers can have boldness and access to God (3:13). Possibly if the Ephesians lost heart, thinking that even such a devout person as Paul could have difficulties, the Christian walk was not worth doing. Paul and Timothy explain that they do not *become weary* or *behave remissly* because, although they have many external difficulties in their ministry, their inner natures are being changed into the Lord's glory (2 Cor. 3:18-4:1, 16). In Luke 18:1 *egkakeo* as well may have a sense of becoming so weary that one behaves badly. Consequently, Jesus ends the parable with a call for

---

[8] Joseph Henry Thayer, *Thayer's Greek-English Lexicon of the New Testament* (2d ed.; Marshallton: National Foundation for Christian Education, 1889), p. 166; Henry George Liddell and Robert Scott, *A Greek-English Lexicon*, ed. Henry Stuart Jones (9th ed.; Oxford: Clarendon, 1968), p. 469.

faith (18:8). Why should anyone behave badly? In this use, because they have not been avenged upon their opponent (18:3).

Luke summarizes the main point of the parable: "it is necessary at all times to pray and not behave remissly/become weary" (18:1). The parable or story which illustrates this point runs through 18:2-5. This parable is one of a few parables where to make everything in the story analogous to the concept is extremely dangerous, as we shall see.

saying, some judge was in some city neither fearing God nor respecting humans (18:2).

Jesus begins his story by introducing a judge. Is he an important judge? No, he is a nameless "some" judge in "some" city. The adjective *tis* can mean "some," "a certain," or any." Jesus does not even tell his listeners if his judge was Jewish or Gentile.

Since the judge does not fear God, Jesus probably has here in mind some Gentile judge. Moreover, he is not only any Gentile judge but a judge in some minor city of the province.

Every city had its own legal organization. Greek cities would have a council (*boule*) of several hundred elected members. Jesus speaks here of an individual judge or magistrate who was delegated by the procurator. The Roman magistrates came from the Senate, either yearly or for a specified time. Since public service was not considered by the Romans to be a profession, magistrates received no remuneration except for expenses such as journeys, special celebrations, and military commands. Since Roman judges received no salary, instead they received homage (and corrupt judges might expect bribes).

The magistrate had the power of *imperium* within his jurisdiction. The *imperium* is the supreme administrative power to interpret and execute the law. During the turn of the century the Romans had few specific criminal laws. Outside of Rome there were no formal juries in court. In contrast, the magistrate dispensed justice by personal *cognitio*, his own discretion. Consequently, the common person in the provinces had little protection against the arbitrary and tyrannical abuse of power except against summary execution. Appeals were elaborate and expensive.

The Roman magistrate could be just or unjust. A wealthy magistrate might in fact be concerned for public service. However, the isolated magistrate receiving no salary and having extensive power in a small area with few guiding laws might easily abuse his power. In addition, Gentiles might or might not believe in God's existence, as the popular Stoic philosopher Epictetus explains:

> Concerning gods there are some who say that the divine does not so much as exist; and others, that it exists, indeed, but is inactive and indifferent, and takes forethought for nothing; and a third set, that it exists and takes forethought, though only for great and heavenly things and in no case for terrestrial things: and a fourth set, that it also takes forethought for things terrestrial and the affairs of humans, but only in a general way, and not for the individual in particular and a fifth set, to which Odysseus and Socrates belonged, who say 'Nor when I move am I concealed from thee' (Epic. I, 12:1-3).

Of what kind of person does Jesus speak? Our judge probably would fit in the first or second set: the divine either does not exist or is indifferent. Jesus stresses whom this judge does *not* fear by saying literally, "*God* not fearing and *human* not regarding" (18:2). This judge respects no one in the universe!

The first verb *phobeo* is the most general word for "fear" or "reverence." The middle voice signifies "to be put to flight, to be seized with fear or terror." *Phobeo* can refer to the fear or reverence that is part of faith as Mary says, "God's mercy extends to those fearing God" (Luke 1:50). Jesus tells his disciples that God is to be feared above all because of God's power after death (Luke 12:4-7). The one criminal on the cross who attained Paradise was the one who feared God's power of final sentencing (Luke 23:40). *Phobeo* can also refer to a fear or terror which may precede faith, have nothing to do with faith, or it may even hinder faith. Angels, the warrior spirits, always seem to terrify their audience (Luke 1:12-13, 30; 2:9; 24:5). When Jesus commands the winds to stop, the fish to be caught, the demons to leave "Legion," the ill to be healed, the dead to be raised, the extent of Jesus' power causes fear among those present (Luke 5:10, 26; 7:16; 8:25, 35-37, 50; 24:37). On the other hand, fear can spur people in the wrong direction. The steward who is so terrified of his master that he buries his money makes a grave error (Luke 19:21-24). The teachers of the law and chief priests want to arrest Jesus because they fear the people (Luke 22:2). Fear is a proper reaction to God and to God's actions because God is all-powerful, however it does not necessarily result in belief or in good deeds.

The judge of our parable either did not fear God ("the God" or supreme God) because he believed the divine did not exist or it was inactive or our judge thought that even God could not harm him. The possibility of the last rationale is supported by the parallel phrase "human not regarding." The judge knew that humans existed, even as possibly the judge knew God existed. *Entrepo*, which literally means "to turn in or towards," means to give heed or regard to, to feel shame, respect, or reverence.[9] As God deserves respect, likewise, so do some humans deserve respect. Children should "respect" their parents (Heb. 12:9). Believers who disobey Paul's letters should come to feel "shame" (2 Thess. 3:14). Paul wants to exhort, not to "shame," the Corinthians because they are like beloved children to him, and, supposedly, not like enemies (1 Cor. 4:14). The tenants in the parable do not "respect" the beloved son of the owner as they should have.[10] Similarly, our judge feels no shame or reverence toward any person. Even as a child should feel reverence to a parent, a good person should feel concern for a widow.

Thus, although the name of the judge and the city were insignificant, the character of the judge is quite significant. The correlated participial phrases ("neither fearing God nor respecting humans") tell the reader that this judge had no moral scruples to which anyone could appeal. Jesus in his story has created the least likely person who would be concerned for justice: a potential tyrant with power in a small city who has no reverence toward anyone.

And a widow was in that city and she was coming to him saying, "Procure justice for me from my opponent" (18:3).

Jesus has set the scene for the widow's appearance. She has to contend for justice with the least likely person to give it: a Gentile irreverent magistrate in some nameless city. Jesus places the widow in contrast to the judge by a partial parallel structure: "(some) judge was in (some) city . . . and a widow was in (that) city." The widow is the protagonist, the leading character in the story. She is clearly dwelling not in any nameless town, but "the" city in which we find our judge. Even as Luke seeks to highlight in his gospel Jesus'

---

[9] Thayer, p. 219; Liddell and Scott, p. 577.
[10] Luke 20:13; Matt. 21:37; Mark 12:6.

concern for the oppressed, Luke makes sure he includes this parable showing Jesus' concern for the state of the widows.[11] The judge should be her advocate, but is acting in conjunction with her antagonist. The *antidikos* (*anti*, "over/against," and *dike*, "justice") is an opponent in a suit of law, properly the defendant, but he could also be the plaintiff.[12] As in the parable of the debtor (Matthew 5:25-26 and Luke 12:58-59), the parable of the widow and the judge is set as a suit of law coming before a judge. The widow, not the opponent, is the person who keeps coming (imperfect tense) week after week to the judge. What does she want? She wants justice. *Ekdikeo* comes from *dikes* or *dikos*, "justice," and *ek*, "out of" or "from." The widow wants "justice from" the judge. She wants to be "protected, defended from" the opponent by the judge deciding the case. She wants vindication of her rights. She goes to the proper authorities. She does not seek vengeance herself. As Peter says, rulers are supposed to punish the ones doing wrong and to praise the ones doing good.[13]

What did the opponent want? We are not told. Together with their daughters, Jewish widows, after their husbands died, had the right to be financially maintained by the heirs in her husband's house.[14] Maintenance included food, shelter, clothing, ransom, medical care, and burial. However, Jesus tells us that even religious scribes were attempting to (and succeeding in) "devouring widows' houses," or stealing widows' properties (Luke 20:47; Mark 12:40). Possibly the widow's opponent was trying to take away her property too. If the widow were Jewish, she would most likely have gone to Jewish judges to decide her case. Even as Paul exhorts Christians not to sue another Christian in the secular law courts (1 Cor. 6:1-6), Jews were formally exhorted to handle their legal matters in Jewish courts. Understandably, a legal matter decided under the auspices of

---

[11] However, the Bible does not represent all widows as good (Isa. 9:17; Luke 4:25-26; 1 Tim. 5:6, 11-15.). Luke includes more references to widows (9) than does any other gospel (Mark - 3; Matthew - 0; John - 0). He also records several devout widows: the prophetess Anna, one of the first evangelists; the widow in Zarephath; and the generous widow (Luke 2:37; 4:25-26; 21:2-3).

[12] Liddell and Scott, p. 155.

[13] 1 Pet. 2:14. See also Rom. 13:4; 12:19; 2 Thess. 1:8; 1 Thess. 4:6. An early document illustrates the unjust treatment of a widow and her vindication by a prefect. When the husband of Aurelia Artemis died (his body was still laid out), Syrion, the owner of a flock of sheep which her husband had tended, burst into her house seizing 60 sheep and goats belonging to Aurelia's husband. After Aurelia's complaint, the prefect ordered that the matter be investigated. G.H.R. Horsley, *New Documents Illustrating Early Christianity*, 3 (Macquarie University: Ancient History Documentary Research Centre, 1983), p. 20.

[14] *m. Ketub*. 4:12; 11:1; 12:3; *b. Ketub*. 11.

the Torah was of more authority than a matter decided by "idolators." For instance, "A bill of divorce given under compulsion is valid if it is ordered by an Israelitish court, but if by a gentile court it is invalid; but if the gentiles beat a man and say to him, 'Do what the Israelites bid thee', it is valid" (*m. Git.* 9:8). Rabbi Tarfon, who was prominent between A.D. 120-140, used to say, "In any place where you find heathen law courts, even though their law is the same as the Israelite law, you must not resort to them since it says, *These are the judgements which thou shalt set before them*, that is to say, *'before them'* and not before heathens" (*b. Git.* 88b). So, is our widow not as devout as we might expect? This is most unlikely since Jesus portrays her as innocent. Perhaps she is a Gentile widow. Or, she is a Jewish widow who has not received satisfaction from the Jewish courts. Possibly her opponent is a well respected pious Jewish member of her community whom the judge would not want to anger. Or, possibly her opponent is a Gentile.

Why did Jesus choose a widow to illustrate a person who needs justice? The Greek *chera*, "widow," is the noun form of the verb *chereuo*, "to be without, lack." Henry Thayer says that *chera* is akin also to *chersos*, which means, "dry land, barren."[15] In a patriarchal society, men become protectors of and providers for their wives. In Hebrew a widow, *'almanah* etymologically, is someone separated (*manah*) from her "strength" or "mighty one" (*'el*). In effect, a widow is a woman "lacking" her "strength." Although ancient women were certainly as capable as women today, a woman (ancient or modern) might not have been prepared to sustain herself economically.

Although we usually remember God's self-revelation in Exodus 34:6-7 ("The Lord, the Lord, a God merciful and gracious, slow to anger, and abounding in steadfast love and faithfulness, keeping steadfast love for thousands, forgiving iniquity and transgression and sin, but who will by no means clear the guilty . . ." RSV), we forget Moses' summary of God's revelation in Deuteronomy 10:17-18:

> For the Lord your God [is] the one who is God of the gods
> and Lord of the lords,
> the Mighty ('el), the Great,
> the Strong, and the Wonderful,
> who does not lift up toward faces

---

[15] Thayer, p. 668; Liddell and Scott, pp. 1989-1990.

(in other words, who is not partial)[16]
and does not take bribes.
[God] executes justice for orphan and widow
and loves a stranger
(or foreigner or visitor)
to give to him food and clothing.

People with power might be tempted to misuse it. However, after God pronounces God's great power and strength, God goes on to declare that this power is used for justice, justice in particular for those people usually in a more defenseless position in society: the widow, the orphan, and the stranger. King David remembers that creed of Deuteronomy 10 in his song wherein he exhorts the righteous to sing to the "Father of orphans and judge of widows" (Ps. 68:5). In God widows can find a righteous judge and an ever-strong "Mighty One."

The Old Testament laws include numerous references to the widow, orphan, and stranger. God commands the Israelites not to wrong or oppress a stranger, not to:

> "afflict any widow or orphan. If you do afflict them, and they cry out to me, I will surely hear their cry; and my wrath will burn, and I will kill you with the sword, and your wives shall become widows and your children orphans" (Exod. 22:22-24).

God is promising to avenge the oppression of any widow, orphan, or stranger. While harvesting, Jews were to leave some food unharvested so that widows, orphans, and foreigners could eat. The tithe of every third year was to go to the widows, orphans, foreigners, and Levite priests in the town if people wanted God to bless their work. Jews were never to pervert the justice due to a widow, orphan, or foreigner.[17] Consequently, God becomes known as One who "upholds the widow" and "maintains the widow's boundaries" (Ps. 146:9; Prov. 15:25).

God has a special concern for widows, measures genuine human piety by action done to assist widows, and promises to punish anyone who oppresses widows. One of the reasons God allowed Israel

---

[16] The Greek New Testament has almost an identical phrase to describe God as impartial: "God does not receive or look into a face" (Gal. 2:6; Matt. 22:16). See also Acts 10:34, John 7:24, and Rom. 2:11.

[17] Deut. 14:28-29; 24:17-22; 26:12-13; 27:19. See also Job 29:13; 24:3, 21; 31:16.

and Judah to fall before Assyria and Babylon was that God's people did not "defend the orphan, plead for the widow" (Isa. 1:16-17).[18] Even the Jews in exile and the Jews returning from exile were exhorted not to oppress the widow, orphan, foreigner, or poor.[19] No wonder the psalmist can call on God to be vengeful toward those who "slay the widow and the sojourner, and murder the orphan" (Ps. 94:6).

When Jesus chose a widow for his story, his listeners should have remembered that their God is a judge, an impartial judge, who throughout the years has promised to remember the rights of the widow and who brought the Jews into exile because they were oppressing the widow. Josephus defends Moses' laws against those who malign them by stating that among the Jews, "A judge who accepts bribes suffers capital punishment. He who refuses to a suppliant the aid which he has power to give is accountable to justice" (*Against Apion* II, [27] 207). The widow was a clear case of an innocent person easily oppressed but who should have had justice. The character of the judge in the parable was in complete contrast to the character of the judge of the living and the dead, the righteous judge, God almighty.[20] The early church did not miss God's concern for widows. Widows in need were fed (Acts 6:1). Dorcas, the renowned disciple, made clothing especially for widows (Acts 9:39). A special ministerial order of widows was begun for prayer (1 Tim. 5:3-16). And James, Jesus' brother, could conclude that the true hearer of God's Word worships purely and undefiledly by visiting orphans (or the friendless) and widows in their troubles, guarding against stain from the world (James 1:27). Even the early second century church declared that the "Way of Darkness" includes those who persecute good, hate truth, do not know "righteous judgement, who attend not to the cause of the widow and orphan, spending wakeful nights not in the fear (*phobos*) of God, but in the pursuit of vice" (Barn. 20:2; Did. 5:2).

Thus, Jesus chose a widow for his parable as a clear example of someone innocent who could be an easy prey. Her presence reinforces the lack of piety of the judge and his contrast to God, who uses power to be impartial and justly to defend the defenseless: the widow, the orphan, and the stranger. God has promised to vindicate the oppressed. Indirectly, the reader can learn that as the widow did, one is not wrong to defend one's own rights. Rather, when someone

---

[18] Jer. 7:5-6; 22:3; Isa. 1:23; 10:1-2.

[19] Ezek. 22:7; Zech. 7:10; Mal. 3:5.

[20] Acts 10:42; 2 Tim. 4:8; Heb. 12:23; James 4:12; 5:9.

defenseless has to defend her/his own rights, as in the case of the widow, other people should be ashamed that they did not do it for her/him. The widow used the only godly weapon she had - perseverance. She kept coming. Believers today need to remember to foster the care of widows and others in need, to advocate for anyone who is being oppressed, and to feed and clothe anyone who is in genuine need.

And he was not willing over a period of time. But afterward he said within himself, "If even I do not fear God nor respect people, on account of this widow bringing me trouble I will procure justice for her, lest she wear me out by coming continually" (18:4-5).

The widow kept coming but the judge kept resisting (both the verbs for "come" and "will" are in continuing action tenses.) Jesus leaves in ellipsis what the judge does *not* wish to do. The judge was not wishing or willing. The reader must supply "to procure justice for the widow from her opponent" from the earlier sentence. By omitting this phrase Jesus accentuates the random stubbornness of the judge. In effect, he simply did not wish to do anything. Jesus gives a sense of continued action over time not only by using the imperfect tense for "wish/will," but also by the prepositional phrase "for a while" (*epi*, "for," and *chronos*, "while"). The root meaning of the preposition *epi* is "resting upon." When *epi* is used to express time, it signifies "of extension over a period of time." *Chronos* itself implies "a period of time."[21] Therefore, Jesus has emphasized how very long that judge kept resisting the widow: the judge kept on not wishing for a long period of time.

In parallel to *epi chronos*, "for a while" or "over a period of time," is another prepositional phrase, *meta tauta. Meta*, like *epi*, is a preposition of time. Although the judge kept on not wanting over a period of time, "but" "afterward" he thought a new thought to himself. *Meta* with the accusative case in the New Testament is an expression of succession in time. The root meaning is "midst." A. T. Robertson explains that *meta* means that: "You pass through the midst of this and that event and come to the point where you look back

---

21 A.T. Robertson, *A Grammar of the Greek New Testament in the Light of Historical Research* (Nashville: Broadman, 1934), p. 600; Walter Bauer, *A Greek-English Lexicon of the New Testament and Other Early Christian Literature*, trans. William F. Arndt and F. Wilbur Gingrich (4th ed.; Cambridge: University, 1957), pp. 289, 896.

upon the whole. This idea is 'after.'"[22] In other words, after the judge had passed through that period of time where he kept on not wanting to procure justice for the widow from her enemy, he looked back at those events (*tauta*, "these things") and said, as it were, one day (*lego* in the aorist tense) something new. *Epi chronos* gives the impression of time resting still because we see it all over a long period. *Meta tauta* gives the impression of change because we see the weekly succession of events as we pass through them.

What does the judge say? To begin with, the judge appeals not to his friends or colleagues, but "within himself." Again we see the judge's incredible power and self-direction. He does not even consult with a superior, such as the procurator. Luke records several parables where Jesus indicates what was happening in the minds of his characters. The wealthy person who had a plentiful harvest after filling already several barns, decided to build large storage bins so that he could enjoy himself for many years (Luke 12:17-19). That decision was a mistake. The judge is very much like the wasteful steward in that his decision was approved. The steward decided to prepare for the future by gaining himself friends by being merciful to the debtors (Luke 16:3-4). Both the unrighteous steward and judge make acceptable decisions although for selfish reasons.[23] In contrast, the midnight friend acts correctly; he gives his friend bread. Although he thinks selfishly he should not answer the door, his friend's importunity or boldness forces him to comply (Luke 11:7-8).

Jesus transmits the fictional judge's inner thoughts, even as in reality Jesus can perceive the inner thoughts of those around him.[24] The judge repeats with the same emphasis on "God" and "human" what had been said about him in 18:2: "If even God I do not fear nor human do I respect." The sentence is a type of conditional sentence where the condition or protasis is treated as fulfilled and real. In this case, the condition is an actual case. The phrase *ei kai*, "if even," introduces the condition "as a matter of indifference." As A.T. Robertson says, "The matter is belittled."[25] The judge not only has no respect for God or for humans, but he himself also knows he has no respect for God and for humans, and he also simply does not see this fact as significant. Ironically, Apollo's oracle, carved on the

---

[22] Robertson, p. 612.

[23] "Within himself" or the preposition "in" with the reflexive pronoun appears also in Luke 3:8; 7:39, 49; Matt. 3:9; 9:3, 21; Mark 2:8.

[24] E.g. Mark 2:8; Luke 11:17.

[25] Robertson, p. 1026.

front of the temple at Delphi, "Know thyself," was an apt description of the judge (*Epictetus* III. 1, 18; *Fragments* I). Although Polonius, lord chamberlain, said, "This above all: to thine own self be true, And it must follow, as the night the day, Thou canst not then be false to any man" (*Hamlet* Act 1, Sc II, 78), the judge in our parable was "false" to this woman because he was "true" to his own self. He knew he was thoroughly without reverence, which tells us that although self-knowledge is a helpful aid toward more enjoyable living, it does not necessarily lead to a moral life or even a repentant one.

The judge decides to procure justice for the widow without changing his totally irreverent attitude. Even he, despite his lack of reverence, decides to comply with her request. Why does he procure justice for the widow? He procures justice for her for the very mundane reason that she causes him trouble. She is a nuisance to him. Jesus begins the apodosis or conclusion with the direct object and with a verb made into a noun, thereby stressing "the bringing to me trouble." The phrase *parecho kopos* occurs a few times in the New Testament. For instance, at Simon's house the disciples trouble the woman who anoints Jesus' head by being angry at her wasting expensive oil.[26] *Parecho* is made up of two words: *para*, "near, beside, to the side of" and *echo*, "have, hold." *Parecho* therefore means "to hand over," or "hold" "to the side of." Someone can cause another to have either something favorable or unfavorable. In this case, the person causes another to have something unfavorable - trouble. The noun *kopos* comes from the verb *kopto*, "cut, strike." *Kopos* literally refers to a "striking" or "beating." In a more metaphorical sense, *kopos* is toil and trouble. *Kopos*, like its verbal counterpart *kopoo*, gives prominence to fatigue.[27] In other words, *parecho kopos* gives the picture of one person continually beating another person until the second person feels weary.

The judge repeats the same idea at the end of the sentence: "lest continually coming she *wear me out*." *Hupopiadzo* is a colorful word which signifies "strike under the eye, give a black eye to." *Hupopiadzo* comes from a compound of *hupo*, "under," and *ops*, "the part of the face under the eyes." *Hupopiadzo* is "to beat black and blue, to smite so as to cause bruises and livid spots" under the eyes.[28] Aristotle cites as an example of a metaphor and hyperbole the description of a man:

---

[26] Matt. 26:10. See also Gal. 6:17.
[27] Liddell and Scott, pp. 978-9, 1338; Thayer, pp. 355, 478, 488; Bauer, p. 631.
[28] Thayer, p. 646; Bauer, p. 856; Liddell and Scott, p. 1904.

> whose eye is all black and blue (*hupopiadzo*), "you would have thought he was a basket of mulberries," because the black eye is something purple, but the great quantity constitutes the hyperbole (*Rhetoric* III, XI, 15).

In Proverbs, although "wisdom is an ornament to the young, but grey hairs are the glory of elders; *bruises* and contusions befall the bad; and plagues shall come unto the inward parts of their belly" (Prov. 20:29-30 LXX). Paul uses the same word to describe the discipline he gives his body, using the metaphor of boxing. Paul does not "beat the air." Rather he disciplines his body by "*beating it black and blue* and bringing it under control" (1 Cor. 9:27). Boxing, the most laborious branch of athletics, as many other Greek sports, was in reality a preparation for war. Blows were confined to the adversary's head. It was invented by the Spartans to learn to ward off blows to the head and to harden the face. So when Paul says he "beats [his face] black and blue," he means that he learns to harden his face so that he can be protected from blows to the head. The boxer would wear *sphairai*, sharp lengthy leather thongs of ox-hide extending from the hand almost to the elbow. In Greek boxing the competitors fought not for a specific time but usually until one or the other acknowledged defeat by holding up the hand. Competitors were not classified by weights, which gave the advantage to heavy-weights. Boxers relied mostly on self-defense.[29] Dio Chrysostom notes that athletes, like soldiers "are overcome more by their exhaustion than by their wounds" (*Discourse* XXVIII.8). He extols the boxer Melancomas, renowned for his self-control and courage, who could box two whole days and defeat his opponent by exhausting him:

> He won all his victories without being hit himself or hitting his opponent, so far superior was he in strength and in his power of endurance. For often he would fight throughout the whole day, in the hottest season of the year, and although he could have more quickly won the contest by striking a blow, he refused to do it . . . but he held that it was the truest victory when he forced his opponent, although uninjured, to give up (*Discourse* XXIX.12; XXVIII, 7-8).

---

[29] E. Norman Gardiner, *Athletics of the Ancient World* (Chicago: Ares, 1930), pp. 197-208.

In other words, the heavy-weight judge had become so weary by the head wounds or the tiring tactics of the widow (her continual coming to ask him the same question - "Vindicate me from my opponent") that he raised his hand to concede the match before he had a total collapse from exhaustion and his face became totally disfigured.

The widow caused trouble or became troublesome to the judge because of the repetition. She won over the judge by her endurance, his weariness. She is like the friend at midnight. He too became bothersome (*parecho kopos*), but for a different reason, because of the impractical hour and situation. The friend came in the middle of the night. Although the householder was already awakened (which was inconvenient enough), now he would have to unlock the gate and wake up all his children sleeping next to him. The friend was "shameless." Like the judge he had no fear of his neighbor's anger. The widow persisted week after week. The midnight friend knocked at a most impractical time.

And the Lord said, "Hear what the unjust judge says: but might not God accomplish the vindication of his elect crying out to him day and night and be long-suffering with them? (18:6-7)

Jesus' parable or story extends through 18:2-5. Luke gives the central point of the parable in verse 1. Now Luke cites Jesus giving the central point. A parable, as any analogy, is similar to its concept only to a certain degree, after which an analogy is "stretched" beyond its original intention. Jesus begins his challenges to his listeners by limiting his analogy: "Hear what the unjust judge says" (18:6). The judge is "unjust" in two ways. First, the judge is literally unjust because he does not want to procure justice for the widow. He has no regard for God or humans. He refuses to give aid, which he has the power to give. An impartial judge is one who will especially defend the defenseless. Second, the judge is unjust because he is probably a Gentile. The plural noun form of "unjust" (*adikos*) was used by Jews to describe Gentiles. For instance, Paul calls all Gentile judges "the unjust," meaning "non-believers": "How can any of you dare when having a grievance against another [believer] go to law before the *unjust* and not before the saints?" (1 Cor. 6:1). Consequently, by calling the judge "unjust," Jesus has set this judge as a contrast to a "just" judge and certainly to The "just" Judge - God, who is a just and impartial judge, especially in the case of widows. What does the *unjust* judge say? "If even I do not fear God nor respect people, on account of this widow bringing me trouble I will procure justice for her, lest she wear me out by coming continually" (18:4-5). The only similarity between God and the unjust judge is that both did procure justice (*ekdikeo*) for the widow. The unjust judge vindicated the widow for selfish reasons. She was a tiresome nuisance.

Therefore, Jesus asks, "but might not God accomplish the vindication of his elect crying out to him day and night and be long-suffering with them?" (18:7). The widow had simply asked for her rights (*ekdikeo*). God now will "accomplish the vindication": the noun form of *ekdikeo* (*ekdikesis*) and the verb "to make" (*poieo*). The verb "make" adds a sense of solemnity and finality to God's "vindication." Jesus uses a double negative, *ou me*, with the aorist subjunctive (the futuristic subjunctive) of "make." In interrogative sentences *ou* always expects an affirmative answer. The second negative, *me*, strengthens the affirmation. In other words, Jesus asks rhetorically, "Will not God surely accomplish the vindication of the elect?" The answer for the future is, "Yes." Again, as in the earlier context of Chapter 17, Jesus speaks about the future. Jesus uses the subjunctive mood instead of the future because in his rhetorical question he wants to express the listeners' doubt, hesitation, anticipation, and hope.

For whom will God accomplish the vindication? Whose wrongs will be made right? God's concern is a necessary one because it is for "his elect, the ones crying out to him day and night." How could God not want justice for those people who had been chosen by God? The Old Testament shows that God chooses the widow, orphan, and stranger. By using the term "elect" instead of "believers" or "saints" or "gathering" or "disciples," Jesus brings out the special relationship the church has with God. One of the things the church is "elected" or "picked out" or "chosen" for is for suffering in behalf of its testimony to Jesus Christ. The widow is like the martyrs with the Lamb or the elect lady or the dispersed church, they were chosen for obedience and "sprinkling with the blood of Jesus Christ."[30] They have had to be persevering or faithful in order to endure innocent suffering.

Although the meek do inherit the earth, God does not require them to suffer in silence. These elect ones have been "crying out" to God. Jesus uses the same word to describe the chosen ones which later will be used to describe Jesus. *Boao* is "I shout" or "I say aloud"

---

[30] Rev. 17:14; 6:10; 2 John 1, 13; 1 Pet. 1:1-2; 2:4, 9; 5:13.

to manifest internal feelings. Jesus *cried out* at the cross in pain and possibly for help: "My God, my God, why have you abandoned me?" (Matt. 27:46-47; Mark 15:34-35). These elect persons continue to shout out as shown not only by the participle, "crying," but also by the descriptive phrase "day and night." "Day and night" is in the genitive case ending, which is used to describe "kind of time" or "time within which."[31] Unlike the widow Anna, who prayed regularly all through the night until the day (Luke 2:37), the elect pray both during the day and during the night. And when they pray, they are shouting aloud in great pain. Might not God accomplish justice for the people God has chosen who are every day crying out in pain? The martyrs who had been killed because of their testimony to God are like our widow. They too cry (not *boao*) in a loud voice for justice (*ekdikeo;* Rev. 6:10). Vindication is very close to revenge, which is why only God should undertake revenge. However, we think vindication is a rare pure act in which someone who has been regarded or treated as in the wrong is now seen to be in the right or truthful. It does not necessarily have to do with another person's punishment. Vindication has to do with truth. Revenge, in its human manifestation, simply is causing another person to be punished in retribution: "an eye for an eye." However, usually what we do is remove someone's head when they have thrown dust into our eye.

Many interpreters would have been delighted if Jesus' rhetorical question had not included the last four words, literally "and is (God) long-suffering or patient with them?" If the answer is "yes," is not "patience" the opposite of "vindication"? And, who is "them"? Some early Christians tried to solve the dilemma by making *makrothumeo* ("long-suffering") into a participle. Jesus then would have said: Might not God vindicate his elect crying out to him day and night and *being long-suffering* against them? In other words, the elect both cry and are long-suffering (or endure) the injustice of "them" (unjust people like the judge). As clear as such a solution might be, the oldest and best quality Greek manuscripts and the most variety of families have *makrothumeo* in the finite verb, the present active indicative.[32]

Other interpreters such as Henry Thayer have kept the best Greek texts but concluded that "them" refers to the unjust people.

---

[31] Robertson, p. 495.

[32] E.g. codices Sinaiticus, Vaticanus (4-Century), Bezae, Koridethi. Only codex Washington (4-5 century), family 13, and later Byzantine texts have the participle.

Jesus, the son of Sirach, has a passage in Ecclesiasticus very similar to Jesus' parable. He recounts that the Lord is a just judge and will hear the prayer of the oppressed, the orphan, and the widow:

> The Lord will not be slow,
> neither will he *be patient* with the wicked,
> until he crushes the sinews of the merciless
> and sends retribution on the heathen;
> until he blots out the insolent, one and all,
> and breaks the power of the unjust
> (Ecclus. 35:18 NEB) (32:18 in the LXX).

The same three words occur in Luke 18:7, "be patient with them" (*makrothumeo epi autois*). The pronoun "them" in Ecclesiasticus refers to the noun following it, "the merciless." Henry Thayer says that Jesus' parable "certainly demands the notion of slowness on God's part in avenging the right."[33] Jesus would then have said, "Might not God vindicate his elect . . . and be long-suffering with [the unjust]?" In other words, God wants to be loving to the oppressed and to the oppressor. However, Jesus has been mainly *contrasting* God's behavior with the behavior of the judge. The judge's slowness illustrates the judge's injustice. Moreover, unlike in Ecclesiasticus, "them" in the parable would most usually refer to the antecedent "elect." Sirach has a similar message to Jesus' in that both of them hearken back to the rich Old Testament revelations of God's concern for the widow. However, Sirach's emphasis is on the punishment of the unmerciful (certainly not God's patience with them) rather than Jesus' emphasis on the comfort of the oppressed and the faith of the true believer. Sirach even stresses how the truly humble person must not "desist" praying until "the Most High intervenes" (Ecclus. 35:17), whereas Jesus stresses how God's very nature is to be sympathetic with the oppressed person.

Walter Bauer recommends that the "difficult to interpret" clause may best be translated, "will he delay long over them?"[34] To translate the second clause in this manner, in effect, the translator must divide the sentence into two questions: "But might not God vindicate his elect crying out to him day and night?" would be answered "Yes" as indicated by the *ou me*. And "will he delay long over them?" would be answered "No." The present indicative question is "rather a rhetorical way of putting a negation than a question of

---

[33] Thayer, p. 387.
[34] Bauer, p. 489.

doubt."[35] Or else, if verse 7 were to remain as one sentence, it would have two different answers: Yes and No. This interpretation is certainly possible. However, it does necessitate ignoring the punctuation of our current Greek texts. Even the third and fourth century manuscripts codex Sinaiticus and papyrus 75 have a brief space only *after* verse 7. Another difficulty these interpreters have to handle is how can God *not* be patient when in Exodus 34:6 one of God's essential attributes is patience.

We think, most likely, the two clauses are parallel ones. God does vindicate the elect and is long-suffering concerning the elect. What then can this mean? Alfred Plummer suggests that God is "long-suffering" in the sense that God is always patient with the elect's complaints: "God listens to the ceaseless crying of His saints with willingness and pleasure." In other words, God "endures" their "cries." Plummer adds, "However long the answer to prayer may *seem* to be delayed, constant faithful prayer always *is* answered."[36] Joachim Jeremias comes to a similar conclusion. He mentions that the change of mood of "make" (*poieo*) in the subjunctive to "is patient" in the indicative (*makrothumeo*) makes the second clause an independent sentence. Literally rendered it reads, "And will not God give judgment in favour of his elect, who cry to him day and night? And he has patience with them." However, he renders the second "sentence" as a relative clause, "Will not God give judgement in favour of his elect, he who listens patiently to them when they cry to him day and night?"[37] However, what would be the point of God vindicating the elect and at the same time being patient to hear their complaints? Justice would quickly end all complaints of the truly oppressed.

What we would like to suggest is another aspect of long-suffering. *Makrothumeo* can mean not only endurance, but it can also serve as a synonym for mercy and compassion. *Makrothumeo* is made up of two words: *makros*, "long, lasting long," and *thumos*, "feeling and thought, esp. of strong feeling and passion." *Thumos* can then also mean "anger forthwith boiling up and soon subsiding again" or simply "glow, ardor." The verb form *thumoo* signifies

---

[35] Robertson, p. 880.

[36] Alfred Plummer, *A Critical and Exegetical Commentary on the Gospel According to S. Luke*, The International Critical Commentary (5th ed.; Edinburgh: T. and T. Clark, 1922), p. 414.

[37] Joachim Jeremias, *The Parables of Jesus*, trans. S.H. Hooke (London: SCM Press, 1954), p. 116.

"provoke to anger."[38] "Long-suffering," therefore, is an apt translation of *makrothumeo*. *Makrothumeo* literally signifies the holding of strong feelings over a long time. *Makrothumeo* can certainly signify "endurance." James, the Lord's brother, writes a similar message to Luke 18:1-8. He comforts his (apparently) poor Christian reader by saying that the rich who oppress their laborers have been condemned (James 5:1-11). The judge will appear at any minute. Therefore, he tells them to be patient or long-suffering (James 5:7, 8, 10). In James 5:11 he uses *hupomeno* as a synonym for *makrothumeo*. *Hupomeno* signifies "endure, stand firm, hold out, bear, remain." In other words, James wants the Christians to continue in their faith in a just God: "Behold we call happy the ones standing firm" (5:11).[39]

Makrothumeo can also have the connotation of "compassion." One of the central self-revelations about God was revealed to Moses at Mount Sinai, "The Lord, the Lord, a God merciful and gracious, *slow to anger*, and abounding in steadfast love and faithfulness" (Exod. 34:6 RSV). The Hebrew phrase, *'erek 'apaim*, like the Greek verb, literally signifies "long anger" or "forbearing." *Makrothumeo* seems to be a synonym for merciful, gracious, and abounding in steadfast love. God holds on to strong feeling over a long time, or is compassionate, which results in mercy. *Makrothumeo* is used in this sense of compassion, as a synonym for mercy, several times in Hebrew literature. According to Proverbs 19:11, "a merciful man is *long-suffering*." The Son of Sirach says, "As a drop of water unto the sea, and a gravelstone in comparison to the sand; so are a thousand years to the days of eternity. Therefore is God *patient* with them (*epi autois*), and poureth forth his mercy upon them" (Ecclus. 18:10-11). Sirach's analogy is similar to Peter's which says that "with the Lord one day is as a thousand years, and a thousand years as one day. The Lord is not slow about his promise as some count slowness, but is *forbearing* toward you, not wishing that any should perish, but that all should reach repentance" (2 Peter 3:8-9 RSV). Again, in both passages, *makrothumeo* is a synonym of mercy. Furthermore, even as Peter mentions God's compassion (*makrothumeo*), followed by a warning that the day of the Lord will come suddenly (2 Peter 3:10), so too Jesus concludes the passage in Luke 18:1-8 with a call for preparation for his return. Sirach again parallels *makrothumeo* and mercy in Ecclesiasticus 29:8: "*have patience* with a person in poor estate, and delay not to show mercy." The writer of 2 Maccabees also

---

[38] Liddell and Scott, p. 810; Thayer, pp. 293, 387.
[39] See also Heb. 6:15; Isa. 57:15.

employs *makrothumeo* as a word of compassion: "For not as with other nations, the Lord waits expectantly *while long-suffering* until they come to the fulness of their sins, does he deal with us" (2 Macc. 6:14). Paul calls *makrothumeo* a characteristic of love, together with kindness (1 Cor. 13:4), and a fruit of the Spirit, together with love, joy, peace, kindness, goodness, and faithfulness, gentleness, and self-control (Gal. 5:22-23). He exhorts Christians to be patient (or compassionate?) with idlers, the fainthearted, and weak (1 Thess. 5:14). Finally, if *makrothumeo* is translated as "compassionate," it clarifies another of Jesus' parables. The laborer who had never paid the fifteen years worth of salary he owed to the king asked him to be patient (or better, compassionate) and he would pay him everything. By granting more time, the king would be merciful (Matt. 18:26, 29). The king forgave the whole debt.

In other words, Jesus would be rhetorically asking his listeners, if the unjust Gentile judge vindicates the widow, do you not think God - the just impartial Judge - will surely accomplish the vindications of those people, such as the widow, chosen by God and especially dear to God who are shouting aloud in pain at all times and be compassionate with them? God will vindicate those whom God loves and be compassionate with them. God will show compassion to the elect by procuring the justice they ask or by being merciful regarding their own sins. The disciple must not only be called and "chosen," but also "faithful" (Rev. 17:14). This story has only a limited analogy with the concept being taught. He employs the Jewish *qal wahomer* rule for evidence - what applies in a less important case will certainly apply in a more important case (*tos. Sanh.* 7:11). As in Luke 11:3, Jesus mainly contrasts human behavior with God's behavior: "Therefore if you (being evil) know to give good gifts to your children, how much more the Father/Parent from heaven will give the Holy Spirit to them who ask him?" Luke 18:6-7 could be rephrased, "If even your unjust Gentile judge can vindicate the widow, how much more will the compassionate just and impartial Judge vindicate people chosen by the Judge who are in pain?"

I say to you that [God] will accomplish their vindication speedily. However, when the Son/Heir of Humanity comes, will he find faith on earth? (18:8)

In case anyone should misunderstand the earlier rhetorical question (we can not imagine how), Jesus answers the question with his definitive pleonasm "I say to you,"[40] "God will accomplish their vindication." If in the earlier question Jesus expresses the listeners' doubt, hesitation, anticipation and hope by using the subjunctive mood, "might accomplish," now he switches to the future tense, "will accomplish." The most common use of the future is predictive, what will happen. Jesus declares authoritatively that God will vindicate the elect. When? The answer is "speedily" (*en tachos*).

Tachos is a noun signifying "swiftness and speed." In the plural *tachos* refers to "velocities." *Tachos* can refer to quickness of temper or apprehension. The adjective *tachus* also signifies quickness of motion as opposed to *bradus*, "slow." *Tachos* is usually translated in the New Testament "quickly, at once, without delay," or "soon, in a short time."[41] For instance, the angel of the Lord told Peter to "rise quickly" from his chains and God warned Paul to get "quickly" out of Jerusalem.[42] When the governor Festus told Paul's adversaries that he intended "quickly" to go to Caesarea from Jerusalem, he did not leave for eight or ten days (Acts 25:4-6). Consequently, *tachos* can signify "soon." Paul tells his Roman readers that the God of peace "will quickly" crush Satan if they avoid the evil people who create dissensions and difficulties (Rom. 16:20). John is told the revelation "will quickly" take place (Rev. 1:1; 22:6). If "quickly" refers to time, then the revelation would probably refer to the end of the Roman persecution. Taken literally, Jesus says that like the unjust judge, God will procure justice, but unlike the unjust judge, God will procure justice quickly. We might wonder if God's sense of "quick" might be different from our "quick" (to us a millenium is certainly not like a day), however, Jesus alludes to no such delay. (Yet the elect have been crying "day and night"!)

While the elect might be tempted to spend their time criticizing or analyzing the degree of speed on God's part, Jesus, as he always does, challenges the listeners with their responsibility. Jesus had been speaking to his disciples and to skeptical Pharisees. Certainly the religious lay leaders of Jesus' time would feel that they were the faithful ones. Jesus' question ("Will the Son find faith on earth?") certainly would be addressed to them. Nevertheless, Jesus does not always tightly differentiate the disciple from the skeptic. When Peter asks if the parable of the waiting servants is "for us or for all," Jesus simply defines a "faithful steward" and allows the listeners to see if

[40] E.g. Luke 11:8, 9; 18:14.
[41] Liddell and Scott, pp. 327, 1762; Bauer, pp. 814-5.
[42] Acts 12:7; 22:18.

they qualify (Luke 12:41-42). The elect might look to the future for their vindication. That vindication might or might not come before the second coming of the Lord. "However" when Christ returns will they themselves be ready? God "will accomplish" vindication but "will [God] find faith? Jesus uses the interrogative particle *ara* which looks forward. It indicates "anxiety or impatience" on the part of the questioner.[43] In Galatians 2:17, *ara* expects a negative answer: "Is Christ then an agent of sin? Certainly not!" When Philip ran up to the Ethiopian treasurer, he asked, "Do you understand what you are reading?" The answer was "no." "How can I, unless some one guides me?" (Acts 8:30-31). So possibly Jesus did not expect a favorable answer. God promises always to be just and compassionate and faithful. Humans are not so consistent.

Jesus reintroduces the concept of faith mentioned earlier in 17:5-10. Faith is something for which the disciples asked. All they needed was the smallest amount of it (17:6). Faith is illustrated by obedience, doing what is commanded, and by appreciation and humility (17:10, 15-19). Faith is remembering to please God instead of being side-tracked onto other goals.

Throughout Luke's gospel, faith is the mental acceptance of a statement of truth which results in behavioral action such as that of the people in the parable who hear God's word, hold it fast in their hearts, and bring forth fruit.[44] Jesus ends the parable of the widow and the judge with our responsibility. Do we remember that when we cry out for justice against someone else, that that self-same justice will be meted out to us? Have we been asking God to help us accept the truth of God's promises? Have we been thanking God for all the benefits God has been bestowing on us? Have we been setting our priorities to achieve the advancement of God's reign? In this parable Jesus has taught a similar message to the one he gave at the temple. Will we be able to endure the cares of this world, ready to stand approved before God's Heir, the impartial but just God (Luke 21:34-36)?

Luke had told us that the parable of the widow and the judge had something to do with prayer. What have we learned? This parable is particularly pertinent to the persons who are suffering unjustly, who are becoming weary and might lose their faith in God because they have not received justice from an opponent. Jesus

---

[43] Robertson, p. 1176; Bauer, p. 103; Thayer, p. 71.

[44] Luke 8:12-15. See also Luke 1:45, 20; 22:32; 24:25.

teaches that in continual prayer, or devout communication to God, these persons express their trust in God. First of all, God is like these suffering persons because Jesus too was on his way "to Jerusalem," the place where he must suffer unjustly and where he would cry out in anguish to God-in-heaven. Second, God is an impartial and compassionate Judge who has a special concern for widows and promises swiftly to punish anyone who oppresses widows. Third, even a Gentile judge who was a nameless tyrant in a small city, respecting no one (and seeing this irreverence as insignificant), acting stubbornly and selfishly, can grant justice. Consequently, we, like the Pharisees, who were looking for signs of God's reign, do not want to be side-tracked by seeking to find out when God will return or bring retribution. We, unlike the widow, do not need to begin a boxing match with God in order to get results. God wants us to share our feelings. God is sympathetic to our needs. God promises results. Rather, we simply need to trust God and then go on to live faithful lives, lives of obedience wherein God's reign has priority.

The Parable of the Tax-Collector and the Pharisee

If the last parable might invite the Pharisees to be an audience, this parable definitely includes them. In some ways the two parables seem very different. Luke introduces this parable by writing "and he also said . . . this parable." The adverb "also" connects the two parables, while the adjective "this" highlights their distinctiveness. The point and audience of each parable are different. In the first parable Jesus creates as the heroine an innocent widow. The second parable has as a hero a sinful tax-collector. Yet, both parables have to do with prayer and its relationship to the last judgment.

And he also said this parable to some relying upon themselves that they are righteous and despising the others (18:9):

This parable is addressed to those people who rely upon themselves. How can anyone with a modicum of Bible training ever identify with this audience? We have been all taught that "Blessed are all who take refuge in God" (Ps. 2:12) and "Trust in the Lord with all your heart and do not rely on your own insight" (Prov. 3:5). The Hebrew warriors in the Old Testament who relied on the Lord were always the ones who defeated their enemies, whereas those people who relied on their weapons and defenses were always themselves defeated.[45] Paul and Timothy learned to rely not on themselves but on God, who raises the dead, through the extensive afflictions they received in Asia (2 Cor. 1:9). Even Jesus, God incarnate, put his trust in God-in-heaven when he came to earth (Heb. 2:13). How can any of us ever identify with those who have been relying and continue to rely upon themselves?

The Greek word for "rely" is *peitho*, allied with the noun "faith" (*pistis*), which comes from "to bind." The transitive verb signifies "to persuade," "to make friends of" from which idea the Greeks created the goddess "Persuasion," an attendant to Aphrodite. The intransitive verb signifies "to trust, have confidence," obey, rely on.[46] A warrior can rely on armor, and without it is defeated (Luke 11:22). In effect, *peitho* in Luke 18:9 has the sense of trusting or having confidence in oneself so as to rely on oneself.

To be self-reliant is truly a Western philosophy no matter how much one chooses to ignore that fact. From Robert J. Ringer's bestseller *Looking Out For #1*, "You and you alone will be responsible for your success or failure," to William Ernest Henley's unconquerable "I am the master of my fate; I am the captain of my soul,"[47] our western culture has lauded the self-reliant person. Self-reliance is an old virtue, as old at least as the Stoics: "No one is free who is not master of himself."[48] Although Epictetus says that when we have lost a brother or son or friend, we are left forlorn, without help:

> But one ought none the less to prepare oneself for this also, that is, to be able to be self-sufficient, to be able to commune with oneself; even as Zeus communes with himself, and is at peace with himself, . . . so ought we also to be able to converse with ourselves, not to be in need of others (*Discourse* III. 13, 6-7).

So, the Christian has two philosophies vying for attention: to rely on yourself is to have Pride and to rely on yourself is to be Mature.

---

[45] Deut. 28:52; 2 Chron. 14:11; Isa. 31:1.

[46] Thayer, p. 497; Liddell and Scott, pp. 1353-1354.

[47] Robert J. Ringer, *Looking Out For #1* (New York: Funk and Wagnalls, 1977), p. x; William Ernest Henley, "Invictus."

[48] Ascribed to Epictetus and to Pythagoras (*Arrian's Discourses of Epictetus*, Fragment 35).

Luke specifies exactly which kind of self-reliance Jesus has been discussing, "that they were righteous." Jesus here disparages not so much self-reliance in general but a very specific type of self-reliance, relying upon oneself for righteousness. Paul discusses the same concept but in different words in Philippians 3:3 when he says that "we do not have confidence in the flesh." The "flesh" for Paul includes such things as would exemplify a righteous Jew: circumcision on the eighth day, Hebrew of Hebrew parents, a zealous Pharisee following the oral law in every detail (Phil. 3:5-6). Christians are trained to repeat after someone praises them, "Not I, but the Lord!" However, no one can escape the responsibility of identifying with some culprit in this parable. If we say (or think) we, in contrast, are not relying on our own righteousness, by saying that, we are in effect treating with contempt those who rely on themselves, thereby being self-righteous! If we finished hearing the parable of the widow and the judge by feeling good about being better than the judge, again this parable would condemn us as self-righteous.

Luke carefully explains the audience of this parable as "the ones relying upon themselves that they are righteous and despising the rest." Relying and despising are participles indicating that these people continue regularly to rely and to despise. *Exoutheneo* can mean "to make of no account, to despise utterly . . . to treat with contempt." Jesus was scorned or treated with contempt when before the crucifixion the soldiers mocked him, crowned him with thorns, and clothed him with a purple robe, kneeled in homage, and spit on him (Luke 23:11; Mark 15:19; Ps. 22:7). The root *exothen* signifies "from without or abroad." The verb form *exotheo* means "to thrust out, force out."[49] In a sense, contempt or scorn comes from treating another person as outside one's own community. Consequently, the soldiers could mock Jesus because he was now "a criminal," even as one jailer once told us that all the inmates at a prison were "animals" and therefore volunteers should not bother with them. Paul speaks several times about despising. He tells Christians not to despise those people who eat only vegetables and not to despise prophesying. He praises the Galatians for not despising Paul himself because he preached to them with a bodily ailment and he urges the Corinthians not to despise Timothy, his representative.[50] Paul's opponents thought Paul's speaking style was contemptible (2 Cor. 10:10). The wonder is that God should choose what the world despises or treats as "outside" to be "inside" (1 Cor. 1:28).

---

[49] Liddell and Scott, pp. 598, 600; Thayer, p. 225.
[50] Rom. 14:3; 1 Thess. 5:20; Gal. 4:14; 1 Cor. 16:11.

If God was scorned and chose those who are scorned, contempt can have no place in God's reign. In effect, the scorned scapegoat which had been driven outside the Israelite camp has become an approved lamb because Jesus has become that goat by taking on the sins of the world.[51] The judge might have been an atheistic irreverent tyrant, however, even he did not despise the widow. Here we have probably the most insidious sin of the synagogue yesterday and the church today: the scorning of those who can not measure up to one's own standards of righteousness.

Two people went up into the temple to pray, the one a Pharisee and the other a tax-collector (18:10).

Jesus does not use the sex-specific term "male" (*aner*), but the generic term "human" or "person" (*anthropos*). However, in 18:13 the masculine pronoun is used for the tax-collector. Moreover, very few women would ever become Pharisees because women were exempt from studying the law.[52] Jesus speaks generically about two men probably because what he says is true of men and women. In addition, whereas in the last parable a woman is the heroine, in this parable a man is the hero.

These two people "went up" to pray in the temple because the temple was built on a hill. Jerusalem itself, built on a plateau 2500 feet above sea level, was surrounded by hills, forcing people to go *up* to Jerusalem.[53] People would go up to the holy city and up higher to the holier temple:

> [Jerusalem] is still more holy [than the Land of Israel or any other walled city in Israel], for there [only] they may eat the Lesser Holy Things and the Second Tithe. The Temple Mount is still more holy, for no man or woman that has a flux, no menstruant, and no woman after childbirth may enter therein. The Rampart is still more holy, for no gentiles and none that have contracted uncleanness from a corpse may enter therein. The Court of the Women is still more holy, for none that immersed

---

[51] See Lev. 16:8-10.

[52] *M. Kidd.* 1:7. For further details see Spencer, *Beyond the Curse: Women Called to Ministry*, pp. 46-57.

[53] Ps. 125:2; Luke 10:30.

> himself the selfsame day [because of uncleanness] may enter therein, yet none would thereby become liable to a Sin-offering. The Court of the Israelites is still more holy, for none whose atonement is yet incomplete may enter therein, and they would hereby become liable to a Sin-offering. The Court of Priests is still more holy, for Israelites may not enter therein save only when they must perform the laying on of hands, slaughtering, and waving (*m. Kelim* 1:8).

Every devout Jew was proud of the temple of Jerusalem, one of the magnificent ancient structures. It was made of white polished marble covered with plates of gold with roofs adorned with cedar and gates covered with gold and silver. Josephus says the temple:

> at the first rising of the sun reflected back a very fiery splendour, and made those who forced themselves to look upon it, to turn their eyes away, just as they would have done at the sun's own rays. But this temple appeared to strangers, when they were coming to it at a distance, like a mountain covered with snow; for as to those parts of it that were not gilt, they were exceeding white (*War*. V. 5. 6).

Not only was the temple on a rocky ascent, but every court was higher as it approached the inner sanctuary. The Gentiles' Court was 14 steps lower than the Women's Court. The Women's Court was 15 steps lower than the Israelite Court (for pure Jewish males), which was lower than the Priest's Court. The sanctuary (*naos* or Holy Place and Holy of Holies) was several steps higher than the Priest's Court. The "temple" (*hieron*) included all the courts and all the temple buildings.

Women were not allowed into the Israelite Court nor impure men nor Gentiles. The Mishnah explains that a man with a third grade derived uncleanness whose "atonement is yet incomplete" may also not enter the Court of the Israelites (m. Kelim 1:8). An "incomplete atonement" would pertain to persons who had passed through the prescribed time of uncleanness, immersed themselves, awaited the sunset, but not yet brought the prescribed Sin-offerings. Would a tax-collector have gone to the Israelite's Court? Probably since uncleanness comes from sin (Ps. 51:2), even if the tax-collector had repented of his sin of robbery, he may not yet have gone through the prescribed ritual of repentance. Moreover, we are told that the tax-collector was "at a distance" (18:13) from (probably) the Priests' Court where he could see the offerings. Probably then the tax-collector was praying in the large open-air Women's Court close to the outside gate which kept out the Gentiles.

Both the Pharisee and the tax-collector went to the temple to pray during one of the three times of daily prayer, where the prayer of the people "ascended up" to God in conjunction with the offerings of people. The morning prayer was shortly after sunrise at the time of the burnt offering. It included the *Tefillah* (benedictions) and the *Shema'*.[54] The afternoon or ninth hour of prayer (3:00 P.M.) included only the *Tefillah*. The evening or sunset prayer included the *Tefillah* and the *Shema'*. A priest would announce these three hours of prayer by blowing the *shofar*, a ram's horn, which was so loud it could be heard as far as Jericho, over 10 miles away (*m. Tamid* 3:8). These two people came up to the temple to pray at one of these three times. They could have prayed at their homes or places of work. However, their piety is shown by their going up to the temple.

The One a Pharisee. Jesus sets up a contrast between these two people by the parallel phrases: "the one Pharisee . . . the other tax-collector." The Pharisees were a devout lay people very influential in the synagogue and in daily life. If God had commanded the priests to be ritually pure during the times of worship, the Pharisees wanted to extend the ritual purity to their daily life. They stressed the authoritative two-fold law: the written Hebrew Scriptures and their own oral traditions. The Hasidaean protestors who developed during the time of the Maccabeans in the second century B.C. probably developed into three groups: the Essenes, the Zealots, and the Pharisees. The Sadducees were the descendents of Zadok, David's high priest. The Pharisees and Sadducees are first mentioned during the reign of Jonathan.[55] They emerge as definite parties during the reign of Hyrcanus II (135-104 B.C.).

"Pharisees" is a Greek transliteration (*pharisaiou*) of the Hebrew *perushim*, "the separated ones." They obtained ritual purity by separation from uncleanness and from unclean persons. For example, Mark explains that the Pharisees:

> do not eat unless they wash their hands, observing the tradition of the elders; and when they come from the

---

[54] The repetition of Deut. 6:4-9; 11:13-21; Num. 15:37-41.

[55] 161-142 B.C.; *Antiquities* XIII, 5.9 [171].

> market place, they do not eat unless they purify themselves; and there are many other traditions which they observe, the washing of cups and pots and vessels of bronze (Mark 7:3-4).

Josephus says that among the different Jewish schools of thought the Pharisees "are considered the most accurate interpreters of the laws, and hold the position of the leading sect." Paul too claims they are "the strictest party" of the Jewish religion (Acts 26:5).

Often in the gospels the Pharisees are the people who evaluate Jesus' theology and the propriety of differing acts of healing.[56] The Pharisees believed good people were resurrected from the dead (Acts 23:6-8). Unlike the Sadducees, according to Josephus, they "are affectionate to each other and cultivate harmonious relations with the community" (*War* II.8.14 [162-166]). Although Josephus claimed that they simplified their standard of living, "making no concession to luxury," Luke claimed they were "lovers of money."[57]

The New Testament describes some Pharisees in laudable terms: the Pharisees who warned Jesus that Herod wanted to kill him; Nicodemus (although he did come by night); Rabbi Gamaliel; Paul; and some early Christian believers. Several Pharisees invited Jesus to dinner.[58] Nevertheless, Jesus' most severe criticisms are aimed at these pious people who, intending all the more by their devotion to the law to glorify God, have neglected the very essence of the law, becoming "whitewashed tombs, which outwardly appear beautiful, but within they are full of bones of the dead and all uncleanness" (Matt. 23:27).

The other a tax-collector. In the last parable the heroine is a widow, someone that the Jews would have considered innocently oppressed. However, in this story the hero will be a tax-collector, one of those persons usually considered to be a robber and a traitor to his country, an oppressor who becomes oppressed by the rejection received.

The *telones* or "tax-collector, tax reformer" was the highest local bidder for the right to collect taxes. Roman censors were

---

[56] E. g. John 7:32; 8:13; 9:13; Matt. 12:14, 24; Luke 5:21.

[57] Luke 16:14; *Antiquities* XVIII, 1, 3 [12].

[58] Luke 7:36; 11:37; 13:31; 14:1; John 3:1; 7:45-52; Acts 5:33-40; 15:5; 23:6; Phil. 3:5.

appointed every four years to collect the direct taxes or *tributum*. They delegated the collection of provincial taxes to a *publicani*, closely associated with the equestrian order, the second rank of Roman nobility from which the cavalry was drawn.[59] The *publicani* would undertake contracts for the Roman government, including collecting taxes, erecting buildings, providing food for armies, and working mines. However, the *publicani* or the king would farm out to private citizens the collection of indirect taxes for a prescribed locale (Antiquities XII. 4.4). For instance, Zacchaeus was the controller of customs for the Jericho area (Luke 19:2-10). Indirect taxes included *portoria*, customs duties on good entering or leaving harbors and city gates (2 1/2% or higher of the value of the good), and *vectigal*, taxes on the rent of state property, public land, mines, and salt-works. The Romans collected land and poll taxes and, indirectly, import taxes. Sales taxes included taxes on slaves when bought (4%) and slaves when freed (5%). If the province had a reigning sovereign, that sovereign might raise taxes. For example, Herod the Great laid his own tax on the land produce and on items bought and sold. The Jews also paid to tax-collectors a yearly tax for the temple or half-shekel (*didrachma*) (Antiquities XVIII, 9.1 [312-313]). Town citizens also paid a "house tax" to build a wall around their town.[60] Since the tax farmers had paid a sum in advance for the right to collect taxes in a certain area, they would then try to make a profit. According to Harold Mattingly, these tax-collectors were "an endless source of corruption and waste." He even concludes, "The final collapse of the West was largely due to the financial exhaustion of the tax-payer."[61]

Although every once in a while a tax-collector is treated with respect (for instance, Josephus speaks of John, the wealthy customs collector at Caesarea in A.D. 66, as someone using his money for the benefit of the Jewish people in *War* II. 14. 4-5 [287-292]), most tax-collectors were detested by Jews and by other nationalities as well. They were considered robbers and robbers of the worst type. They robbed their own people by selling their services to a foreign oppressor. They were robbers and traitors! Philo says of Capito, the tax-collector for Judaea, that he:

---

59 Beginning with Augustus, the emperor could assign *equus publicus* to any man of free birth, blameless character, and a census of 400,000 sestertii.

60 *m. B. Bat.* 1:5; *Antiq.* XIX.6.3 [299].

61 M. Cary and others, eds. *The Oxford Classical Dictionary* (Oxford: Clarendon, 1949), 363; 720; 747; 939; 336.

> cherishes a spite against the population. When he came there he was a poor man but by his rapacity and peculation he has amassed much wealth in various forms (*Embassy to Gaius* XXX. 199).

In the Mishnah, the collection of the earliest Jewish oral laws, tax-collectors were grouped together with murderers and robbers as persons to whom one could lie (*m. Ned.* 3:4). Alms or change for money could not be taken from excisemen or tax-collectors while they were working because their money was considered stolen money (*m. B. Qam.* 10:1). If thieves entered a house, only where they touched was unclean. However, if tax-collectors entered a house, the whole house became unclean. Imagine how "unclean" Jesus would be by eating with "many" tax-collectors at the home of a tax-collector, Levi Matthew.[62] If the term *exoutheneo* in Luke 18:9 has the connotation of treating someone as an outsider, a tax-collector would epitomize such an outsider. No wonder Jesus metaphorically describes the treatment which should be given to someone who refuses to listen to the congregation's testimony as the same treatment given to "a Gentile and a tax-collector" (Matt. 18:17). Even Jesus does not approve of tax-collectors as a class. He parallels tax-collectors with non-believing Gentiles who love only those who love them (Matt. 5:46). John the Baptist exhorts tax-collectors, "Collect no more than is appointed you" (Luke 3:12-13). Yet these extorters were some of the very people who responded graciously when they were asked to change their lives and begin to become citizens of God's reign by doing God's will. The tax-collectors and prostitutes are like the elder son who said he would not work in the vineyard but afterward changed his mind and went. Jesus said to the chief priests and elders that because of their belief in John, "Truly, I say to you, the tax-collectors and the harlots go into the kingdom of God before you."[63]

The Pharisee, having stood by himself, these things was praying, "God, I thank you that I am not as the rest of the people, greedy, unjust, adulterous, or even as this tax-collector (18:11):

Jesus first introduces the two characters of his story without telling the listeners anything about them. However, the groups with which these two people were associated would immediately conjur up positive and negative connotations. The Pharisee had the appearance

---

[62] *m. Tohar.* 7:6; *m. Hag.* 3:6; Luke 5:27-30.
[63] Matt. 21:31. See also Matt. 9:10-11; 11:19; Luke 7:34; 15:1-2.

of piety not only by his association with the Pharisaical movement but also because he stands by himself, calls God "*the* God," showing that he believed in the supreme God, not in idols, and he begins his prayer with praise for God. God and God's creatures love thanksgiving (*eucharisteo*). Amusingly, the Pharisees' prayer is God-centered, not human-centered.

Nevertheless, even though the Pharisee has learned to do all the proper forms of religion, he begins to go amiss when he renumerates the reasons for this thanksgiving. He does not thank God for the provisions God has given him (Matt. 15:36; Mark 8:7). He does not thank God for healing someone (John 11:41-43; Luke 17:11-19). He thanks God because he is different from everyone else. He is not greedy, unjust, nor adulterous. His prayer is like the words of a bride we once saw who as she processed forward to be married, although her body and face were directed forward, her lips and eyes were sidewise as she gave instructions to her father. The Pharisees' prayer was directed to God as he glanced sideways toward his human colleagues.

Greed, lack of righteousness or justice, and adultery are three negative traits. Lack of righteousness or justice (*adikos*) is a general term which can refer to unbelievers such as the judge (Luke 18:6) or to Jews who did not obey all the laws of cleanness (*Am-Haaretz*). Greed (*harpax*) and adultery (*moixeia*) cover both economic and sexual sins. Indeed, Paul uses these same two terms, among others, to describe those people who will not inherit God's reign. He also tells Christians not to associate with other Christians (*not* true of unbelievers) who are immoral and greedy (1 Cor. 5:10-11; 6:10). The adjective *harpax* is used here as a noun. It is related to the verb *harpazo,* signifying "to seize, carry off by force, snatch away." It connotes the overpowering of another. Jesus usually uses it in a negative sense, but the rest of the New Testament includes some positive uses. Still, wolves "snatch away" or "devour" sheep, as do false prophets (Matt. 7:15; John 10:12). Even one species of wolf is an *harpax*. Goods can be "snatched away" or robbed. Ironically, Jesus elsewhere claims that the Pharisees themselves look clean outside, but inside they are full of "plunder" and violence (Matt. 23:25). In a positive sense, however, the Spirit "snatched up" Philip, God "snatched up" Paul to the third heaven, and some can be "snatched up" out of the fire.[64] In summary, *harpax* has the sense of one who

[64] Matt. 12:29; 13:19; Heb. 10:34; Acts 8:39; 2 Cor. 12:2; Jude 23.

snatches away other things or other people, which can be in robbery or plunder.[65]

The Pharisee was saying he was not one who snatches away others' belongings. He was not a robber or an extortioner. He was not like a Gentile. No wonder his head turned to the tax-collector, symbolic of the worse kind of robber, an unpatriotic robber. This Pharisee would agree with Josephus' claim that he lived simply. He was no lover of money.

In effect, the Pharisee is proud that he has fulfilled several of the ten commandments: "You shall not commit adultery," "You shall not steal," "You shall not covet your neighbor's house; . . . nor anything that is your neighbor's," and "you shall have no other gods."[66] Since Jesus is later to ask the rich young ruler if he obeyed the ten commandments (Luke 18:20), he should have seen this Pharisee as quite exemplary. Jesus had condemned as an "adulterer" even the person who divorces a spouse (except for unchastity) or who marries a divorced person (Matt. 5:32). However, Jesus continually taught that people need to renovate not only their actions but also their thoughts. If adultery begins with a lustful look, how can any adult escape the need for forgiveness?[67]

I fast twice a week, I give a tithe from all which I acquire (18:12)

If the Pharisee first begins by thanking God for his not succumbing to negative acts such as economic and sexual sins, he then goes on to enumerate his positive traits: he fasts twice a week and separates ten percent of all that he acquires. He is no more devout than any other Pharisee or "associate." Devout Jews were known to fast on Mondays and Thursdays, which is why some later Christians chose to fast on Wednesdays and Fridays.[68] The disciples of John the Baptist used to fast regularly, as did the prophetess Anna (Luke 2:37; Matt. 9:14). The tractate *Taanith* explains how the Jews would have community or national fasts at times of any public distress, such as when there was a drought or a plague. If there was no rain by early November, especially pious persons would fast for three days. If rain did not come by late November, everyone had to

---

[65] Liddell and Scott, pp. 245-246; Thayer, pp. 74-75.
[66] Exod. 20:3, 14-15, 17.
[67] Matt. 5:27-28; 15:19.
[68] *Didache* VIII. 1; *m. Ta'an.* 2:9.

pray three days up to thirteen days (*m. Ta'an.* 1:3-6). Although Jesus did not have his own disciples fast regularly, he instructed them on how to fast (joyfully) and he himself fasted for forty days (Matt. 4:2; 6:16-18).

Consequently, fasting was a devout act. The Pharisee was as devout in this respect as any other Pharisee. He certainly was not as rigorous as Anna or as one of the three-day fasters or as Jesus.

Simply to know how to tithe, what to tithe, and when to tithe was incredibly complicated, which is possibly why the "people of the land" (*Am-Haaretz*) probably did not abide by all the rules for tithing. According to the Old Testament the "first fruits" were given to the Levitical priests since they had no land, even as Abram had given Melchizedek, the priest, ten percent of his spoils.[69] Another ten percent of the grain, wine, oil, and cattle was saved up and eaten by the household at a sanctuary (Jerusalem) to which Levites were invited.[70] Every third year, instead of the tithe being used at Jerusalem, it was given to the Levites, strangers, orphans, and widows in the town.[71] If God's laws were not complicated enough, the human laws made them immensely cumbersome. The tractate *Maaseroth* or "Tithes" elaborates exactly when a fruit was liable to tithe (e.g. "peaches - after they begin to show red veins," *m. Ma'as.* 1:2). Yet if a fig tree overhangs a neighbor's garden, that neighbor can eat the figs and be exempt from tithes (*m. Ma'as.* 3:10). Another tractate, *Demai*, is devoted to what to do about "doubtful" produce which has not definitely been tithed before receiving it. The scrupulous observer of the law would tithe it again.

Our Pharisee would not try to tithe only part of his produce but he would tithe all the Rabbinic requirements, including the "doubtful" produce. He was certainly obeying God's laws. However, although Jesus approved of tithing as did the church approve of generosity (e.g. 2 Cor. 8:14-15), Jesus was very angry with those Pharisees who tithe even the smallest herb yet forget the underlying principles behind all of God's laws - justice and love:

> But woe to you Pharisees! for you tithe mint and rue and every herb, and neglect justice and the love of God; these

---

69 Deut. 18:4-5; 26:1-15; Gen. 14:20. See also *m. Bik.*

70 Deut. 14:22-27; 12:6-7, 17-18. See also *m. Ma'as. S.*

71 Deut. 14:28-29; 26:12-15; Num. 18:21.

you ought to have done, without neglecting the others (Luke 11:42 RSV).

What is so terrifying about our Pharisee when we look at him clearly is that he errs in the very process of trying to be pious. He had the right name for God. He avoided greed and adultery, the overpowering of others economically or sexually. He gave of his time and his wages to God's work. He was aware of the need for holiness. Basically, he remembers God's covenantal laws without remembering God. Where is his compassion (*makrothumeo* 18:7)? Where do love and mercy fit in? He is not unjust, but is he just?

If the Pharisees of the Sermon on the Mount prayed to be seen (Matt. 6:5), this Pharisee prayed to see. Why did he pray where he could see the tax-collector? If the tax-collector was in the Women's Court, why was not the Pharisee in the Israelites' Court? He must have been at least near the Israelites' Court. Was he temporarily unclean? Or, was he in the Women's Court because he came too late to get into the smaller Israelites' Court? Or did he remain in the larger Women's Court in order to see and be seen? There is his mistake. The Pharisee is like Soren Kierkegaard's ethical (but not religious) person who has virtue but not repentance (e.g. *Either/Or*). His righteousness was determined by comparison with other people's, not by comparison with God's. His prayer, although perfect in form, was not directed to the God who sees and rewards in secret. When he should have been concerned about what was inside him, instead he was concerned with what was outside him. Nevertheless, to Jesus' listeners our Pharisee would exemplify most the pious person of their time.

But the tax-collector who had been standing at a distance was not wishing to lift [his] eyes toward Heaven, but he was beating his chest saying, "God, have mercy on me a sinner" (18:13).

Jesus now goes on to describe the "other" one, the tax-collector whom the Pharisee was pleased not to be, the unpatriotic thief. Both of them were standing in the usual posture of prayer. The tax-collector had been standing for a while. But he was "far off," probably meaning far away from the Priests' Court. He was not standing near others, easily seen and easily seeing. His place of prayer showed that his central concern was communication to God. But unlike Jesus and other devout persons (Mark 7:33-34), the tax-collector did not feel he could look up into heaven. He did not feel that he was acceptable to God. Rather, he kept on beating his chest.

"Beating" or "striking" (*tupto*) one's chest was a sign of mourning or contrition done with the fist or hand. Great depth of feeling is involved. When the crowds experienced the eclipse of the sun and Jesus' death, they went home "beating their chests" (Luke 23:48). They too felt contrition and sorrow.

Before a word is heard from the tax-collector, the listener already has seen two vivid contrasting pictures. Both men stand. One is standing where he can easily see others praying to God, sharing his satisfaction about himself. The other is standing far away from others, by looking down and beating his chest, showing that he feels penitent. His words utter what his actions perform: "God, have mercy on me a sinner." Like the Pharisee, he addresses God as "the God," the supreme God. However, if the Pharisee says, "God, I thank you," the tax-collector says, "God, (you) be merciful with me."

Hilaskomai ("be merciful, gracious," in the passive form) comes from *hilaos* or its Attic form *hileos*, "gracious, gentle, happy." Literally, the verb *hilaskomai* means "to make friendly, gracious, or favorable."[72] *Hilaskomai* translates the Hebrew *kapar*, "to cover, forgive, atone for," closely related to the noun *koper*, "cypress-flower, ransom." Both the Greek and Hebrew verbs flow from the imagery of making someone friendly by appeasing that person with gifts as Jacob tried to appease Esau's anger by sending him costly gifts (Gen. 32:20), or as a wise person might appease a king's wrath (Prov. 16:14). Even more specifically, *kapar* can signify a payment made in lieu of death. According to the Old Testament laws, if a person was killed by an ox which has been accustomed to gore in the past, the ox and the owner both should be put to death. However, the owner can pay a *ransom* for his own life.[73] In other words, the money, offering, or gift "covers" or protects oneself from possible death.

The adjective *hilasterios*, as does the Hebrew *caporeth*, refers to the mercy cover over the ark of the covenant. The pure gold mercy cover (2 1/2 by 1 1/2 cubits)[74] had at its two ends two gold cherubim

---

[72] Friedrich Buechsel, *"hileos, hilaskomai, hilasmos, hilasterion," TDNT* (1965), III, 300, 314. Thayer, p. 301.

[73] Exod. 21:30; 30:12; Num. 35:31-32; Deut. 21:6-9.

[74] A middle size cubit was 6 handbreadths (*m. Kelim* 17:9). The mercy cover is described in Exod. 25:17-22 and Heb. 9:3-5. Herbert Danby, *The Mishnah* (Oxford: Oxford University Press, 1944), p. 629, n. 14.

facing each other with wings spread out. The ark, a chest, had within it the ten commandments. The mercy cover and the ark, as well as the golden altar of incense, the golden urn with the manna, and Aaron's rod that budded were all in the Holy of Holies in the sanctuary. This holiest of all places was entered only once a year at the day of atonement by the high priest bringing in a blood sacrifice for his own and the peoples' wrongdoing (Heb. 9:7; *m. Kelim* 1:9). In effect, the blood represented the "cover" or "ransom" (atonement) for the lives which the people should have lost. That blood was sprinkled on the mercy cover. When their wrongdoings were "covered" the people were pardoned.

At the mercy cover God would appear in a cloud: "There I will meet with you, . . . above the mercy seat, from between the two cherubim that are upon the ark of the testimony" (Exod. 25:22; Lev. 16:2). The tax-collector alludes to God's mercy cover, to God's merciful and compassionate nature, the *makrothumeo* toward the elect (Luke 18:7). He feels that he deserves death and his gift of appeasement is his humility.

Mercy or pardon is always something a sinner needs. If God met people at the mercy cover, Christ becomes the mercy cover, the covering of the law by mercy. Christ met the demands of the law making possible divine mercy. God sent the Savior, a "means of atonement" (*hilasmos*) for the sins of the whole world.[75] Jesus is the blood, the mercy cover, and the high priest (Heb. 2:17). He intercedes for the people's sins in order that they might be forgiven and he becomes the means by which they are forgiven. People can easily appreciate Jesus as divine interceder; however in this parable we see the other side. People may not so easily appreciate the need for them to ask forgiveness. Jesus does not complete his office without people asking for forgiveness. This tax-collector has done just that.

Often people confuse approval and acceptance. Neither Jesus nor the tax-collector approve of the tax-collector's behavior. The tax-collector calls himself a "sinner." Although the Pharisees and scribes called all tax-collectors and all persons who did not observe all the laws "sinners,"[76] this tax-collector probably did not simply collect his due. Like Zacchaeus he too must have collected far beyond his allotment. He could simply have ignored the appelation "sinner"

---

[75] Matt. 5:17-18; Luke 16:17; John 19:30; Eph. 2:15; 1 John 2:2; 4:10; Rom. 3:25.

[76] Luke 15:2; 19:7.

as not applicable. Yet he was deeply penitent. A sinner can refer to any person since everyone in some way "misses the mark"(*harmartano*), misses or wanders from the path of righteousness or God's laws.[77] For example, Simon Peter called himself a "sinner" in comparison to Jesus who is able to garner nets full of fish when none were around (Luke 5:8). A sinner as well can refer to someone especially wicked, a criminal, or a prostitute (Luke 6:32-33; 7:37). The tax-collector did think he was especially wicked.

We, the readers, know who of the two, the Pharisee, the tax-collector, would become acceptable in God's sight. However, Jesus' listeners when they first heard this parable did not know. If you heard of someone pious who had worked on growth so much that he or she could be thankful to God, would you not think that person would be in better place before God than someone who had simply understood that what this one was doing was not pleasing to God and regretted these actions? Jesus tells his listeners exactly how to evaluate these two persons, to the chagrin of some and to the delight of others.

I say to you, this one went down justified into his house rather than the other one; since everyone lifting himself will be humbled, but the one humbling himself will be lifted (18:14).

Jesus repeats the authoritative "I say to you" (18:8) before the significance of his story. The two humans had ascended up the Temple mount, up to the Temple courts to pray. Now the effects of those prayers in their lives are symbolized by their descent from the Temple mount into their homes. Their prayers, according to Jesus, had to do with justice. The widow sought justice for herself. She wanted justice to come forth in the open (*ekdikeo;* 18:3, 8). Jesus now evaluates whether the Pharisee or the tax-collector received justice (hiddenly - at the present) from the perfect Judge of judges. *Dikaioo* means "to put into a right relationship," "show to be right." The person who is justified is declared guiltless, acquitted of a charge.[78] As the Old Testament law explains, the judge must decide a dispute between two people, acquitting the innocent (justifying the righteous) and condemning the guilty (Deut. 25:1). The tax-collector, who is clearly guilty, by asking for pardon becomes acquitted. The Pharisee, who appears righteous, by not seeing his own guilt and by assuming

---

[77] Thayer, p. 30.
[78] Thayer, p. 150.

his own innocence becomes condemned. What great irony is here! The person who looks to be acceptable because he spends his time comparing himself with others in reality is unacceptable to God (Luke 16:15).

Why was the tax-collector acquitted while the Pharisee was condemned? Jesus explains the reason in the final clause, "since everyone exalting himself will be humbled, but the one humbling himself will be exalted." The earlier context preceding both parables is the day of Christ wherein Jesus warns that "whoever seeks to gain his soul will lose it, but whoever loses will gain it" (17:24, 33). Jesus' two parables have come full circle back to the same theme - the final judgement. These two parables on prayer concern themselves with prayer and its relationship to judgement. The decision of the last judgement is already made today based on current action.

What is true of one tax-collector and one Pharisee is true for all people. Each is a synecdoche, a part representing a whole. The Pharisee is one who continues to "lift up" himself. *Hupsoo* means to "lift high, raise up." When planets mount to the north of the eclipse, they are at the "highest." The noun *hupsoma* is a hill, a height on which a fort could be established, as was the Acrocorinth in Corinth to which Paul probably alludes in 2 Corinthians 10:5.[79] Sovereigns often would sit on an elevated throne, awaiting the captives presented as gifts (Ps. 68:18; Eph. 4:8-10). Metaphorically, the literal idea of "raising up" could also signify "exalting." One of God's names is "the Most High" or "the Highest" because God like ancient sovereigns rules the world.[80] If mercy has to do with "covering" oneself with presents, exaltation has to do with approaching the sovereign or judge without presents because one considers that none are necessary. The image is of two subjects approaching a sovereign on a hill or raised platform or pedestal. The Pharisee "exalted" himself because he thought he had no guilt. He was righteous. He was self-reliant. He was pleased he was able to meet the standards of goodness of his day unlike some other people. As the one "lifting," he continues to be pleased with his own ability to be special.

What the Pharisee did regularly ("lift up") will be terminated suddenly (future). The opposite of "raising up" is "leveling" (*tapeinoo*). *Tapeinoo* literally refers to "not raising far from the ground," of a place or of stature. Metaphorically, the person who is

---

[79] Liddell and Scott, pp. 1910-11.

[80] Isa. 57:15; Luke 1:32, 35, 76; 6:35; 24:49.

"leveled" is "humbled" or "abased in power or pride."[81] In other words, the hill which is now "elevated" (*hupsoo*) will be made "level" (*tapeinoo*). *Tapeinoo* and its noun and adjective counterparts (*tapeinosis, taipeinos*) comprise an extremely significant word family. Jesus describes himself as "gentle and *lowly* in heart" (Matt. 11:29). Paul describes his behavior toward the Corinthians as "humbled" in imitation of Christ's gentleness and meekness (2 Cor. 10:1; 11:7). Jesus, God, in becoming human and allowing himself to be killed "humbles" himself (Phil. 2:7-8). Christians, likewise, instead of being selfish and conceited, in "humility" should consider other people's interests more important than their own interests (Phil. 2:3). Those who want to enter God's reign must "humble" themselves as do children (Matt. 18:4; Luke 18:15-17). Even as God chooses the outsider, the scapegoat, the repentant tax-collector, so does God regard positively those who are innocently oppressed. As Mary says, in response to God's favor, "My soul praises the Lord, and my spirit is extremely joyful over God my Savior, since [God] looked at the *lowly state* of [God's] slave" (Luke 1:46-48). God's favor is toward those people who acknowledge their need for God's forgiveness and help, even as earlier Jesus exhorted his disciples to be themselves forgiving (Luke 17:3-4). Mary taught this to her own son, Jesus, because God clearly revealed this truth in the earliest confessions: "The Lord, the Lord, a God merciful and gracious" and "the Lord your God . . . who . . . executes justice for orphan and widow and loves a stranger" (Exod. 34:6; Deut. 10:17-18). The Messiah about whom Isaiah prophesizes is one who is in a state of "humiliation," he is afflicted (Isa. 53:7-8 LXX). No wonder Jesus believes in humility! Everything he models is "lowly."

If the person who exalts himself will be humbled, on the other hand, the person who humbles himself will be exalted. These two principles are ones which occur and reoccur in Jesus' teachings both in concept and in word. The last clause in this parable appears almost identically word for word in two other contexts in Jesus' teachings. A form critic might say that Jesus said this sentence once and the gospel writers set it in three contexts. However, what would be more natural than a Jew repeating a teaching more than once at different times in order to teach a very difficult concept? The Jews taught by repetition (as even contemporary teachers do from any nationality).

---

[81] Liddell and Scott; pp. 1756-1757.

In this parable the "exaltation" is justification. The Pharisee who said he was "not unjust" became the one who is not just. The tax-collector became the one who is just. Was the Pharisee too honest? Does God not want to hear our self-praise? Both the Pharisee and the tax-collector were honest. However, the Pharisee measured religiosity by limited external behavior and by comparison with other humans' behavior.

In the parable of the places of honor at a wedding feast, the person who "exalts" himself seeks a reward of recognition now rather than seeking a reward from God (Luke 14:11; Matt. 6:1, 6). The host who honors the guest by making the guest take a higher place is like God, who will reward people in due time. Similarly, the people who "exalt" themselves by accentuating their authority ("calling yourself rabbi, father, master") are not being the kind of leaders Jesus wants. The leader who serves will be rewarded or "exalted" by God in due time (Matt. 23:12). All three teachings have to do with the proper place of others to determine our behavior. In Matthew 23:12 and Luke 14:11, Jesus teaches his disciples that their behavior should not be determined by the assessment of other people's behavior. In Luke 18:14 Jesus teaches his disciples that their assessment of themselves should not be done by comparison to other people. Jesus does not here say that people can not honestly acknowledge their strengths. Self-effacement or modesty is not necessarily humility. Someone could counter every compliment with a negation and think that (s)he is more humble than anyone else. As Uriah Heep, the clerk, says, "I am very 'umble" (Charles Dickens' *David Copperfield*). Rather, what Jesus here wants are people who acknowledge the ways they do not please God. The only way to do so is by looking to God, not by rating one's neighbor. If that neighbor is asking God for mercy and you are not, that neighbor will become acceptable to God and you will not.

Jesus here pronounces that great teaching on position reversal. As Hannah prayed, "The bows of the mighty are broken, and they that stumbled are girded with strength" (1 Sam. 2:4), and as Mary prayed, "God removed rulers from thrones and exalted the lowly" (Luke 1:52), so too Jesus teaches and prays that those who appear to be on top will go to the bottom and those who appear to be on the bottom will go to the top. The Father's blessings are revealed to babies (Luke 10:21). The poor, captive, and blind are liberated (Luke

4:18; 7:22). The poor, hungry, mournful will receive God's blessings, while the rich, full, and happy will receive God's cursings.[82]

Summary

As Jesus "set his face to go into Jerusalem" to enter the place where he would be crucified, he takes with him all the other outsiders, the oppressed and the forgiven. He speaks about the last judgement to those whose faith begins to wear out because they have not seen justice and to those whose faith in themselves should be wearing out. Both parables concern themselves with possible errors of the pious. The widow and the tax-collector received justice. Both parables on prayer bring out the importance of remembering the nature of God as one communicates to God. To the widow, Jesus says, God is just. Although you might need to enter into a boxing match with other humans, God needs no fight to pronounce a just sentence. Continue to trust God. Do not be side-tracked by oppressors. To the tax-collector, Jesus says, God is merciful. Rely on God to raise you up. Be honest with your failings. Do not be side-tracked by missing crucial priorities. In other words, when we pray, we need to remember above all to whom we pray. We pray to the just and compassionate Judge who sees in secret. We communicate to God. Our reward (or our punishment) will come from God. Therefore, we should not evaluate our own piety by comparison to other people's. To have the right form of prayer is fine, but God looks beyond the form to our hearts. We need to be honest with ourselves and with God and to hold firmly to God's self-revelation: "The Lord, the Lord, a God merciful and gracious . . . who is not partial and takes no bribe."

---

[82] Luke 6:20-25. See also 2 Cor. 11:7; James 1:9-11; 2:1 ff; 4:6-10; 1 Pet. 5:5-6; John 3:14; 8:28; 12:32-34.

4

Jesus' Covenant of Prayer

(Whatever You Ask -- Believe)

True Child of Abraham, the second Adam, the new Melchizedek, the high priest fulfilling at last the perfect sacrifice of God's holy law, Jesus makes his prayers no less than covenantal communications with the one true holy God. Much has been written about covenants since the time that God cut them with ancient Israel out under the numberless stars that would someday represent Jacob's children, there above the blood-drenched plains of quaking misty Mount Sinai in tablets of stone, and afterward at the limp feet of a dead man in sacred blood that would soon write a covenant forever on living human hearts. A covenant, we know, is an agreement, a pact made between two parties. God uses the image of the marriage bond, a sacred connubial trust that must not be broken. Pacts and treaties between countries form alliances that the despicable crime of treason alone breaks. The Reverend Paul Bricker likens God's covenant to that offer the Mafia makes which cannot be refused. Power, benefit, threat of consequences are all implied in a covenant agreement. God's covenant with Israel, and with any Moabite like Ruth or Canaanite like Rahab or even Uzzite (Edomite?) like Job who entered it, always was conditional. If the conditions God laid down were not met, if faithfulness and set-apartness and honesty and charity were not maintained, the most dire consequences were visited by God upon God's people: plague, famine, defeat, and captivity. So too Jesus taught a communication of prayer that was conditional and therefore covenantal.

The Old Testament covenants were characterized by the faithfulness of God. God could always be counted upon to fulfill God's part of the agreement no matter what God promised to do. In the same manner Jesus established a conditional covenant of prayer that assures if certain conditions God demands are fulfilled, God will answer prayer. Matthew 7:7-12 to which we alluded briefly in our chapter on the Lord's prayers shows this conditional prayer covenant which relies on the security of knowing that God, at least, will keep God's promises. The passage reads literally:

> Ask, and it will be given to you; seek, and you will find; knock, and it will be opened to you. For everyone asking receives and the one seeking finds and to the one knocking it will be opened. Or, what person is there among you who his son asks bread - he will not give him a stone? Or also a fish he will ask - he will not give him a snake? Therefore, if you being evil know good gifts to give to your children, how much more your Father, the one in the heavens, will give good (things) to those asking him. Therefore, all which you may wish that people do to you, in the same way also you do to them, for this is the law and the prophets.

Truly "for this is the law and the prophets." This is , after all, the point of all the old covenants of God. If God's people would only be loving and faithful to God and to each other, their loving Parent would shower good gifts upon them. And that is all in our best moments we ask of our own children - to be kind to each other and faithful and obedient and loving to God and us. But unlike us in the moments that sin makes us impatient or cruel or unjust parents, the longsuffering ever-merciful God patiently tends the covenant people long after God's emissaries throw up their hands in exasperation.

Ask/Believe

While the faithfulness of God may be the point of these illustrations, today most of us, especially since the advent of the "Health and Wealth" gospel, tend to focus on the asking and getting what we want part. Can we really ask God for anything and if we believe hard enough, that is if we really, really, rea-ll-lll-lly believe, we will get it? Anything? Anything at all? A cursory reading of the relevant Scripture passages certainly seems to suggest that conclusion to many people world-wide today.

Shifting Mountains and Uprooting Trees

Early on in Jesus' ministry his miraculous power over nature became poignantly evident to his disciples. At his first miracle common water turned into the finest wine, elusive fish leaped into nets at his command or fetched coins to his hand. The quaking disciples found howling wind and crashing waves grow placid at his direction. And often he would couple these incredible demonstrations with the encouragement that the disciples' own faith could produce equal and finally greater works! One of the most provocative incidences occurred at the end of his ministry when confrontation had finally come and the deadly slide into open war would leave him at the cross a slain and defeated commander. Mark 11:12-25 records this puzzling and to many of us bizarre incident:

> And on the morrow when they came out from Bethany, he was hungry. And having seen a fig tree from a distance having leaves, he went (to ascertain) whether he could find anything in it, and coming upon it nothing he found except leaves; for the time was not of figs. And when he responded, he said to it, "No longer into the ages (nevermore) out of you will anyone eat fruit." And his disciples heard.

We may pause here to marvel with so many critics about this incident. How many scholars have pointed out that the tree was not at fault! This, we are told specifically, was not the time for fruits, yet Jesus cursed the barren tree. Why? Was Jesus indeed the spoiled maniac some would paint him to be, petulantly wanting his own way in everything and ultimately being silenced by mature people as a general annoyance? Or is there a deeper, more sinister meaning in this incident, applying directly to the nature of the kind of prayer he is teaching and the character of the covenant he is bringing?

Let us examine where and when this incident took place. The account is interjected into the record of the cleansing of the temple. It answers a question that was generally being asked after the triumphal entry: Where was Jesus? Jesus was using Bethany as a base, commuting back and forth to Jerusalem. He raises Lazarus, enters Jerusalem triumphantly, goes to the temple, is dismayed, goes back to Bethany, returns, curses the fig tree on the way back to the temple, which he now enters as Judge, scourging the temple clean. Triumphal entry is now contrasted with ferocious judgement. Jesus will either be received as king or suffered as judge. Like the fig tree the temple which does not bear fruit will no longer be permitted to attempt to bear fruit, no one will commune there. Then the passage continues:

> And going by early in the morning they saw the fig tree withered out of the root. And having remembered, Peter says to him, "Rabbi, see the fig tree which curses have withered." And when he answered, Jesus says to them, "If you have faith in God, truly I say to you that whoever might say to this mountain, 'Be lifted up and be thrown into the sea,' and does not judge in his heart but he might believe that what he says comes, it will be to him. On account of this I say to you, all which you (plural) pray and ask, believe that you receive, and it will be to you. And whenever you stand praying, forgive if something you have against anyone, in order that also your Father, the one in the heavens, might forgive you your trespasses (Mark 11:20-25).

A sinister context, indeed, for this supposedly "Health and Wealth" teaching! Jesus tempers it with a teaching on forgiveness to show that the point here is not the cursing. We humans are supposed to forgive so that we will be forgiven, for the point for us is to avoid God's curse.

The lessons are painfully obvious here. God's people are unfaithful because they are unproductive. The temple is like the fig tree, it is going under God's curse. The temple of God has been turned into a supermarket. Mammon is the deity worshipped here. There may be a kind of faith present, but it is not a faith producing right actions. The temple is like a beautiful tree full of leaves on display but when one comes to eat there is no spiritual sustenance. Jesus curses this den of thieves just as Paul will later reprove women in prayer, glitteringly adorned without spiritual substance. Truly as Jesus' earthly brother interpreted this truth, a faith that does not produce good actions is dead (James 2:17).

The second lesson is also a terrifying one. Like Jesus, the disciples have the power to curse, even to move mountains because of their faith: a specific kind of faith which produces good fruit which nourishes others with spiritual sustenance. Verse 25 shows us one of these exemplary spiritual fruits - forgiveness. This is not irony when Jesus juxtaposes cursing and forgiveness together. This is dismay, an indication of the reason why he cries over Jerusalem. How long has he held out his hand or piped his song for Israel to dance (Matt. 11:17; Luke 7:32) but was rejected? People like his disciples are always to forgive, because final vengeance is God's (Rom. 12:19; Heb. 10:30). Yet, a time comes when judgement falls, the terrible day of the Lord dawns. When the temple of Jesus' body is destroyed, the veil of the earthly temple is torn in two. The Old Covenant with Israel is ended. The glory of God's presence departs.

Mark 11:23 sets in the singular the fact that what happens in one's will affects the results, as when your (singular) faith has made you whole. As James says, to gain God's favor we cannot have envy and selfish ambition in our hearts (James 3:13-18). But Mark 11:24 moves to the plural. When two or three are gathered in Jesus' name results occur. While you yourself have to be genuine (you cannot be a child of perdition), you are a part of a community of faith. Your prayer melded with the prayers of your community is acceptable to God and therefore powerful. Communal prayer keeps prayer from being individually selfish prayer or essentially magic, bending the will of the deity to one's own personal will. Praying in community, the gathering of two or three, augments the faith of one while keeping the prayer subject to a group and therefore helping steward it away from selfishness. James in 5:14-15 counsels the prayer of healing is given to the elders of the Church. Having a chronic disease, one of the authors has several times called in the elders of various churches and noted that the extent of each healing experience seemed proportional to the faith of the elders who were making the request. One group of skeptical suburban elders received a perceptibly little result from their "well-here-goes-nothing" prayer, while a fervent group of store-front pastors and male and female urban lay leaders knocked out one flare-up of the disease in a single evening. Empirically, as John in his testimony in I John 1, the authors know from personal experience the augmented prayer of faith of faithful godly elders is rewarded by the loving God.

"A gathering of two or three" is a comfortingly flexible term God has given us. Matthew 18:18-20, a passage which also amplifies the points under discussion, expands the flexibility of this teaching:

> Truly I say to you, whatever things you may bind by law and duty upon the earth will be bound in heaven and whatever you may loose (or destroy) upon the earth will be loosed (or destroyed) in heaven. Again I say to you that if two (literally have a symphony, have voices together) are in agreement from among you upon the earth concerning every matter which if they may ask, it will come to them from my Father, the one in the heavens. For where there are two or three assembling (or gathering) in my name, there I am in the midst of them.

Interestingly, as in the case of the teaching about forgiveness following immediately upon the viewing of the results of the cursing of the fig tree, this passage is followed by the parable of the unforgiving servant. Before and after this passage the text has to do with actions and the need to be forgiven and reconciled.

Both verses 18 and 20, we see, deal with the decisions of a gathering or assembling of believers, that is with the church. A two or three member body confirms that one's request is in Christ's name and so establishes it is concordant with the will of Christ. This decision is submitted to God as a kind of legislation and God decides whether to sign it into law or not. Maybe prayer for healing by faithful elders also fits in with this understanding. God requires two or three witnesses, the established elders of the church. Like legal witnesses, they agree and present the petition to God through prayer and God chooses how to respond. True, some are given the gift of healing. They can exercise that gift for the good of the assembly. But all of us have access to healing through the faithful elders' sometimes more cumbersome machinery. Francis MacNutt in *The Power to Heal* uses this principle to organize groups of the faithful who work along with doctors, learning the diagnosis and praying specifically for the exact physical place where illness lodges. The praying and medical communities cooperate as God heals through the concerted good actions of both.

While forgiveness figures in this passage, cursing is present too. That which is loosed or discarded or destroyed on earth, like the fig tree, is unbound or destroyed in heaven. In verse 15, which precedes our cited passage, a petition to a sinning person is discussed. If a person refuses to respond and repent before all the different requests of the levels of the church, that person becomes as a tax-collector and Gentile, an outcast from the covenant. But God's faithfulness is contrasted to a sinning person's lack of faithfulness. Thus we, with godly persistence, keep praying to the merciful God for the sinning person. So prayer ties in with church decisions and church discipline. Further, the teaching is in the context of parables about those who sin and do not relent. Forgiveness, the need to repent and be forgiven, and the need to forgive are all tied into the right actions required from a faith whose prayers can get results. And all of this action occurs within the *ekklesia*, the Greek group assembled to obtain a legal decision, which is the way the church is presented here. God as the judge receives our testimony and our pleas and makes a decision. God as president, the one who presides, receives the legislation from the duly appointed representatives and considers whether to make it a part of universal law - the action of the universe.

We see how poignantly these teachings tie into Jesus' urgings for oneness in John 17. If we fail to respond and relent, as the sinning person does in Matthew 18:16-17, we indicate we do not want Christ redemptively present and we become outsiders. We are not one with Christ and God and the church. In the same manner in Matthew 18:21 and following, a failure to forgive means Christ is not redemptively present and God does not forgive. But when brothers and sisters agree, Christ is not only redemptively present but great results also occur. Whatever we ask, God's power is present to fulfill. Since former combatants are now one together, we become one with Christ and the Father, who are one. We receive Christ's perspective and Christ's Parent's answers. All of us are in unity. We might posit the Father is the generator of the power source we plug into through Christ. The church is a series of extension cords extending throughout the earth. If a person becomes estranged, that connection is broken, that person is cut off from the power source. No wonder her or his light goes out.

That is why two or three in agreement, the *ekklesia*, becomes so important. The decision-making group for Jesus *is* the agreement of Christians. This agreement is the church, the body of Christ on earth for Jesus.

The beauty of this definition is that Jesus uses the term *ekklesia* to indicate whatever is a duly elected political group for us, whatever is the group that we have designated to make our decisions. By the time the Book of James is written such a designated group already exists. James simply calls them the elders, the older ones, for Jesus has not established titles and positions. Jesus does not seem to care what we decide to call them. He allows us this freedom. Jesus does not unreel a great corporate chart like Bruce Barton's *The Man Nobody Knows* might have done and tack it up on the wall of heaven, while we sit in our corporate replica boardrooms on earth trying to intuit what the next move or takeover of the corporation of God, Inc. ought to be. If we have deacons instead of elders, trustees instead of deacons, bishops or executive presbyters or district supervisors or overseers, Jesus' flexibility teaches, in whatever group we organize to make our decisions, there he will be.

The point at issue is the kind of faith that this asking group has. Do they have a faith whose asking produces the results of answered prayer? Faith, after all, is a gift similar to that commissioned in the parable of the talents. You bury it in the backyard, it does not grow. But if you use it, it multiples and provides riches. Like a little-used muscle, when flexed and exerted, it begins to get larger and more powerful.

So we are moved back poignantly to Jesus before the withered fig tree teaching about a kind of asking that can uproot trees and move mountains. Matthew 21:18-22 gives us one more rendition of this singular account:

> And early in the morning, returning into the city, he was hungry. And having seen one fig tree on the road, he went to it, and he did not find anything in it except only leaves, and he says to it, "No longer from you will come fruit forever." And the fig tree withered immediately (Matt. 21:18-19).

In Mark 11's account we noted Jesus curses the fig tree, goes into the temple, and he and his disciples see the tree withered on their return. Here he seems to be cursing it after the temple incident. Matthew, we should note, tends to group events together. His is not a chronological biography primarily but a theological one. He is less interested in when events occurred as what occurred. Mark spells out what happened chronologically, faithfully showing the temple events occurred in between the cursing and its results. Matthew groups result with event for in his proleptic vision the fig tree began withering when Jesus cursed it just as surely as Adam and Eve lost immortality and began dying when they disobeyed. Later and ever after until it snapped off and blew away and was ground beneath feet and hooves into dust the tree's withered condition proclaimed the full result of God's curse.

Matthew 21 continues:

> And having seen, the disciples were amazed, saying, "How so quickly did the fig tree wither?" And when he answered, Jesus said to them, "Truly I say to you, if you (plural) have faith and you (plural) do not doubt (judge), not only might you (plural) do to the fig tree, but also to this mountain you might say, 'Be lifted up and be thrown into the sea!' It will happen." And all which you (plural) may ask in prayer believing, you will receive (Matt. 21:20-22).

Clearly we see the point of including the teaching on prayer here. No matter how high our own self-confidence quotient we would doubt that we could pull off such a miraculous event without prayer. Only God could do such a thing. Yet in Luke 17:6 after his teaching on forgiveness when the disciples entreat Jesus to increase their faith, Jesus replies, "If you (plural) have faith as a mustard seed, when you said to this mulberry tree, 'Be uprooted and be planted in the sea,' also it would obey you." Jesus does not introduce prayer in this reply. He does not say pray five times a day and your faith will increase. Rather, he chides, if you had the faith the size of a tiny mustard seed, a teeny wimpy-sized faith, you could rip trees out of the earth by command and have them reroot themselves in the water. What a curious reply. The disciples keep asking for more faith while Jesus keeps responding with behavioral statements: forgive each other, exercise your faith. What is happening here? Jesus is paralleling the activity of God and the activity of people demanded by the covenant. God is faithful to the covenant and will respond answering prayer, giving good gifts to people. When the disciples ask to be faithful, that is when they ask for more faith, Jesus responds by describing the ways they can be faithful to their part of the bargain, fulfilling the commandments of the covenant. Do they want more faith? Do *we* want more faith? Fulfill the human's part of the covenant. Act with forgiveness and compassion toward people and humility and obedience toward God and that will be the faith required, the faithful response. If the disciples uphold by their actions their part of the bargain, God will surely uphold God's. The sad point Jesus is making is our commitment to the covenant, our faith, is not even the before-sized faith in a before and after advertisement. It is smaller than the size of about the smallest seed in the farmer's seed box. But if it were simply teeny we could do great physical wonders. Yet, frankly, outside of a circus sideshow act or a

Las Vegas magician's who would want to do that? Moving trees by command is a basically useless activity. Jesus by example curses a tree and it withers. He points out his disciples could not only do that but rip a whole tree out of the ground and move it around if they had the faith.

Yet such an activity would be of no earthly good to anybody, except for showing off or removing the need for people to have to work communally to change the crust of the earth for building habitations and the roads to link them together. The point is obviously not moving mulberry trees or mountains. The point is that if even a tiny-sized faith can move what looks like immovable physical objects, think what it can do with diseases, with other people, with bringing in the reign of God, with altering great events, with things that count for Christ. The disciples ask to have their faith increased. This is the same plea the father of the boy plagued by demons will make in our next section. But Jesus is counseling them to act on the faith they have. They ought not to worry about having more because a little faith, a mustard seed-sized faith, goes a long way. And like a mustard seed planted in the earth, we have noticed, a faith that is planted in Christ does begin to grow and increase. As we use it it gets greater.

This drives us back to considering the source of faith. Perhaps Jesus does not need to mention prayer in the Luke 17 passage because the point of needing to rely on the omnipotent God for such a breathtaking kind of power in our own lives is self-evident. Certainly the co-occurrence of the fig tree incident with the temple scourging underscores the power of Jesus' authority. By the temple cleansing Jesus' authority is demonstrated to the temple officers, just as in the fig tree incident Jesus' authority is demonstrated to his disciples. In macrocosm and in microcosm Jesus as judge who cleanses the world, Jesus as gardener who prunes off the unfruitful branch, is potently established. Interestingly, the Pharisees, unlike today's doubters who have the luxury of two millenia to obscure the facts, do not doubt the occurrence of Jesus' miracles. They cannot deny them, so they try to assign them to Beelzebub, an absurdity, we will see, when Jesus confronts the powers of hell over the prize of a child. But the point to the disciples is plain. If one wants to have the power and authority Jesus had, one had better remain plugged into his power source.

Remaining at One with the Authoritative God

The bearing of fruit and the cursing of the fig tree for not bearing fruit become particularly significant when we parallel to the fig tree incident the teaching of Jesus in his last discourses to his disciples. In the famous John 15 teaching about the vine and the branches he notes:

> I (myself) am the true vine, and my father is the vinedresser. Every branch in me not bearing fruit, he removes it, and each bearing fruit he prunes it in order that it may bear more fruit. Already you yourselves are clean on account of the word which I have spoken to you. Remain in me, and I in you. As the branch is not able to bear fruit from itself if it does not remain in the vine, in the same way neither (can) you yourselves if you do not remain in me. I myself am the vine, you yourselves (are) the branches. The one remaining in me and I in him, this one bears much fruit, because apart from me you (plural) are not able to do anything. Unless someone remains in me, he is thrown outside as the branch and withers, and they gather them and they throw (them) into the fire and it burns up. If you (plural) may remain in me and my words in you (plural) may remain, whatever you may wish, ask and it will come to you (1-7).

Now the analogy of the non-fruit bearing fruit tree becomes more personally and poignantly significant. Not simply the temple but we ourselves individually are depicted as either fruit bearing or non-fruit bearing branches. If we do not bear good fruits we are destroyed like the fig tree and the temple, cut off from God and destroyed. If we are good branches, Jesus' words clean us, prune us for greater service. The conditional phrasing that runs all through these verses comes into play. "If you remain in me" is so phrased that its fulfillment is in doubt but with some expectation of realization. We see here the anxiety which makes Jesus ask if there will indeed be faith on earth when he returns (Luke 18:8). But if this condition is met, if they remain in him, whatever they wish they will get. There is a strong sense of the "will happen" here. Jesus does not set up what is called a first conditional clause herein, a condition determined as fulfilled. His question, "And if I by Beelzebub cast out demons, your sons, by whom do they cast them out?" (Matt. 12:27) assumes the reality of the condition. This is not a second class condition where conditions determined as unfulfilled or contrary to fact are mentioned. "Lord, if you had been here my brother would not have died," realized Martha (John 11:21). And this is not a fourth class or least probable condition with little prospect of realization. Instead, as a third class condition with doubt but some prospect of realization Jesus sets up what is called a chiastic thought development to describe the conditions that determine the fate of the bad branches and the good branches: either answered fruitful prayer from remaining in the tree or destruction. In a chiasm, in a way similar to that in which we just set up the preceding sentence, the two middle parts of Jesus' sentence relate as do the two end sections: A B B A. So the bad is described, then the good. The good get rewarded and the bad get burned. Both, in a sense, get their requests answered. The bad ask by their unfruitfulness to get cut off and destroyed. The good by bearing fruits ask to get their prayers answered so that they may bear more fruits. So the point of answered prayer, then, is the bearing of good fruits. Whatever prayers serve to help the good bear more fruits, these are prayers built upon the good remaining in God and they are answered. And we see by the examples that these prayers have a power that can unearth the Andes or root up an unbearing fruit tree and fling it into the sea.

That Jesus should command us to ask for whatever we want as long as we remain in God's will would be quite unfathomable to many Greeks. Epictetus, the slave who popularized the survival philosophy called Stoicism, quotes a prayer:

> Have I been discontented with any of these things which happen, or wished it to have been otherwise?...for what Thou hast given I am grateful also. The length of time for which I have had the use of Thy gifts is enough for me (IV. X. 15-16).

But Jesus does not teach such a fatalistic approach to God's doling out of gifts and answers to prayer requests. Instead by using the third class condition Jesus denotes that if certain conditions are met, God will fulfill the prayer. What Jesus leaves in doubt is whether we will truly ask in God's name. As we noticed when we studied the first three imperatives in the Lord's prayer, wherein the agent who will do the requested actions was unclear, our Lord Jesus is not certain that we will remain in him and in God.

Therefore oneness, remaining in God, is the focus in John 15:7. Why should the Father give us whatever we ask we are wondering? Because the Father is glorified when we are fruitful. What is in this for us? Asking in God's will means our Parent will give us whatever good things we ask for.

And how are we fruitful? Well, what exactly does it mean for us to remain in Jesus? We will see in Jesus' great prayer for the church in John 17 that it means remaining in Jesus' words. As he teaches in John 14:15, "If you love me, you will keep my commandments." We remain in the obedience to his commandments and his words remain in us. Then we ask for the things that help us remain and be profitable for God's reign and so we become Christ's disciples. John 15:8 summarizes this teaching, "In this is (was) my Father glorified that you may bear much fruit and you may become my disciples." This use of the past tense, called the aorist, is peculiar here. One would suppose a present tense ought to be used. Of course, this may simply be a Hebraism as Hebrew has only repeated and punctiliar action, the aorist standing for the latter. Dana and Mantey in their grammar put it under the category of the gnomic aorist. As well, it may be a culminative aorist or a "timeless aorist" as A. T. Robertson suggests.[1] The force of the culminative is cumulative - a conclusion is drawn from the acts in their entirety: "By all this being done my Father is glorified." The gnomic aorist describes a truth so generally accepted, a fact so universal that it is put in what is called the general or, sometimes in English, the eternal present. "Whenever this is done my Father is glorified." These acts produce an always true, timelessly true fact. This is how God is glorified. The verse teaches, "In this is my Father glorified, when you bear much fruit and you become my disciples."

W. Bingham Hunter from the Talbot School of Theology in his paper "What Does It Mean To Pray In Jesus' Name" and the book from which it is derived, *The God Who Hears*,[2] makes a clever use of algebraic equations to parallel the phrase "In Jesus' name" with "according to God's will." Therefore, only things asked according to God's will are truly asked in Jesus' name. The earliest recorded Christian sermon that we have extant after the close of the Book of Acts, called *the Second Epistle of Clement*, seems to support this equating of God's will with God's name. The author writes:

---

[1] H. E. Dana and Julius R. Mantey, *A Manual Grammar of the Greek New Testament* (New York: MacMillan, 1955), pp. 196-197; A. T. Robertson, *A Grammar of the Greek New Testament in the Light of Historical Research* (Nashville: Broadman Press, 1934), pp. 836-837.

[2] W. Bingham Hunter, *The God Who Hears* (Downers Grove: InterVarsity, 1986).

> For the Lord says, "Continually my name is being blasphemed (scoffed at) among all the nations," and again, "Alas for him through whom my name is blasphemed." How is it being blasphemed? In your not doing what I want" (II Clement 13:2-3).

Asking versus Challenging

Jesus follows his teaching in John 15 with a prophecy about what oneness with God will mean. "And in that day," he promises in John 16:23, "you will not challenge me for anything (*erotao*). Truly, truly I say to you (plural), whatever you may ask (*aiteo*) the Father in my name he will give you." When Jesus is challenged by his home town compatriots in Luke 4:22ff. he does not produce results. We are commanded over and over not to challenge God or Christ but to ask. We notice that *aiteo* can either mean asking for a matter or for an action. First, the word is used in Scripture simply for requesting something like alms (Acts 3:2) or a tablet (Luke 1:63) or water (John 4:9-10). Normally one human asks another as in Matt. 5:42. When we ask God, we are calmly petitioning, not frantically doing so (Matt. 6:8; 7:7-10). We ask as a child does a parent, calling out in our night, knocking on the office door. Martha knows that the perfect child of God asks in this way in John 11:22, whatever Jesus asks God will do, even to be able to alter God's time for Lazarus to die. James in 4:2-3 cautions against asking for what is not needed. Instead we should ask for spiritual needs (Col. 1:9) and for the wisdom of God asked in faith (James 1:5-6).

Some of these examples already suggest the second definition, asking for a favor as a subordinate to a superior. Joseph asked Pilate in this way for the body of Jesus (Matt. 27:58) and Herodias' daughter of Herod for the head of John (Matt. 14:7). The mother of the sons of Zebedee knelt before Jesus and asked him in Matthew 20:20, and in this way we, like Paul, ought to ask God for us not to lose heart (Eph. 3:13). A further aspect of this second category is asking for a resolution about a person or thing, as in requesting a disciplinary action. The crowd was persuaded to ask Pilate the procurator for Barabbas in Matthew 27:20 and also Luke 23:23. In I Corinthians 1:22 we see being asked in this way can be requesting a kind of sign to prove one's superiority. So two or three agreeing humans ask God in this way in Matthew 18:19. A superior can also call one to account for one's hope in I Peter 3:15 and can require a duty as does the head of the household who expects much from a servant to whom he or she has given much (Luke 12:48). So this is the kind of asking with believing which Jesus teaches humans to do at the fig tree incident (Matt. 21:22). Ephesians 3:20 assures us God has the power to do above what we ask. God hears and gives us our requests (not demands = *erotao*) in I John 5:14-16 because we are asking while keeping his commandments and pleasing God (I John 3:22).

This attitude of asking not challenging or demanding is part of what being one in Christ and God means. It is part of remaining at one with Jesus in Jesus' name, following his commandments, bearing fruits of godly actions, becoming disciples. If they adopt this attitude, the disciples are now invited by Jesus to begin a new relationship in John 16:24, "Until now you have not asked anything in my name; ask and you will receive that your joy may be complete."

The Reasons for Asking

When we look at the reasons Jesus provides to motivate us to ask we certainly see a striking contrast to the constipated holiness in the magnificent film-maker Franco Zeffirelli's portraits of Jesus, Mary, and St. Francis or the bizarre grotesqueness of holiness depicted by Flannery O'Connor and Graham Greene. These artists paint the picture of holiness that the world sees, a weird repulsiveness to those being lost. But Jesus sees what the eyes of the faithful see--productive, burgeoning joy. So in John 14:13-14 we ask things in Jesus' name so that the Father may be glorified in the Son. Whatever we ask in this context in Jesus' name he will do. In John 15:7-8 we ask so that the Father is glorified, we bear fruits, we become disciples, if we remain in Jesus. Now in 16:24 we ask the Father in Jesus' name so that our joy may be complete. We can conclude our joy is complete because we are not cut off as unfruitful branches, instead we bear fruit and so become disciples. We are commanded to ask (*aiteo*), seek, and knock. We will find what we want because God is faithful to God's promises. The God we entreat as a superior is like a loving parent. We can see God's care reflected in our own actions toward our children. If we can give them good gifts, God will certainly give good gifts to those who ask in the right way.

We see that asking implies remaining at one with God through obeying the commandments Jesus gave, having a life of fruitful good action for the reign of God and becoming disciples. We must be fulfilling the law and the prophets by doing actions to people which we would want done to ourselves. The behavioral response of forgiving others and of seeking their forgiveness and of doing good actions to others is always coupled as a condition with getting what we want from God. This behavioral response shows we are at one with God and makes our prayer acceptable. In true religion, unlike in magic, the end not the formula is significant to God. We can see why this is so when we examine the innuendos involved in that dramatic scene wherein Jesus' disciples are confronted by a demoniac they cannot cure and Jesus shows the battle with evil is a subtle struggle where remaining in God is imperative, the right ends are crucial, and asking for anything but what God wants can mean cataclysmic trouble. Obviously the early church did not understand this lesson because it added a formula to Jesus' words we still add to the text today, an adjuration to fast while praying. What is the precise truth about prayer and fasting?

Prayer--and Fasting?

Earlier we cited the sermon called II Clement, which was written sometime between A.D. 120 and 174, within a few decades of the death of John the apostle. In 16:4 this sermon teaches, "Good, therefore, is charity (almsgiving, kind deeds) as is repentance from sin; better (more profitable) is fasting than prayer, and charity than both." Fasting is better than prayer! Polycarp, the great disciple of John, heartily commends fasting and praying in his letter 7:2. The earliest worship and discipline manual which we introduced in our chapter on the Lord's prayers counsels, "The teaching of these words is this, 'Bless the ones cursing you and pray on behalf of your enemies, (but) even fast on behalf of the ones persecuting you'" (Did. 1:3). Before baptism both the baptizer and the one being baptized are instructed to fast for one or two days and any others who can join them are urged to do so as well (7:4). Fasting was popular among the faithful Jews, so the Didache instructs Christians to do it on Wednesdays and Fridays to contrast themselves with the Jewish faithful's fasting on Mondays and Thursdays (8:1). Fasting was an integral and highly valued practice in the early church. It was so highly valued in fact that it was added back to the words of Jesus just as the doxology was appended to the Lord's prayer of Jesus in the Didache 8:2. Let us look at the event as Scripture presents it and, for those interested, in the footnotes we have traced where early church practice was added to Jesus' teaching in later manuscripts.

Confrontation in Mark 9:14-29

The glorious transfiguration has just taken place and the awe-struck inner circle disciples are stumbling down the mountain to find a great crowd in the heat of controversy with the rest of Jesus' band:

> And when they came to the disciples, they saw a great crowd around them and scribes disputing with them. And immediately all the crowd, having seen him, were completely amazed, and running up, they greeted him. And he asked them, "What are you arguing about with them?" And one out of the crowd answered him, "Teacher, I bore my son having a dumb spirit to you. And wherever it seizes him, it dashes him down, and he foams at the mouth and gnashes his teeth, and he becomes stiff. And I told your disciples so that they might cast it out, and they were not able." But answering them, he says, "O unfaithful generation, how long will I be with you? How long will I tolerate you? Bring him to me." And they bore him to him. And having seen him the spirit immediately convulsed him, and having fallen upon the ground, he rolled about foaming at the mouth. And he asked his father, "How long has it been like this with him?" And he said, "Since childhood. And often even into the fire it has thrown him and into water in order that it might destroy him. But if you are at all able, help us, having compassion for us." But Jesus said to him, "If you are able to do it - all things are able to be done by the one believing" (Mark 9:14-23).

Amidst the writhing, shrieking convulsions of the afflicted young man, Jesus turns the plea of a father back upon him. The father asks Jesus in verse 22 to help if "you" are at all able. Jesus replies, "You can get what you want, you can help if *you* are able." The father like the disciples in our last section is asking for Jesus to increase his faith. But Jesus' reply to the father echoes that reply he gave to the disciples. If faith is even as small as a mustard seed....The responsibility for that faith is the father's. Like the disciples and the father, we like to shirk our responsibility, emphasizing Jesus' acting, God's part of the covenant. We are God's tools. But we sin blithely enough, expecting God continually to overlook our behavior and hold up God's end of the bargain. But

Jesus is always turning back the responsibility. *Your* faith has made you whole he says over and over again. Maybe this is why we oppress and cheat and wage war, baptizing our selfish ambition with sanctified terms as we outdo the world in sin glazed over with a pious veneer: cheat a widow and orphan out of their pittance for Jesus, oppress an underdeveloped country for Christ. Jesus says *your belief* makes things possible. The father gets the point, even if we do not. "Immediately shouting the father of the child said, "I believe; help my unbelief!" (Mark 9:24). The father screams in desperation for help with his faith.

Jesus knows he can heal the child, but Jesus' focus is also on his disciples, on the father, and on the crowds. And further, Jesus wants to save this young man not only from the demon but from the grip of hell, from his possession and also from his sins. So Jesus challenges the faith of his hearers and then acts as an example on their behalf.

> And Jesus, having seen that the crowd was running together, rebuked the unclean spirit, saying to him, "Dumb and deaf spirit, I myself command you, come out of him and no longer enter into him. And with cries and many convulsions he came out. And he became as one dead, so that many were saying that he died. But Jesus, when he had stretched out his hand, raised him, and he arose. And when he came into a house, his disciples privately asked him, "Why were we not able to cast it out?" And he said to them, "This kind by nothing is able to come out except by prayer" (Mark 9:25-29).

So reads the uncorrected manuscripts of both Sinaiticus and Vaticanus, the authoritative Alexandrian documents of the New Testament from the early 300's. As well reads the old Latin, the Italic from around 400, as also does the Georgian, the later Caesarian manuscript from the area between the Black and Caspian seas. This is also the reading used by the scholarly early church father Clement of Alexandria, circa 215. So a variety of manuscript family types and three strong manuscript witnesses attest to this reading.

What happened, then? Correctors' hands are clearly seen changing the authoritative codex Sinaiticus, adding the phrase "and fasting." The corrector of Sinaiticus is not the one who did it before the manuscript left the scriptorium where it was copied. Rather

Sinaiticus was already in circulation when it was altered.[3] A host of later Byzantine and Western manuscripts follow the change. Members of less reliable text families, Alexandrinus, which is Byzantine in the gospels, the palimpset Ephrami (C), and the often bizarre Codex Bezae of the Western type follow, supporting what is clearly an addition. Clearly "and fasting" has been appended to Jesus' charge to pray at a date later than the early 300's. Throughout the 8th and 9th centuries this new addition now becomes the authoritative reading in a host of manuscripts. And this reading is prevalent today. But why was fasting added?

The usual argument is that the early church imitated Jewish practices of fasting and so this addition of a prevalent practice crept into the text. But, really, who of the truly faithful would dare add words to Jesus' mouth for such a superficial reason? The early church had set forms of baptism, too, but they did not add these back into the text of Jesus' command to baptize. Coupling prayer and fasting must have meant something much deeper to the early church to be regarded as self-evident enough to be Scripture. Perhaps, the church itself was simply ascetically bent. The bridegroom was gone and the feasting was over. Jesus, the accused winebibber and glutton, was clearly not ascetic. He was a partygoer who enjoyed life. But he did promise when he was gone the party would be over for the faithful, and persecution at his end and very shortly throughout the early church did still the celebration and slaughter the joyful. A time of persecution called for a time of stern discipline, soldierly bootcamp training to withstand the war with evil through suffering. Fasting was a form of training. Like a boxer the church was getting in shape and this, as we saw in our opening quotation, became to them at least

---

[3] While P^{45} is credited in the apparatus with having the words "and fasting" in Mark 9:29, a check of the manuscript reveals that the words may not appear there at all. *Vid* or *ut videtur* is what the notation reads (*propter spatium*, or on account of space, in Kenyon), in other words, enough space is missing or difficult to read to have included the eighteen letters that comprise the Greek words "and fasting." How then can P^{45} be summoned up as a witness? The missing words are being read back from 5th century manuscripts. Twenty lines are missing in the end of the previous verse. So, it is surmised, they could easily be missing here as well. But suppose they are not? Suppose the text simply ends at the end of a line and leaves a gap, which we have noticed sometimes happens? Suppose the text read something else? The inclusion of "and fasting" in even an early papyrus must remain a theory only. Stronger is the evidence from the original codices Sinaiticus and Vaticanus that the words were not original. See Frederic G. Kenyon, *The Chester Beatty Biblical Papyri Descriptions and Texts of Twelve Manuscripts on Papyrus of the Greek Bible: Fasciculus II, The Gospels and Acts* (London: Emery Walker Limited, 1933), p. 11.

as important as prayer. So to them, when Jesus waged war against evil, he recommended training for battle fitness for his disciples, fasting as well as prayer. In this context, then, in a similar manner to the doxology appending itself to the end of the Lord's prayer for liturgical reasons, fasting attached itself to prayer waged against a major encounter with evil.

Interesting, of course, to note is that Jesus himself does not even pray in this passage, not to mention fast. What can this mean? Jesus advises that this kind of (persisting) devil does not come out in any way but by prayer and yet Jesus does not himself pray, he simply commands. Of course, Jesus could have uttered a prayer which was not recorded. More likely we have on hand the inverse of the scene when Michael the Archangel tells Satan, "The Lord rebuke you" (Jude 9). The Lord himself has to be enlisted to deal with powerful demons. Since Jesus is the Lord he did not need to invoke himself, in which action, if the disciples were listening, they would have seen further proof of Jesus' authority and power. We, as the disciples, need to enlist Jesus.

What about demons? Do they really exist? When the present authors were in college, enjoying the tail end of the rationalistic scientistic materialistic mindset that characterized the later industrial-expansion age of the early decades of the twentieth century, the question of a self-directing conscious source of evil seemed to be a vestigial shadow from the nearly dead pre-scientific superstitious past. Such an attitude was maintained by the United States' global insularity and the absence of any developed means by which to test attitudes prevalent in the minds of North Americans. Further, what the rest of the world thought, particularly what the third world thought, we hardly cared. What *we* actually thought we did not know, judging by the naive assessment of contemporary perspective made by the God-Is-Dead movement. A number of factors brought new information to the forefront of our national consciousness. The late 1960's and the so-called dawning of the Age of Aquarius introduced a new astrology that would have seemed laughable if twenty years later our technologically educated children were not still as deeply immersed in the New Age mixture of theosophy, spiritism, and the occult. From respected thinkers like Dr. Elisabeth Kubler-Ross to popular entertainers like Shirley MacLaine the philosophy has run rampant through the minds of upwardly mobile young scientists, engineers, and technicians. While the New Age philosophy may not emphasize supernatural evil it does concentrate on the interrelation of the natural and supra-natural.

Evil came into prominence with a vengeance in the blockbuster movies "Rosemary's Baby" and "The Exorcist" and the brood of demonic movies they spawned. The dark side of the spiritual revival of the 1960's revealed a full-fledged Satanic Church operating under the guidance of one Anton LaVey. News from Germany revealed a full gamut of occult activity through the research and ministry of Christian psychologist Dr. Kurt Koch. A parallel witchcraft, both white and black, was assaulting the women's movement, and was emanating not only from California but also from centers in Salem, Massachusetts, New Jersey, Colorado, even Oregon. Along with the waves of Cambodian and Vietnamese refugees came blatantly open instances of possession. In the Spanish-speaking sections of major United States cities Santeria and other mixtures of the occult and Christianity thrived. Seances, fortune reading, alleged astral projection, "the force," "spiritual vibrations" became a part of common parlance and consciousness and their inverse bad trips, bad vibrations, curses, black magic and the demonic overlords will make the 1970's and 1980's look like a national epidemic of "Dungeons and Dragons" to historians of the future. To the uninitiated future scholar we may look like an age that has hopelessly confused fact and fiction, but to the present minister the darker forces of the universe have simply poked their elbows through the pasteboard backdrop that serves as a facade for our material world.

The authors have done over twenty years of city ministry among third world people and the United States poor, working, and middle classes and we have seen at least three clear instances of possession. What can be believed in the safety of the college classroom (as long as one avoids the library and its revelations of lives like Aleister Crowley's) cannot be maintained on the streets. Only those who have not ministered can question whether conscious malignant evil exists. Only those who have not pondered whether the explanation for Auschwitz can be glibly encompassed by the cumulation of human evil can hold such an ignorant viewpoint. Only those who have never met a battered wife, seen a neo-Nazi or Klan demonstration, treated a child who is a victim of abuse or, more to the point, seen pure malignant evil suddenly leer out of the eyes of some gibbering unfortunate who prophecies, wallows in depression, and has lost the will to eat and live can so utterly blind themselves to what everyone else has been plainly acknowledging all around us in this age of the technological potential of nuclear destruction. The ancients of Jesus' time recognized the activity of evil when they saw it. So Jesus, confronted by active evil, wields his authority and counsels his followers to appeal to him by prayer when they confront systematically strong pervasive evil.

We have been examining Mark's presentation of this event, but Matthew has also recorded it in 17:14-20:

> And when they came to the crowd, a person came to him falling to his knees before him and saying, "Lord, have mercy on my son, because he is an epileptic and suffers badly; for often he falls into the fire and often into the water. And I brought him to your disciples, and they were not able to heal him. And when he answered, Jesus said, "O generation faithless and perverted, how long will I be with you? How long will I endure you? Bring him to me here. And Jesus rebuked him, and the demon came out from him and the child was healed from that hour. Then the disciples, having come to Jesus privately, said, "Why were we not able to cast it out?" But he says to them, "On account of your little faith; for truly I say to you, if you may have faith as a seed of mustard, you will say to this mountain, 'Pass over from here to there, and it will move; and nothing will be impossible to you."

In this fascinating rendition of the account the father does not identify the boy as being possessed. The boy's father simply identifies him as having lunacy (being moonstruck) or epilepsy, the word employed stands for both. Jesus is the one who puts the name to evil and commands the demon to leave. Jesus, who is always interchanging "rise up and walk" (the physical, the material) with "your sins are forgiven" (the spiritual) is confronted with a physical diagnosis and gives a spiritual therapeutic. Interesting also is the fact that the tense shifts between verses 19 and 20. Verse 20 moves from the past to the present tense, a peculiar occurrence. Since this is the moral of the story, the eternal truth Jesus presents from the temporal incident that all have just witnessed, Matthew slips the entire final verse into the present, the presentation of Jesus of a true and timeless truth.

As in the parallel passage in Mark, here, too, we have a case where something has been added to the text, but now not simply "and fasting" has been appended, but an entire sentence, "But this kind does not come out except in prayer and fasting," has been added as a verse 21. The text is then made an echo of Mark's version. But the manuscript evidence is even more strikingly against such an addition being genuine. Now all the authoritative witnesses for this passage line up on the side of omission.[4]

What are we to conclude? No doubt Jesus himself fasted as a good Jew would (e.g. Matt. 4:2), though apparently he was not ascetic enough to please the sticklers. The New Testament itself speaks positively of the practice of fasting (e.g. Matt. 6:16-18) so we may infer

---

[4] Basically, the distribution looks like this: To omit verse 21 we have the original Sinaiticus, Vaticanus, another Alexandrian manuscript from the 300's that lies protected in the Vatican, Koridethi, a Caesarian text-type manuscript from the 9th century, 33, another 9th century Alexandrian manuscript, called the "Queen of the cursives," and one of the best of the gospel minuscules, that is the small letter editions. Even 892, a 9th or 10th century manuscript with a number of remarkable readings of an early type, is here, as well as the Old Latin Codex Palatinus from Africa, a 5th century Western manuscript, the third earliest family; the Old Syriac, Western texts which were copied from manuscripts perhaps as early as the late 100's or early 200's; a Christian Palestinian Caesarian Syriac text (Aramaic) from probably the 400's and the Coptic's Sahidic, Bohairic from the 3rd and 4th centuries. Finally the mixed type of text which is largely Byzantine of the Ethiopic^{RO} is here and the Georgian Caesarian text 897 (Adysch). Attesting to the wide distribution in so many text-types is the fact that the earliest church historian Eusebius, who made a career of gathering up and treasuring omitted accounts and missing words of Jesus, does *not* include this verse as genuine.

And what have we on the other side, the side of inclusion? Verse 21 has only been included in codex Ephraemi, the 5th century largely Byzantine palimpset, which we have seen also includes the phrase "and fasting" in Mark 9:29; the wildly aberrant codex Bezae, that unique 5th or 6th century Western manuscript which we saw also appended "and fasting" to the text in Mark 9, the 9th or 10th century Byzantine manuscript K; L, which is codex Regius, which ironically usually agrees with Vaticanus, but not herein; Washingtonianus, a 4th or 5th century manuscript like codex Bezae where the Byzantine text is mixed through all of Matthew 17; and a number of other late Byzantine texts like 9th century Sangallensis and Petropolitanus. Interestingly, the Syriac Peshitta version has it. This manuscript from the beginning of the 5th century is close to the Byzantine text-type and this encourages us to speculate that the reading might have originated among the Syrian people. Certainly *the Didache, the Lord's Teaching to the Gentiles by the Twelve Apostles*, appears to have originated in Syria and, as we have seen, it adds words to Jesus' model prayer and claims it is comprised of the preserved words of Jesus to the apostles themselves. Later disciplinary manuals from Syria followed this practice, even having the apostles recorded as speaking in their own voices, so the theory makes good historical and chronological sense. From the teaching that produced *the Didache* it spread to the Coptic, to the minuscules, to various georgian, coptic, ethiopic and other versions. We see the reading influenced the Armenian and the Diatessaron of Tatian, a Syrian follower of Tertullian who later fell into heresy. Since these manuscripts are Syrian based or influenced, they strengthen the case for Syria for the source of the inclusion of the verse.

believers did it. We have seen the early church regularly fasted and prescribed fasting. But as widespread as the practice was, it was not a prerequisite prescribed by Jesus for a bout with the forces of evil. Rather like those British sea captains of the 1700's and 1800's Jesus seemed to send his troops well-fed into war. Spiritual support and sustenance was what they needed and this they got by turning to the Lord in prayer.

Summary

Ask believing, knock expecting to have the door opened, exercise faith the size of a tiny seed and great events physical and spiritual can occur for you. These powerful teachings seem to provide a commentary on the breathtaking statement that Jesus suddenly fires at his followers in John 14:12, "Truly, truly I say to you, the one believing in me that one will do the works which I do and greater than these he will do, since I go to the Father."

Scripture abounds with the examples of Old Testament heroes with whom God discussed God's plans and to whom God turned for the doing of mighty acts on earth. These were faithful fulfillers of the human side of the great covenant God cut with God's people. Jesus introduces to his new followers in his new era a new covenant. If we followers remain at one with him and with his Parent and with the Holy Spirit, if we remain at one with each other, submitting our requests to the constituted counsel of Christ's body on earth, if we bear fruit, that is do good actions that serve the reign of God, if we glorify God on earth and the Christ that God sent, if we through thought and action become disciples through following Jesus' commandments, forgiving one another, and acting on the gift of even a mustard-seed-sized faith, the Lord will be pleased to answer our prayers in most magnificently powerful ways to the glory of God and to our most fervent joy.

PART II

THE LORD PRAYS

5

The Words for Prayer

As a child rotating a kaleidoscope, delighting in the ever-changing colors and symmetrical patterns caused by the reflections of the one pattern, so too as adults we can delight in and learn from the manifold aspects of prayer in Jesus' prayer-life. The many Greek words which describe communication with God in heaven illustrate the many dimensions of prayer. These many dimensions of prayer can educate us, even as they educated the earliest disciples, helping us to be like our teacher. As Jesus says, "Every disciple fully trained will be as the teacher" (Luke 6:40). Jesus' prayer gives instruction on both prayer and Jesus. Jesus' prayer-life reflects Jesus' full humanity and, surprisingly, Jesus' full deity.

What words for prayer are used by Jesus and used to describe Jesus? Over twenty words can be found in the New Testament in regard to Jesus and prayer. Prayer is forceful request for needs (*deomai*), asking something of someone or challenging someone (*erotao*), looking up [to heaven] (*anablepo*), lifting up [the eyes] (*airo, epairo*), sighing (*stenazo*), rejoicing exceedingly (*agalliao*), publicly praising (*exomologeo*),singing in praise (*humneo*), giving thanks (*eucharisteo*), blessing (*eulogeo*), calling down blessings (*kateulogeo*), making a sacred vow to God (*proseuchomai*), speaking (*lego*), speaking loudly (*phoneo*), crying aloud (*boao*), crying out (*anaboao*), a formal supplication (*hiketeria*), weeping silently (*dakruo*), and a shout (*krauge*).

Forceful Request for Needs (*Deomai*)

Deomai, coming from *deo* "I want, need," signifies "I stand in need of" or "I want for myself." It can simply refer to parts (as of a chariot?) needing repair or to begging for something from a person. The noun *deesis* signifies "entreaty, petition; want, need." The emphasis is on petitionary, personal need. For example, when Paul entreats the tribune to let him defend himself before the Jerusalem crowd or when he urges Agrippa and Bernice at Caesarea to listen to him, his entreaty is *deomai* (Acts 21:39; 26:3). Paul also uses this same verb to urge the Corinthians and Galatians, his most rebellious congregations, to be reconciled to God (2 Cor. 5:20; 10:2; Gal. 4:12). *Deomai* is a forceful urging in regard to some need. To pray in *deesis* is to pray forcefully when we have need or to request fulfillment of needs by God.

What a relief to know that to pray for needs is possible because that is precisely what we humans normally do! And Jesus certainly encourages us to ask. What new perspective does Jesus shed on this area? The types of things Jesus tells us we need are totally different from those we thought we needed. When Jesus saw the crowds, worried and helpless as sheep without a shepherd, he was moved with compassion to the depths of his inmost self. Then he told his disciples that:

> On the one hand the harvest is great, but on the other hand the workers are few; therefore pray to the Lord of the harvest in order that [the Lord] may drive out workers into his harvest (Matt. 9:37-38).

Jesus feels a concern for the many people with their own spiritual and physical needs. The way Jesus resolves their needs is by praying for more workers like himself even as he finds and designates those workers. Jesus commissions the twelve disciples after he tells his disciples to pray for more workers (Matt. 9:35-10:5). Luke records that he had prayed all night before he chose that first group of twelve (Luke 6:12-16). Consequently, Jesus most likely spent the night following his own advice: praying for helpers and discussing the possible persons with God in heaven. Jesus repeats this command to pray for workers *after* commissioning the seventy-two[1] disciples (Luke 10:2). They were to precede Jesus in every town to prepare the way for him.

Jesus does not seem to think that we can have too many ministers. Moreover, his prayer does not simply ask God to fulfill the spiritual and physical needs of people. Rather, Jesus commands his disciples to pray for the means (workers) by which the goal (to help the crowds) can be reached. Since Jesus commands his largest commissioned group to pray for more workers (as far as our gospels record), we can safely conclude that his command continues appropriate for today.

The prayer is perfectly understandable. To whom do we pray? We pray to the Lord of the harvest. The owner of the farm is certainly interested in the harvest of the crops. If the crops are not harvested, they will spoil or go to seed on the vines, be eaten by bugs and birds and squirrels, or be damaged by frost and rain or wind. In other words, the need we request is one in which the Supplier of needs also has interest. (Is this what it means to pray in the Lord's will?) And

---

[1] A number of good quality ancient manuscripts support both 70 and 72 in Luke 10:1, 17. Both numbers have early careful Alexandrian text-types ("70" is supported by fourth century codex Sinaiticus) and a variety of text-types ("70" is also supported by codex Alexandrinus, which is the oldest Byzantine text, and family^{1,13} which are Caesarean text-types). However, seventy-two has support from the earliest texts with the most variety of text-types (papyrus^{75}, a second century Alexandrian manuscript, third century papyrus^{45}, fourth century codex Vaticanus, fifth century Western codex Bezae, and the earliest translations of the Greek text - old Syriac, the earliest Sahidic, Armenian, which is Caesarean, Old Latin, and Vulgate). Many of the Greek manuscripts which have seventy also add an additional "two" later: "Jesus sent them two by two *by two*" (א, A, C, f^{1}, f^{13}, L, W, ψ, S). Consequently, an early scribe may have accidentally omitted the "two" from "seventy" and added it after the later "two" because his eye wandered from one line to another.

Jesus' symbolism in choosing seventy-two disciples is difficult to ascertain. The seventy-two disciples were not from the interested but not completely committed followers recorded in Luke 9:57-62 (10:1 "others"). These seventy-two disciples were to precede Jesus. Jesus could have been alluding to the elders chosen by Moses (Num. 11:16,24-26; Exod. 24:1), the nations of the world (Gen. 10-11), Jacob's offspring (Exod. 1:5; Hebrew = 70, LXX = 75), or the Sanhedrin. Different manuscripts attest seventy or seventy-two nations (Septuagint = 72; Hebrew = 70), seventy plus one or seventy-two members of the Sanhedrin (*m.Sanh.* 1:5; *m.Yad.* 3:5; 4:2). If Jesus was alluding to the elders, he might have been including Eldad and Medad who, unlike the other seventy elders, prophesized among the Israelites in the camp.

what will the Owner of the harvest do? The Lord will *drive out* workers into the harvest. In order to answer our need, which is also God's need, laborers will not simply be sent out, they will be thrown out!

Every once in a while, we have been all alone in a difficult ministry and we have remembered Jesus' command. And when we have prayed for more workers, every time Jesus has sent at least two of them. None of us need ever hesitate to ask for workers. Jesus' answer to the great need was not our usual answer - work more and more hours! Possibly if we empathized with people more, came to perceive and to learn about their needs, enjoyed working in community, and were not so jealous to guard our financial returns, we might be praying the prayer for workers more frequently. Will we be ready to welcome them?

At times the first century Christians prayed for needs which were ones which they were sure God affirmed and they had resounding results. After Peter and John boldly refused to keep silent about Jesus before the Jewish governmental authorities, they were released. Peter, John, and their friends and neighbors then loudly prayed for continued boldness to speak (Acts 4:31). And when they prayed for boldness, the place in which they were standing began to shake like a tossed ship at sea and all of them were filled with the Holy Spirit and spoke the word of God with boldness. Paul prayed that he might personally see the Roman Christians for the first time and the Thessalonian Christians for the second time in order to meet their needs face to face (Rom. 1:10; 1 Thess. 3:10). The Lord made both visits possible.

Jesus not only tells his disciples to pray for the need of others, but also for their own need. Again, the need that Jesus singles out may not be the one we consider lacking. Do we have the strength to endure? Jesus will return someday to earth in a cloud with power and much glory. In the meantime we can lose our vision through the excessive regular use of alcohol or through anxiety about everyday matters. As Jesus asks in the parable, when the Son of Humanity comes, will he find faith on the earth (Luke 18:8)? Consequently, he commands us to be alert (or not to fall asleep) at all times, while praying that we might have the strength to escape all that is to come -- our own loss of vision and world-wide disasters -- and stand approved in Jesus' presence (Luke 21:34-36). Our goal should be to be happy to see God at the day of judgment because our Judge will be our Defense Attorney and not our Prosecutor! Jesus will set us free only if we have not become an oppressor ourselves either of others or even of ourselves. Consequently, we need strength to persist. The One toward whom we persist can give us that strength if we ask.

Jesus prayed this prayer for endurance for Simon Peter (Luke 22:31-32). He prayed that Simon's faith might not give out (literally, suffer a full eclipse). Peter's faith did suffer a partial eclipse. But Jesus was so confident of Peter's return to faith that he commands him to strengthen his brothers and sisters once he turns back. In effect, Jesus interceded in Simon's behalf. Even now Jesus continues to help any people who are tempted by strengthening them and pleading for them (Heb. 2:18; 7:25 *entugchano*).

Ask (*Erotao*)

Although *erotao* simply means "I ask," the word shows Jesus in his capacity as intermediary. *Erotao* comes from *eiro* which means "to say, speak, or tell." It can signify "to ask something of someone or about something" or more specifically "to question or challenge a person," as a sentry does or as a debater questions an opponent in order to refute his answers.[2] Greek has several different words for "ask," two of which are contrasted in Jesus' conversation in John 16, *erotao* and *aiteo*.[3]

In the gospels humans request (*erotao*) of one another or of Jesus, but only Jesus requests of the Father. (In contrast, John uses *aiteo* and *erotao* as synonyms to refer to human requests of God in 1 John 5:16.) For example, some Gentiles wanted to see Jesus, so they asked (*erotao*) Philip if they could see him (John 12:21). Paul requests the "true yokefellow" help Euodia and Syntyche (Phil. 4:3). These people are requesting that someone do something. In the same way, Jesus tells his disciples that he will ask (*erotao*) the Father and another Advocate (the Holy Spirit) will be given to them to be with them forever (John 14:16). Prayer here is very similar to *deomai* and *entugchano*. Jesus intercedes in behalf of the needs of others.

Why must Jesus *ask* for the Spirit to come? Jesus tells his disciples that he will return after his ascension through the means of the Spirit (John 14:16-19). Verse 15 clarifies the point of Jesus'

---

[2] Henry G. Liddell and Robert Scott, *A Greek-English Lexicon* (9th ed.; Oxford: Clarendon, 1940), p. 696.

[3] For biblical definitions see ch. 4 "Asking versus Challenging."

request. If the disciples love Jesus, a love which is shown by obedience to Jesus' commands, then Jesus will as well ask the Father to give the Holy Spirit to dwell in them. Jesus has set up a conditional sentence. The disciples' love is potential love. If it becomes actual, then the presence of the Spirit will also become actual. Jesus is the intermediary, looking at our love and requesting another Advocate to assist us. Jesus' request, consequently, is based on evaluating the disciples' actions, actions which today continue to be evaluated. Jesus' request of the Father is always answered affirmatively by the Father because they are in total agreement on the prerequisites.

In John 16 Jesus employs *erotao* in its more specific sense, to question or challenge. If Jesus can intercede for us and evaluate our actions, as well Jesus can *challenge* our requests. Jesus says:

> In that day you will ask for yourselves (*aiteo*) in my name and I do not say to you that I myself will ask (*erotao*) the Father concerning you (pl); for the Father himself loves you, because you have loved me and you have believed that I myself came from God" (John 16:26-27).

Jesus' words become almost meaningless if he is not contrasting *aiteo* and *erotao*. The passage is clear if *erotao* signifies to question or challenge. When Jesus has ascended to God in heaven, Jesus' disciples will be able to ask (*aiteo*) for things to be given in Jesus' name (John 16:23). Jesus will not question or challenge (*erotao*) the Father concerning us *if* we love Jesus and believe he came from God. In other words, answers to our requests are based on the type of relationship we have toward the Giver. Jesus intercedes not only in our behalf, but also in behalf of the Godhead. Furthermore, only Jesus is on an equal footing with the Father sufficient to question or challenge human requests.[4]

Jesus uses *erotao* again three times in John 17, the lengthy prayer after Passover which will be discussed at length in two later

---

[4] In John 16 *erotao* implies that Jesus "who asks stands on a certain footing of equality with him from whom the boon is asked, as king with king (Luke xiv.32)...our Lord never uses *aitein* or *aiteisthai* of Himself, in respect of that which He seeks on behalf of his disciples from God; for his is not the *petition* of the creature to the Creator, but the *request* of the Son to the Father" Richard C. Trench, *Synonyms of the New Testament* (Grand Rapids: Eerdmans, 1953), p. 145.

chapters. Jesus again intercedes for his disciples and those who will believe in Jesus through the first disciples (the disciples' disciples). His earlier command to us to pray for workers (*deomai*) is exemplified by Jesus and developed in Jesus' concern for his own workers. Even as he wants us to pray for strength to persist (Luke 21:36), Jesus also prays that we be kept from the evil one. We have already seen how Jesus prayed specifically for Simon to be kept from the evil one (Luke 22:32). Jesus also prays that all his disciples become one in imitation of the One God, an overwhelming need we all have. Paul reiterates Jesus' prayer in Romans 15:5-6, asking God to give the Romans one mind in Christ Jesus.

An everyday word like "ask" reveals much about Jesus' unique nature. Jesus asks even as we do, however, only Jesus is in a position to screen out requests made to the Father. Jesus can challenge our requests as they come up to God because he evaluates our love, faith, and obedience.

Summon Help (*Parakaleo*)

The gospel writers do *not* describe Jesus' prayers of intercession with the word one might have expected, *parakaleo*. *Parakaleo* means "I call for," "I call to my side, summon," as one summons one's friends to attend one as witnesses in a trial. The noun form, *parakletos*, is used of the Holy Spirit. In contrast the Greeks often used *parakaleo* for communication with the gods. In the New Testament Paul uses *parakaleo* to describe his three appeals to the Lord to remove his thorn in the flesh (2 Cor. 12:8). Jesus does use the verb once. At his arrest he tells the disciple who had a sword to put it down: "Do you think that I am not able to appeal (*parakaleo*) to my Father, and he will send me at once more than twelve legions of angels?" (Matt. 26:53). Jesus has not resorted to any intercession for his personal behalf, although at Gethsemane he discusses this possibility with the Father.

Look Up to Heaven (*Anablepo*) and Sigh (*Stenazo*)

So far Jesus pleads for human needs and challenges human prayer. As well as in words, prayer also can be done simply with a look or an inarticulate sound. Except possibly in two recorded instances (Mark 7:33-34; John 11:41-42), Jesus normally effects change in humans or in nature by word of command rather than by prayer. For instance, having stretched out the leper's hand, he touches him saying, "Be clean" (Matt. 8:1-3). Having risen from his seat on the boat, Jesus rebukes the winds and the sea and there is a great calm (Matt. 8:26). He tells the demons, "Go" and they leave (Matt. 8:32). Frequently, he touches people or commands them to act on their healing (Matt. 12:13). Sometimes he touches the specific part of the body that needs healing (Mark 8:22-25).

When Jesus travels in the region of the Decapolis, a deaf man with a speech impediment is brought to Jesus. Jesus places his fingers in the man's ears and touches his tongue. And then "after looking up into heaven (Jesus) sighed and says to him 'Ephphatha,' which is, 'Be opened'" (Mark 7:33-34). In effect, Jesus' prayer is a deep sigh. Like the Holy Spirit, who intercedes with sighs too deep for words (Rom. 8:26), Jesus too "pray(s) sighing".[5]

Stenazo is to express grief by inarticulate or semi-articulate sounds. Paul tells us that all of creation sighs together (*sustenazo*) and suffers great pain together as a woman in childbirth until now. And not only does all of creation sigh but also we ourselves who have the first fruits of the Spirit sigh to ourselves as we wait for adoption as heirs (Rom. 8:22-23). Paul also says we sigh longing to put on our heavenly dwelling (2 Cor. 5:2,4). Paul uses *stenazo* to express both the groaning from the burdens of a suffering world and the yearning for a perfected world. *Stenazo* can also mean to groan in complaint (James 5:9) or to groan from being over-burdened (Heb. 13:17).

What kind of sigh did Jesus express in the Decapolis? He took the man aside privately because God's proclamation of release is usually only for those with faith (Mark 4:10-12; 7:6-8). Did he sigh because of the crowd's lack of faith? Later, Mark records another of Jesus' sighs. When the Pharisees wanted a sign from heaven, Jesus sighs deeply (Mark 8:12). He draws a sigh up from the center of his being (*anastenazo*) because of his exasperation with the combative belligerent spirit of the religious leaders of the time. Or, did Jesus sigh because he was himself tired of healing? Did he sigh because of the severe physical limitations this particular man had to endure? Or, did he sigh because of the suffering in this world while yearning for its redemption? Mark does not specify. However, Jesus' sigh does indicate how Jesus totally identified with suffering persons. If Jesus' sigh was both a groaning and a yearning, in line with Paul's use of *stenazo*, then it was a full albeit inarticulate prayer. Jesus was both

[5] *Thayer*, p. 587.

calling attention to need (groaning) and pleading for satisfaction (yearning).

Jesus did sigh *after* he began to look up into heaven. His sigh, therefore, was a communication to God. As well, Jesus' *look up* was also the prayer. Eliphaz the Temanite says that when you delight yourself with the Almighty you will look up cheerfully to heaven (Job 22:26). In the Apocrypha when the disreputable elders accused Susanna, she "looked up to heaven through her tears, for she trusted in the Lord" (Daniel and Susanna 35 *NEB*). King Solomon too spreads out his hands into heaven although "heaven and the highest heaven cannot contain thee" (1 Kings 8:22,27). God is somehow "in all" as well as "over all" (Eph. 4:6). Yet to look up can be to address God. Jesus follows a similar sequence when he blesses the five loaves and two fish. After he looked up into heaven, he blessed the food.[6] A prayer which is only a look and a sound without words shows how close was Jesus' communication with God in heaven.

Rejoice Exceedingly (*Agalliao*) and Public Praise (*Exomologeo*)

At least eight different Greek words are used to express thanksgiving to God in prayer: *agalliao, exomologeo, humneo, eulogeo, kateulogeo, eucharisteo, aineo*, and *doxazo*. The first six words are used in the New Testament to describe Jesus in prayer. *Agalliao* is found previous to its use in the New Testament only in the Greek Old Testament.[7] The more common Greek word is *agallo* meaning "glorify, exalt" and especially "pay honour to a god."[8] The believers in the one God apparently felt so much joy they added extra vowels of emphasis for *agalliao*, "rejoice exceedingly" or "rejoice extremely." The verb form, *agalliao*, which translates eight different Hebrew words, occurs frequently in the psalms, as in Psalm 9: "I will be glad and *rejoice exceedingly* in thee" (v. 2) and "rejoice exceedingly in your salvation" (v. 14). Hosts at feasts even had an "oil of extreme gladness" with which to anoint their guests (Ps.45:7; Heb. 1:9). Similarly, in the New Testament, *agalliao* is often used in pleonasm (repetition of words of similar meaning) with another word for "rejoice," *chairo*. For instance, Jesus commands his disciples to rejoice and *be extremely joyful* when they are persecuted and falsely

---

6 Luke 9:16; Matt. 14:19; Mark 6:41. See also John 11:41 *airo*; 17:1 *epairo* "lift up the eyes".

7 Bauer, p. 3.

8 Liddell and Scott, p. 5.

condemned on Jesus' account because their reward is great in heaven (Matt. 5:12). Also, the great multitude in heaven exclaims that it must rejoice and *be exceedingly glad* and give God the glory for the marriage of the Lamb has come and the Bride is ready (Rev. 19:7).

Earlier Jesus had probably prayed for more laborers and had commanded his disciples to pray for more laborers (Matt. 9:38; Luke 10:2). The laborers had come. The 72 had left and returned. They had returned with joy (*chara*) because of the power they had had over the demons in Jesus' name (Luke 10:17). Jesus had agreed with the disciples that they had authority and power over the enemy because he had given those things to them. However, he reprimands them for rejoicing because of their power. Rather, he says, they should rejoice because their names are recorded in heaven.

In that hour Jesus too rejoices, and he rejoices *exceedingly* (*agalliao*). *Agalliao* takes the dative case of the thing in which the joy originates. The one who causes Jesus' joy is the Holy Spirit. (Some ancient manuscripts omit "Holy," however, the earliest and best manuscripts, papyrus[75], codices Vaticanus and Sinaiticus, include it.) Luke 10:21 shows the oneness of the Deity and proper joy. The Holy Spirit causes Jesus to rejoice and consequently Jesus praises (*exomologeo*) the Father.

Jesus begins his prayer with *exomologeo*. It is made up of *omologeo*, "confess, profess" or, literally, "say the same thing" as another, and *ex*, "out of." Jesus speaks forth from the heart, freely, openly, publicly. *Exomologeo* signifies more specifically "acknowledge openly and joyfully," "make grateful acknowledgements, give thanks, sing praises." The Holy Spirit causes an extreme inner joy which flowed out from Jesus into a public grateful acknowledgement to God the Father. Unlike his disciples did, Jesus does not rejoice in his power over the enemy. Rather, Jesus rejoices over the fact that only the powerless, "the babies," receive God's revelation: "I publicly praise you, Father, Lord of the heaven and the earth, for having hidden these things from wise and intelligent people and having revealed them to babies; yes, Father, that such a choice was pleasing to thee" (Luke 10:21). Paul repeats in 1 Corinthians 1:18-2:5 what Jesus has revealed. God did not want wisdom and intelligence to become means toward gaining salvation in order that no human being might boast in God's presence. Those whom Paul calls "foolish," "weak," "low and despised," Jesus calls "babies."

The extreme joy that Jesus experiences recaptures the joy of the announcement of his own birth. Mary, Jesus' mother, had rejoiced in God her Savior for the same reason that her Son did, God has regard for the "low estate" of the slave (Luke 1:46-48). The angel Gabriel tells Zechariah that he "will have joy and *gladness*" and many will rejoice at the birth of John the Baptist (Luke 1:14). The unborn babe John the Baptist leaps for *joy* when Mary's greeting comes to Elizabeth's ears (Luke 1:44). As with Jesus, their knowledge of God's concern for the meek and their participation in God's work causes a great joy which resounds into public praise.

Jesus' prayer changes from the first person, "I gratefully acknowledge you" (Luke 10:21), to the third person: "Everything has been given to me by my Father, and no one knows who is the Son except the Father, and who is the Father except the Son and to whomever the Son may wish to reveal" (Luke 10:22). Has Jesus broken the mandate sometimes given to preachers that praying should not revert to preaching? *Exomologeo* explains Jesus' words. This whole prayer is a public profession. Consequently, Jesus naturally moves from the first to the third person. Jesus publicly and gratefully praises the Father in the presence of his disciples (v. 21). Then he speaks about their relationship in the third person, "Son and Father" (v. 22). Finally, he speaks directly to the disciples (vv. 23-24).

Jesus goes on to express his solidarity with the Father and the value of what the disciples have just overheard. The Son gratefully acknowledges the Father but then the Father hands over *everything* to the Son. Solely the Father and the Son have full knowledge of who each is. Such knowledge of God is extended only by the Son. In his prayer Jesus has explained the interrelationship of the one God as God speaks to self: by means of the Spirit, to the Father, revealed by the Son.

Jesus then turns to the disciples (v. 23), probably turning away from heaven and away from the unbelievers (v. 25). Privately he tells them how providentially blessed they are. They are blessed at least for two reasons. One, they are blessed because they have heard that God is concerned for the powerless and, consequently, they are the ones privileged to hear God's message. Two, they are blessed because they have seen and heard God in the person of Jesus.

Matthew records additional words Jesus said at the end of this prayer: "Come to me everyone working hard and loaded with burdens, and I will give you rest. Take my yoke upon you and learn from me, for I am gentle and lowly in heart, and you will find rest for your souls; since my yoke is easy and my burden is light" (Matt. 11:28-30). Not only does God choose the powerless and Jesus command the disciples to pray for workers, Jesus here helps us learn that those who hearken to God's drive are already workers, hard workers and over-burdened. Jesus identifies with the lowly because he sees himself as lowly in heart. He is gentle and will give rest to the powerless. Working for Jesus will have its yoke and its burden but, Jesus promises, it will be light and restful compared to the previous burdens.

Jesus' joyful prayer of public profession raises at least two questions of application. Are our reasons for joy ones which flow from the Holy Spirit? Are we lowly, thereby having cause to rejoice? The New Testament affirms all rejoicing because God is concerned for the lowly. Rejoicing should be part of the Christian's initial, present, and future life.[9] Certainly, God expresses and exemplifies the emotion of joy, an extreme joy.

Sing in Praise (*Humneo*)

Hidden away in the Letter to the Hebrews is another word for praise as prayer. If prayer is indeed communication to God by a human, Jesus prays by singing as well as by conversational words and by inarticulate looks and sounds. The writer of Hebrews exhorts the Italian Christians not to succumb to the ways of the old covenant by showing how the new covenant is superior. In Chapter 2 the author describes how Jesus was a perfect high priest and sacrifice because he was fully human:

> For it was fitting by him (God), on account of whom are all things and through whom are all things, by bringing many sons (or heirs) into glory to perfect the pioneer of their salvation through suffering. For also the One purifying and the ones being purified are all from one (origin); for which reason he is not ashamed to call them brothers (and sisters), saying:
>
> > "I proclaim your name to my brothers (and sisters),
> > I *sing praises* to you in the midst of the church";

---

[9] See also Matt. 5:12; Acts 2:46; 16:34; 1 Pet. 1:6,8; 4:13; Jude 24; Rev. 19:7.

and again:

"I (myself) will trust him";

and again:

"Behold (here am) I and the children whom God gave to me" (Heb.2:10-13).

The first Old Testament quotation contains the verb *humneo*. Jesus is described as singing praises to God in the midst of a gathering of his "brothers." (Since "brothers" is often used generically to signify "siblings," we can add the word "sisters" to communicate the intent of the Greek.) In Hebrews 12:23 *ekklesia* ("church" or "gathering") is also used but there the writer specifies that it refers to the gathering "in the heavens." Since the point in chapter 2 is Jesus' humanity and perfection through suffering, *ekklesia* in 2:12 most likely refers to an earthly gathering of believers. Jesus, the pioneer of our salvation, has the same humanity we have which he received in the incarnation. Therefore, although from a divine standpoint to have kinship with humans is an "emptying of oneself," becoming a "slave," Jesus now being human is not ashamed to call us "family." The Messianic Psalm 22 (v.22) is quoted to express Jesus' sentiments wherein he calls us "brothers and sisters" and his "gathering."

Possibly the three quotations in Hebrews 2:12-13 may summarize Jesus' life: Jesus' proclamation (v. 12), Jesus' trust amidst his sufferings, and Jesus' completion of his mission (v. 13). "Behold here am I and the children whom God gave to me" is reminiscent of John 17:6 where Jesus reviews his work on earth before his arrest. Jesus is a model to all humans of proclamation, trust, and accomplishment.

Humneo is a synonymous verb for *apaggello*, "I proclaim" or "I confess." The praise of *humneo* since it is in the midst of a gathering of other people, therefore, is a type of proclamation or public testimony about God. Jesus not only is not ashamed to call humans "brothers," but he is also not ashamed to call God "Parent," praising God "in the midst of the church." ("In the midst of the church" is emphasized in the clause because it is situated first in the clause in Greek.)

Humneo, the verb, and its noun *humnos* are the Greek basis for our transliterated English noun "hymn." A *humnos* was a common Greek word for a song in praise of gods or heroes. For example, the Philistines "sang in praise" (*humneo*) of their god Dagon when they seized Samson (Judg. 16:24). Epictetus, the first century Stoic philosopher, says that:

> Why, if we had sense, ought we to be doing anything else, publicly and privately, than *hymning* and praising the Deity, and rehearsing His benefits? Ought we not, as we dig and plough and eat, to sing the *hymn of praise* to God? "Great is God, that He hath furnished us these instruments wherewith we shall till the earth. Great is God, that He hath given us hands, and power to swallow, and a belly, and power to grow unconsciously, and to breathe while asleep" (*Discourses* I.16,16-17. See also III.26,30).

A hymn would celebrate or commemorate the gods, a famous person, event or place.[10] After the Passover meal, Jesus and the disciples sang in praise of God the Hallel ("praise thou" as in Hallelujah; Pss. 113-118 in Hebrew).[11]

Humneo has a rich Old Testament background. When David first appoints Asaph and his kin to the new Levitical order of praise, they are to "Sing to (the Lord) and sing praises (*humneo*) to (God)" (1 Chron. 16:9). Wisdom's loud proclamation is called a "hymn" (Prov. 1:20; 8:3). Isaiah prophesies a future day wherein God's people will say, "Sing praises (*humneo*) to the Lord, call God's name" (Isa. 12:4). And indeed singing praises to God becomes a significant topic in Ephesians and Colossians.

In Colossians 3:16 and Ephesians 5:18-20 Paul uses *humnos* in combination with several other synonymous nouns. He explains that Christ's word can fully dwell among us if we communicate in melody to one another and to God:

> in all wisdom teaching and exhorting one another in psalms, hymns, spiritual songs, in thanks singing in your hearts to God (Col. 3:16).

---

[10] Liddell and Scott, p.1849; Zion Ps. 137:3.
[11] Matt. 26:30; Mark 14:26; Bauer, p.844.

Our teaching and exhorting are done not only by hymns or "songs in praise of God," but also by psalms and spiritual songs.

But can *humneo* really be a type of prayer? Paul could simply be using singing to describe an attitude, a way of life, a celebration and enjoyment of life because one loves God and loves those made in God's image. As the Psalmist asks, "May my mouth be filled with praise that I may sing in praise (*humneo*) of your glory" (Ps. 71:8). For Paul to emphasize song and music is remarkable in light of the fact that he writes Colossians and Ephesians while he is under house arrest in Rome. Nevertheless, Paul demonstrates at Philippi in Macedonia that what might very well be an attitude is also an action. At Philippi Paul and his coworker Silas are imprisoned as if they were the most dangerous of criminals. They were beaten by the soldiers, placed in the inner cell, and chained by their feet. Luke tells the reader that down around midnight Paul and Silas were "praying-singing to God" while the other inmates listened (Acts 16:25). Most translations render the phrase "praying and singing" in order to have a smooth English rendition. However, the second participle "singing" (*humneo*) appears to serve as an adjective to describe the first participle "praying." Paul and Silas were praying in the form of songs of praise to God. The New English Bible version renders the sentence, "About midnight Paul and Silas, at their prayers, were singing praises to God." Paul and Silas, like their Lord, Jesus, were singing in praise of God in the midst of a gathering (in this case an unwilling gathering - inmates) and thereby proclaiming God's name to other humans. The power of their testimony is shown by the fact that when the ground shook and the doors of the prison were opened, none of the inmates left. We are not told if any of the other inmates became believers in this all-mighty God, however, the jailer ignored his duties that night and brought Paul and Silas home to hear more of their message.

If singing to God can be prayer, then prayer is indeed a broad category. If singing to God can be prayer, then our singing itself needs to be done more thoughtfully. When hymns are addressed to God, then we need to sing such hymns as prayers, musical prayers. If songs of praise can be prayer, may also playing on a stringed instrument (*psallo*) be a prayer? As Psalm 150:3 reads, "praise God with lute and harp." Then, could dancing be a prayer? "Praise God with tambourine and dance" (Ps. 150:4)? Can "everything that has breath praise the Lord" (Ps. 150:6) in prayer?

The voice, the face, the hands, the body can all be used to communicate to God and to teach and proclaim to other people. Jesus, we are told, sang in praise of his heavenly Parent proclaiming God's name to other believers. May our prayers as well be sacred songs to our hero - God! Moreover, may our whole lives be songs of praise!

Give Thanks (*Eucharisteo*), Bless (*Eulogeo*), and Call Down Blessings on (*Kateulogeo*)

The Lord taught his disciples to ask for bread. The response to the fulfillment of that request is thanksgiving for bread received. Jesus many times is shown giving thanks for food. Two different Greek words are used to describe Jesus' "grace" at meals. *Eucharisteo* comes from *eu*, "well," and *charis*, "gift," "that which affords joy," "thanks." A good gift necessitates a hearty thanks. The Lord's Supper is called the Eucharist because Jesus, following his custom, thanks (*eucharisteo*) God for the bread before he passes it around to his disciples (Luke 22:19). We continue in thanksgiving to participate in the meal. Even after his resurrection, Jesus continues to bless (*eulogeo*) bread before passing it around to be eaten (Luke 24:30). *Eulogeo* from which comes "eulogize" is derived from *eu*, "well," and *logos*, "a word." To eulogize, literally, is to give a good word or to celebrate with praises. It is also a blessing called down from heaven (*kateulogeo*). *Eucharisteo, eulogeo*, and *kateulogeo* are used synonymously to describe the benedictions given at mealtimes. Jesus not only blesses God for food, but he also blesses people. He blesses (*eulogeo*) his disciples before he is carried up to heaven and he blesses (*kateulogeo*) even children brought to him.[12]

Jesus takes the five loaves and two fish the disciples had in the wilderness, looked up to heaven (*anablepo*), and he blessed (*eulogeo*) the food and, having broken the bread, he gave them to the disciples and the disciples gave the food to the crowds. Five thousand men and their families were fed (Matt. 14:19; Mark 6:41; Luke 9:16). Later, Jesus takes seven loaves of bread and a few small fish and, having given thanks (*eucharisteo*), he broke them and gave them to the disciples and the disciples gave them to the crowds (Matt. 15:36; Mark 8:7). Four thousand men and their families at this time were fed.

---

[12] Luke 24:50-51; Mark 10:13-16.

To thank God for meals was not unusual for Jews. *The Mishnah*, which records Jewish traditions before and after Jesus' times, has a tractate entitled "Benedictions" (Berakoth) which records early rabbinic directions for prayer. If people are reclined around a table, one person is encouraged to say the Benediction for everyone (*m.Ber.* 6:6). The Jews had a different benediction for different foods as well as for different occasions. Over bread a person was obligated to pray, "Blessed art thou, [Adonai our God, king of the world], who brings forth bread from the earth." Over wine a person was obligated to pray, "Blessed art thou...who *creates* the fruit of the vine" (*m.Ber.* 6:1). To bless a variety of foods that do not grow from the earth a person's obligation would be fulfilled if he prayed, "Blessed art thou...by whose word all things exist" (*m.Ber.* 6:3). Another benediction was said after the meal was eaten, which changed depending on the size of the gathering. For a gathering of a thousand the leader would say, "We will bless the Lord our God, the God of Israel of whose bounty we have partaken." For a gathering of ten thousand the leader would elongate the benediction, "We will bless the Lord our God, the God of Israel, the God of hosts, who sitteth between the Cherubim, for the food which we have eaten" (*m.Ber.* 7:3). Although women, slaves, and minors were required to recite the after dinner benediction, the "Common Grace," they were not included in the count of total persons. Possibly, for this reason, the disciples did not include the women and children in the total count of persons present at the meals (Matt. 15:38; Mark 8:9; *m.Ber.* 3:3; 7:2). The New Testament does not record the Common Grace at these meals nor the content of Jesus' benedictions. Jesus does appear to give a prayer of thanksgiving at the time usually allotted to the Common Grace during the last Passover meal.[13] Possibly, Jesus used a prayer similar to one recorded in the Mishnah. However, although Jesus might have thanked God as his contemporaries might have, he had incredible results. Thousands of people were fed from very small quantities of food. Jesus exemplified his own teachings. He asked for bread. Should not we dare to pray likewise?

Jesus also expresses thanksgiving in his prayer before he commands Lazarus to be raised from the dead:

> And Jesus raised up (*airo ano*) his eyes and said (*lego*):
> "Father, I thank (*eucharisteo*) you that you heard me.
> And I myself had known that always you hear me, but

---

[13] Luke 22:17-20 included by the best ancient manuscripts; possibly also Matt. 26:26; Mark 14:22.

> on account of the crowd standing around I spoke (*lego*), in order that they may believe that you yourself sent me." And having said these things with a loud voice he shouted: "Lazarus, come outside" (John 11:41-43).

Here is a prayer which is audible in order to be educational. Jesus begins by looking up. Giving such a look was sufficient for the Son to communicate with the Father.[14] Furthermore, why would Jesus then follow his look by thanking his Parent for having heard him? Jesus' prayer was already heard by the time he spoke audibly (v. 41b). By using the pronoun "I" Jesus emphasizes that *he* himself knows that always his Parent heard him (v. 42). However, the crowd standing around him did not know God in heaven always heard the human Jesus.

Jesus' words raise several questions. Should we be thankful to God for hearing us and fulfilling our requests? Did Jesus have a unique communication with the Father that we can never (or *should* never) attempt to reduplicate? The reason Jesus thanks God for hearing him is so that the crowd might believe that Jesus was sent by God (v. 42). Does God *always* hear us even as God always heard Jesus? If God always heard Jesus without audible words, why should we ever pray aloud?

First of all, appreciation is an essential ingredient of communication with God as it is an essential ingredient of communication with humans. How many of us are like the nine lepers who asked to be healed, were healed, but never returned to praise God (Luke 17:11-19)? Naturally we all say we are like the tenth leper who as he was walking along suddenly noticed that he was healed. He turned back. And with a very loud voice glorified (*doxazo*) God and fell down on his face at Jesus' feet and thanked him (*eucharisteo*). This Samaritan leper was not only physically healed, he became spiritually healed as well. When we thank God, our thanks are in effect a profession of belief in God. Thanksgiving (*eucharisteo*) is close to confession of belief (*exomologeo*) and glorification (*doxazo*) (Rom. 15:9).

From *doxazo* comes our "doxology," a word (*logos*) of glory (*doxa*). *Doxa* can simply be an opinion, but in the Bible *doxa* is always a good opinion. *Doxa* is a translation of the Hebrew *kabod*, "splendor, brightness." *Kabod* is properly used of the light from the

---

[14] Mark 7:33-34; 6:41; Luke 9:16; Matt. 14:19.

sun, moon, and stars. It is the equivalent of the Shekinah glory of the Lord, the bright cloud which enveloped the Tent of the Meeting (Exod. 40:34-38). Glory is part of God's essence. To glorify is to cause the dignity and worth of some person or thing to become manifest and acknowledged.

Glorification is often done by actions. Believers glorify the Father by the "fruit" they produce (John 15:8;21:19; Matt. 5:16). The gospel writers rarely record Jesus using *doxazo* as a word of praise in prayer to the Father. Rather, the Son and the Father glorify each other in their actions. While on earth Jesus glorified God in heaven, not so much by words, but by accomplishing the work God gave him. As God, Jesus also appropriately should be glorified. Jesus is glorified by everyone when he teaches in the synagogues in Galilee, when he raises to life the widow's son at Nain, and when he heals the bent woman, leper, blind man, and paralytic.[15] That glorification culminates in the crucifixion (Luke 23:47; John 7:39; cf. 21:19). After Jesus enters Jerusalem, he begins to dwell upon his own death, "the hour of glory" (John 12:23), and he is disturbed. His prayer to the Father flows out of his talk with Andrew and Philip about death and life:

> Now my soul is disturbed. And what shall I say? Father, deliver me out of this hour? Rather, on account of this I came into this hour. Father, glorify your name" (John 12:27-28).

How will the Father glorify The Name? God will glorify God by Jesus' crucifixion (John 12:23; 13:31; 17:1,4). The Son's command to the Father that the Name of God be glorified is immediately answered and the answer is heard in some form by the crowd: "And I have glorified and again I will glorify" (John 12:28).[16]

Glorification can also be praise or celebration. Consequently, when we thank God, we recognize the magnificence and goodness of God. Moreover, that glory which envelops God we can enjoy also in God's word and God's ministry and in each other (1 Cor. 12:26). In return we impart, as it were, a tithe back to God in a word of praise. Therefore, we should always be thankful to God for fulfilling our

[15] Luke 4:15; 7:16; 5:25-26; 13:13; 17:15; 18:43; Matt. 15:31.

[16] The New Testament records two other instances where God chooses to allow humans to hear communication within the Godhead: Jesus' baptism (Matt. 3:17; Mark 1:11; Luke 3:22) and transfiguration (Matt. 17:5; Mark 9:7; Luke 9:35).

requests and showing love for us by hearing us. As Paul says, "And whatever you may do in word or in action, [do it] all in the name of the Lord Jesus, while thanking God the Father through him" (Col. 3:17). As much as we enjoy giving thanks, nevertheless, we still notice that if in one day we should receive good news and bad news, the bad news is what we remember. We forget to thank God and God's emissaries for the good. In addition, although thanksgiving is essential, not everything is cause for thanksgiving. For instance, the religious Pharisee who thanked God he was not like the disreputable tax-collector praying next to him was not the justified person (Luke 18:10-14).

Second, does Jesus' prayer before Lazarus' tomb indicate that Jesus had a unique communication with God? Could all Christians say that if God "hears" (to hear is to do) them then they have been sent by God? Jesus has a unique relationship with his Parent. They are one in a literal sense as well as in a more metaphorical sense. In other words, Jesus is God. We humans are not God. Consequently, the effectiveness of our prayer does not show we are God, which is the import of Christ's words to the crowds. Jesus' prayer before the tomb is part of an overall plan to help humans believe that if any of them trust in Jesus as the full incarnation of God, then they too as Jesus will be resurrected (John 11:4,15,25-26, 45). Jesus makes his prayer audible for the sake of the crowds standing around him (v. 42). Often Jesus does not even allow unbelievers to be present at a healing. However, at this time, Jesus' first focus is fully to manifest who he is. The crowd often has many unbelievers. Even with Jesus' explanation of his actions, some of those seeing the marvel of Lazarus walking out alive from the tomb still feared their own loss of political power and decided that Jesus must be killed (John 11:45-53).

However, although this prayer shows the uniqueness of the Son's relationship to the Father, a relationship we can never reduplicate, yet Jesus has promised us that as close as we become to God and learn how to ask properly, then too we can be assured of God's affirmation (John 15:7). God will hear and do. God does always hear us. Words certainly are not necessary. Yet they may be expedient. We may pray aloud so that listeners today may come to know that God hears prayers. We might also pray aloud so that listeners may hear our own confession. Prayers recited aloud were the more usual practice among Jesus' Jewish contemporaries (*m.Ber.* 2:3). Audible words, though, are not a necessary ingredient of prayer.

Finally, although this prayer might seem to indicate that Jesus prayed for healing, in effect he does not do so. Again, Jesus commands the healing. In that sense, his authority is his own. Yet, Jesus appears continually to be in intimate communication with the Father.

Make a Sacred Vow to God (*Proseuchomai*)

Proseuchomai reveals more about Jesus' customary prayer habits than any other word of prayer. *Proseuchomai* comes from two root words: the preposition "to" (*pros*) and the verb "wish, vow, or pray" (*euchomai*), literally signifying "pray to." *Proseuchomai* stresses the One addressed. It is "prayer addressed *to* God." In the New Testament *euchomai* usually refers to a vow or wish. At Cenchreae Paul shaved his hair because of an *euche* (noun form of *euchomai*; Acts 18:18). Paul *wishes* that everyone would be a Christian as he was (Acts 26:29). *Euchomai* occurs a few times with God as the object. Paul prays to God (*euchomai pros*) that the Corinthians not do wrong, but rather improve (2 Cor. 13:7,9). The "prayer of faith," which will heal the sick is literally a "vow of faith" (James 5:15). Probably James wants to highlight that if the elders pray with "faith," in effect their prayer is like a vow. If they trust God as able to heal, their prayer has assurance of results.

The sense of a vow is retained in *proseuchomai*, words dedicated to God. However, *proseuchomai,* being limited to God, emphasizes the sacred nature of the act. *Proseuchomai* was another common word among the ancients for prayer to the gods. The noun form *proseuche* signified not only "prayer," but also "a place of prayer" (Acts 16:13). Jews, especially from Egypt, commonly used *proseuche* as a synonym for a synagogue. Philo from Alexandria, Egypt frequently employs *proseuche* to name the Jewish places for prayer and meetings set in the midst of the Jewish neighborhoods (e.g. *The Embassy to Gaius* XX.134).

After Jesus overturns the tables of the moneychangers at the temple of Jerusalem he chastises the people for forgetting the original function for the temple: "'My house shall be called a House of Prayer', but you make it a den of robbers" (Matt. 21:13; Mark 11:17; Luke 19:46). As well as to the prayers we are exhorted to make for our persecutors,[17] *proseuchomai* can refer to customary prayers. For

[17] Luke 6:28; Matt. 5:44.

example, a multitude of people were praying outside the temple when Zechariah entered to burn incense (Luke 1:10). *Proseuchomai* is used for prayer in the temple and at the customary hours outside the temple (Luke 18:10-11; Acts 22:17; 10:9,30). Luke describes the prayers of Cornelius, the devout and generous centurion, as prayers for needs (*deomai*). However, the angel describes Cornelius' prayers as sacred ones (*proseuchomai*; Acts 10:2,4). The same word continues to be used of prayer by men and women in church worship.[18]

Jesus' practice of prayer prompted the disciples to ask him how to pray (Luke 11:1). He taught them what is now called "the Lord's Prayer." What were the disciples seeing in Jesus' prayer life? Jesus prayed publicly, privately, at usual and unusual times. We have seen how Jesus' prayers in public were often of thanksgiving, public praise (Matt. 11:25-26), blessings called down on children (Matt. 19:13-15), or blessings for food. After Jesus was baptized, Luke records that he continued in prayer (Luke 3:21). We have here a rare opportunity to see and hear the presence of the Truine God. As Jesus prays the Spirit descends bodily, descending on Jesus as a dove might descend, and a loud voice (*phone*) comes from heaven, "You are my Son, the beloved one, in you I am pleased" (Luke 3:22; Mark 1:11; Matt. 3:17). John the Baptist is an eyewitness (John 1:32-34). Here we see the Son's communication with the Father immediately answered. The Father confirms the Son's identity and expresses approval.

As well as praying in public, Jesus also prayed by himself. In the Sermon on the Mount, Jesus exhorts his listeners whenever they pray to enter an inner room and shut the door to pray because the God who can perceive what is secret will see and hear what is said in secret (Matt. 6:6). Jesus' own examples of prayer show that he envisioned many occasions where prayer in public was appropriate. However, Jesus practiced himself what he exhorted others to do, pray in secret.

After Jesus had blessed the five loaves and two fish, a blessing which multiplied them for more than five thousand people, Jesus made the disciples get into the boat to cross the Sea of Galilee while he sent away the crowd. After the crowds had been sent away, Jesus went up a mountain near the sea to pray privately. When evening came, he was there alone (Matt. 14:22-23; Mark 6:46). Since Matthew indicates Jesus was alone "when evening came" possibly a few disciples had joined Jesus earlier in the day. Nevertheless, by

---

[18] 1 Cor. 11:4,5,13; 14:13-15; 1 Tim. 2:8; Acts 12:5.

evening he was alone. Apparently, after the extended miracle of the day, Jesus wanted (and needed?) an extended time of peace and empowerment.

Luke as well records how at another time after he had healed a man with leprosy, great multitudes of people came to hear Jesus and to be healed of their infirmities. Instead of constantly teaching and healing them, Jesus himself withdrew from the city to go to the uninhabited region and pray. Luke writes, literally, "And he himself was withdrawing in the uninhabited region and praying" (Luke 5:16). Apparently, Jesus would regularly leave his work to go to a place where people could not ask him for help, and he would regularly pray. Jesus would schedule his day so that he could be in regular communication with the Father, a communication particularly needed after Jesus' power was being drained through extensive teaching and healing (e.g. Luke 8:46). The gospel records several other instances when Jesus withdrew to an uninhabited region or a mountain. When Jesus heard that John the Baptist was killed, he withdrew with his disciples to a lonely place (Matt. 14:13; Mark 6:32; Luke 9:10). Could they have gone there to pray? When Jesus was ministering in Jerusalem, during the day he would teach in the Temple, at night he would leave the city and lodge on the Mount of Olives (Luke 21:37). Could he have prayed on that mountain every night? Later we see Jesus praying there privately, but near some of his disciples, before he was betrayed and arrested (Luke 22:39-46). Jesus prayed privately regularly.

Jesus did not have only two extreme possibilities for prayer: public versus private prayer. Luke records the amusing oxymoron, "And it happened while he (Jesus) was praying alone the disciples were with him" (Luke 9:18). Jesus was praying *alone* with people! Several times the gospel writers would describe Jesus as "alone" even though he was with a few or many disciples (Mark 4:10). The gospel writers make a contrast though between the disciples and the crowds.[19] Some teachings are limited to the ears of the disciples.[20] Sometimes, the disciples would hold their questions for times when they could ask Jesus privately (Mark 13:1-4). Also, Jesus would heal at times only in the presence of some of his disciples (Mark 5:37). In effect, Jesus could feel comfortable praying in the midst of a sympathetic group. Even as Jesus could not heal many in Nazareth because of their unbelief, similarly Jesus can not pray intimately in

---

[19] Mark 7:33; 8:23, 34; Luke 10:23; 12:1.

[20] Mark 10:32; Luke 9:43-44; 18:31; 22:14-16; Matt. 20:17.

the midst of people who are questioning his identity (Mark 6:5-6; 14:33).

People who are testing Jesus' claims not only limit Jesus' prayer, but they also are not privileged to see Jesus in intimate prayer. After the disciples had seen Jesus praying, he asked them who he was (Luke 9:18-22). Being in Jesus' presence during prayer, the disciples made possible an occasion for Jesus to ask them about his identity. How did this opportunity come about? What happened when Jesus prayed? About a week later, Jesus took Peter, John, and James with him up into a high mountain to pray (Luke 9:28). We are told that "as he was praying" the outward appearance of his face and his clothes changed. Matthew and Mark indicate that Jesus was transformed or "transfigured" (*metamorphoomai*) before the disciples. Matthew uses two similes to try to describe Jesus' new form: "his face shone like the sun, and his garments (*himation*) became intensely white as the light (*hos to phos*)" (Matt. 17:2). These same similes had been used earlier by the psalmist to describe the majesty of God:

> "Bless the Lord, O my soul.
> Lord my God, thou art very great;
> with praise and majesty you clothed yourself,
> robing yourself with light as with a garment
> (*phos hos himation*),
> spreading out the heavens as a curtain" (Ps. 104[103LXX]:1-2).

In effect, Jesus is described by the same words, indicating the same magnificence of the one unique God. When Jesus prayed, he began to receive again some of the divine glory he had in his pre-existent state as God. Outwardly he revealed his true nature as God. Matthew's and Mark's use of *metamorphoomai* ("transform") is very enlightening because *morphoomai* often signifies an external appearance which reflects the essential or permanent nature of an individual. For instance, Gaius Caligula, the Roman Emperor, used to dress as the god Apollo. Philo, the first century Jewish philosopher and statesman, reprimands Caligula for dressing like Apollo without having any of Apollo's virtues. He concludes, "Let him cease once for all to mimic the true Paean, for a divine form (*morphe*) cannot be counterfeited as a coin can be" (*The Embassy to Gaius* XIV [110]). Caligula could imitate the outward appearance. However, Caligula's outward appearance did not reflect the respective inner nature.

The Transfiguration (or transformation), consequently, was an historical event in reverse to the Incarnation. According to Philippians 2:6 Jesus was in the form (*morphe*) of God. In other words, before the incarnation Jesus' outward appearance reflected his essential nature as God. When the Son chose to come to earth, the Son did not choose to appear to the inhabitants of earth with the divine majesty ("he considered not a treasure to be hoarded the being equal to God"). Rather, he took on the form (*morphe*) of a slave, in other words, he became human. Outwardly Jesus on earth looked as a slave, an outward appearance which reflected his essential nature. Jesus is always God and slave. However, for a moment Jesus allowed a few select people to see the divine glory, a glory present with Jesus in prayer.

When did Jesus pray? We have seen how he prayed alone in the evening at one occasion (Matt. 14:22-23). We also see how he prayed all through the night before he appointed the twelve: "And it happened in those days he went out into the mountain to pray (*proseuchomai*), and he was spending the night in prayer (*proseuche*) to God. And when day came, he called his disciples, and selecting from them twelve, whom also he named apostles" (Luke 6:12-13). The phrase "in those days" indicates that Jesus was regularly going into the mountain to pray during these times.

Jesus did not limit his prayer to evening. At an earlier time, Mark and Luke record, Jesus healed many sick and demon-possessed persons in Capernaum. And then in the "early morning while it was still dark (Jesus), having risen, left and went out into an uninhabited region and there he prayed" (*proseuchomai*; Mark 1:35). (Luke mentions Jesus' departure to the uninhabited region but not the prayer [4:42].) Instead of prayer in the evening, Jesus here prays in the very early morning. But apparently he always chooses uninhabited regions for prayer.

To find an uninhabited place is not always that easy. At Capernaum Simon and others searched diligently for Jesus until they found him because the people of the city were all seeking him. They did not want him to leave. However, Jesus does not do what the people want him to do. He tells them that his calling is to preach the good news of God's reign also to other cities. One consistent pattern of Jesus' prayer is that he prayed in the midst of a very busy schedule under the urgency of many people ("everyone"!) seeking him out. Also, in this instance at Capernaum prayer apparently helped Jesus maintain the focus and direction of his work. His own calling was to preach the good news of God's reign to cities. He would also pray in a quiet place at a time when he would not be disturbed. The Gospels record more evening than morning prayer. Although Jesus is like the sons of Korah who "call for help by day" and "cry out in the night" (Ps. 88:1,13), Jesus is even more like the "servants of the Lord, who stand by night in the house of the Lord!" (Ps. 134:1) or David when "the lifting up of his hands" is an "evening sacrifice" (Ps. 141:2).

To what extent were Jesus' times and contents of prayer simply prayers customary for a devout Jewish man? And, can knowledge of early Jewish prayer help us obtain further knowledge of Jesus' own prayers? Joachim Jeremias in *The Prayers of Jesus* points out that Jesus was brought up in a devout Jewish home and he was accustomed to go to the synagogue on the Sabbath.[21] Devout Jews of the first century would pray three times a day. The *Shema'* ("Hear") had to be recited by men in the morning and evening to coincide with the temple sacrifices. The morning time was after sunrise, the time of the burnt offering. "Morning" could be as soon as "one can distinguish between blue and white." Rabbi Eliezer said morning was as soon as one can distinguish between "blue and green" and the *Shema'* had to be finished before sunrise. Rabbi Joshua thought morning could be as soon as "the third hour," the time when kings rise (*m.Ber*. 1:1-2; 4:1). The evening time was sunset. According to Rabbi Eliezer the "evening" *Shema'* should be recited from the time when the priests enter the temple to eat of their Heave offering until the end of the first watch. Other rabbis say the *Shema'* could be recited as late as midnight or, according to Rabbi Gamaliel, even up to the rise of dawn, since the fat is burnt throughout the night (*m.Ber*. 1:1). According to the Mishnah, women, children, and slaves were exempt from reciting the *Shema'* (*m. Ber*. 3:3). Rabbi Eliezer ben Hyrcanus, who was prominent around A.D. 80-120, even defines an Amharitz or a "common" person as a free adult male who does not recite the *Shema'* two times a day.

The *Shema'* begins with Deuteronomy 6:4: "Hear, Israel, the Lord our God is one Lord." It includes Deuteronomy 6:5-9:

> and you shall love the Lord your God with all your heart,and with all your soul, and with all your might. And these words which I command you this day shall be upon your heart; and you shall teach them diligently to your children, and shall talk of them when you sit in

---

[21] Luke 2; 4:16.

> your house, and when you walk by the way, and when you lie down, and when you rise (*RSV*).

The *Shema'* concluded with the recitation of Deuteronomy 11:13-21 and Numbers 15:37-41. Possibly other benedictions were added (*m.Ber.* 1:4). Jesus certainly knows the *Shema'* and is aware of its recital among his countrymen. The lawyer who asks how to inherit eternal life is asked not only "what is written in the law?" but also "how do you recite?" (Luke 10:25-26). The lawyer answers with the beginning of the *Shema'* (Deut. 6:5).

The morning and evening recitation of the *Shema'* would be combined with the *Tefillah*, literally, "The Prayer" (the Eighteen Benedictions or *Shemoneh Hesreh'*), the most important Jewish prayer. "The Prayer" was also recited at the ninth hour, around three in the afternoon, the hours of prayer for Peter, John, and Cornelius (Acts 3:1; 10:30). An additional Tefillah was said on Sabbaths and festival days to correspond to the additional offering. The *Tefillah* was to be said by all people, including the women, children, and slaves (*m.Ber.* 3:3), in their entirety, or in abbreviated form (*m.Ber.* 4:3). Sometimes more benedictions were added (*m. Ta'an.* 2:2). The *Tefillah, Shema',* and benedictions could be prayed in any language (*m. Sota* 7:1). During the early part of the first century *A.D.* at least the first six benedictions were part of "The Prayer." By the end of the first century eighteen benedictions were recited. The first and probably the oldest benediction reads:

> Blessed art thou, Lord our God and God of our fathers, God of Abraham, God of Isaac and God of Jacob, great, mighty and fearful God, most high God, who bestowest abundant grace and createst all things and rememberest the promises of grace to the fathers and bringest a Redeemer to their children's children for thy Name's sake out of love. O King, who bringest help and salvation and who art a shield. Blessed art thou, Lord, shield of Abraham.[22]

Both the *Shema'* and the *Tefillah* were often recited in public. The rabbis even suggested regulations for when the recitation could be interrupted for greetings. According to Rabbi Meir, "Between the

---

[22] The eighteen benedictions with the later nineteenth Babylonian benediction are found in *The History of the Jewish People in the Age of Jesus Christ (175 B.C.-A.D.135)*, Emil Schuerer, eds. Geza Vermes, Fergus Millar, and Matthew Black, II (2d ed.; Edinburgh: T. & T. Clark, 1979), pp. 456-459.

sections [Benediction and *Shema'*] he may salute a man out of respect and return a greeting; but in the middle [of a section] he may salute a man [only] out of fear of him, and return a greeting" (*m. Ber.* 2:1). Craftslaborers could recite the *Shema'* even on the top of a tree or on top of stones (*m. Ber.* 2:4). In effect, prayers were to be a part of everyday life if the reciter concentrated on the prayer. Jesus' complaint about hypocrites is not that they prayed in public ("in the synagogues and at the street corners") but that they "loved" to pray "in order that they might be seen by people" (Matt. 6:5). Their goal was not praise of God but praise from humans.

Some of Jesus' prayers have been prayers of adoration similar to prayers given by his peers. Also, he said "grace" before meals. Like the first benediction of the *Tefillah*, the Lord's prayer begins with praise of God and recognition of God as the Reigning One able to provide all things necessary to humans, including food and forgiveness. The Lord's prayer is much simpler, more succinct, and more universally applicable. Jesus did not teach his disciples to pray to the God of Abraham, Isaac, and Jacob, "God of our fathers." Rather, they prayed simply to their "Father" or "Parent." In the ninth benediction, prayer was made for the produce of the "year," whereas in the Lord's prayer, prayer is for bread for the day. In the sixth benediction, people prayed for forgiveness. In the Lord's prayer they also pledged forgiveness to others.

Jeremias points out that Jesus prayed regularly at the three prayer times: morning, afternoon, and evening.[23] We have no extant record of his use of the *Shema'* or *Tefillah* at those times. Certainly, Jesus might have prayed the *Shema'* or *Tefillah*. Jesus was unusual in that he deliberately left public places for hills or secluded places. He did not simply have a brief time of prayer. He stretched the morning and evening times. He was praying once a *great while before* sunrise (Mark 1:35). More than once his prayer began in the evening and extended to dawn (Luke 6:12). He prayed before and up to the evening (Mark 6:46-47). Possibly at this time he could have ascended to the mountain at the three p.m. prayer time but he stayed there until dark. In other words, Jesus did not so much adhere to the three prayer times as that he prayed for such a length of time that he prayed *through* two prayer times.

---

[23] Joachim Jeremias, *The Prayers of Jesus*, Studies in Biblical Theology, 6 (London: SCM Press, 1967), pp. 73-75. Jeremias cites convincing reasons to show that Jesus was acquainted with the *Shema'* and *Tefillah*.

Devout Jews like Jesus were conscious of prayers which flowed from a contrite heart rather than from an uninterested mind. Both Rabbis Simeon and Eliezer exhorted their students not to make their prayer "a fixed form, but (a plea for) mercies and supplications before God" (*m. Abot* 2:13; *m. Ber*. 4:4). Nevertheless, Jewish prayers did tend to follow certain prescribed words. In contrast, the prayers of Jesus which have been recorded are all everyday words, brief and personal prayers to God.

The early western church (early second century) came to imitate the three daily Jewish prayer hours but substituted the Lord's Prayer for the *Shema'* and the *Tefillah* (*Didache* 8:2-3). In contrast, in the earliest church, Paul the Apostle exhorted the church to pray frequently rather than commanded the specific times and words of prayer. Paul told the Thessalonians: "At all times rejoice, constantly pray (*proseuchomai*), in everything give thanks (*eucharisteo*); for this is God's will in Christ Jesus among you" (1 Thess. 5:16-18). Ephesians 6:17-19 explains how prayer infuses all of the Christian's life: "And take the helmet of salvation and the sword of the Spirit, which is the word of God, through all sacred prayer (*proseuche*) and prayer for needs (*deomai*) praying (*proseuchomai*) in every time in the Spirit, and for this being alert in all perseverance and prayer (*deesis*) concerning all the saints and concerning me." Paul's exhortations for constant prayers follow from Jesus' example. However, the individual Christian is allowed to be free to organize and verbalize his/her own prayer.

Speak (*Lego*), Speak Loudly (*Phoneo*), Cry Aloud, Cry Out (*Boao, Anaboao*)

So far we have discussed a variety of aspects of prayer. The most common New Testament word emphasizes prayer as reverent or dedicated. Other words highlight prayer as verbal request (forceful request for needs, asking something of someone or challenging someone, summoning help) or appreciation (rejoicing exceedingly, public praise, giving thanks, singing in praise, blessing, calling down blessings). Prayer can also be a non-verbal act (looking up to heaven, lifting up the eyes, and sighing). Near the end of his physical life on earth, Jesus' prayers become cries of anguish, at times less verbal. On the one hand, his prayers are introduced with the everyday word for speaking, *lego*, as they are in John 11:41: "And Jesus raised up his eyes and *said*." *Lego* had meant "to lay with, count with; to enumerate, recount, narrate, describe" as one does a tale and it came to mean "to say," in other words, "to put word to word in speaking, join words together."[24] The use of *lego* in prayer directly shows that all words addressed to God are prayers.

On the other hand, the words which Jesus formulates near his death are loud shouts and cries. At times the New Testament indicates when Jesus speaks louder than usual. *Phoneo* or the noun *phone* may simply be to "produce a sound or tone" as in our "telephone," but usually the verb *phoneo* is used for people who speak loudly or clearly. For instance, Luke points out that at the end of the parable of the sower Jesus calls out in a loud voice, "The one having ears to hear, hear!" (Luke 8:8). After some people rebuked the blind man for yelling out to Jesus, Jesus calls for him loudly (*phoneo*; Matt. 20:32; Mark 10:49). Luke describes this loud call as a "command" (18:40). Unclean spirits would often come out of someone with a very loud voice.[25] Jesus commands Lazarus to come out of the tomb with a loud voice (John 11:43; 12:17). Paul calls out loudly to the Philippian jailer, "Do not harm yourself!" (Acts 16:28). The crow of the rooster is a loud and clear sound.[26]

Similarly, Jesus' last words on the cross were not whispers or even sighs but very loud shouts. At the ninth hour (about 3 p.m.), the hour of prayer (Acts 3:1; 10:3-4, 30), Jesus calls out to God in his despair, "For what reason have you abandoned me?" (Matt. 27:46-47; Mark 15:34-35). Jesus' question is not only loud, Matthew and Mark also describe it as an exclamation. Mark describes it with *boao*, "to cry aloud, shout." The Greek translation of Isaiah 40:3 has *boao* to describe the high, strong voice of the one in the wilderness (quoted in Mark 1:3; Matt. 3:3; Luke 3:4; John 1:23). Outside of the New Testament *boao* is even used of the roar of the sea and the howl of the wind. *Boao* can more specifically be a cry of joy or of pain, as the cry of joy of the barren one who will "break forth and *shout*" because she will have many children (Gal. 4:27). The cry of pain can be the cries of the oppressed harvesters or the cries of the unclean spirits (James 5:4; Acts 8:7). It can also be a cry for help (Luke 18:7,38; 9:38). All these possible meanings are united by a common "cry out as a manifestation of feeling."[27] At the cross, Jesus cries out in pain and possibly for help, manifesting his feelings of loneliness.

---

[24] Thayer, p. 373.
[25] Mark 1:26; 5:7; Luke 4:33; 8:28.
[26] Matt. 26:34, 74; Mark 14:30, 72; Luke 22:34, 60-61; John 13:38; 18:27.
[27] Thayer, p. 104.

Matthew heightens his description by adding a prefix to make *anaboao*, literally, "cry upwards." *Anaboao* is "I cry, shout aloud," especially as a sign of grief or astonishment.[28] Jesus cries out and upwards. His question is really an exclamation. Jesus' loud cry to God in heaven appears to be the culmination of his earlier feelings of trouble and sorrow in Gethsemane. Before Jesus dies, Matthew, Mark, and now Luke also record his very loud final shout.[29] Luke records those last words, "Father, into your hands I entrust my spirit." In these two shouts we see reflected loud despair and loud affirmation. Apparently, Jesus' exclamation of abandonment was answered because Jesus dies feeling confidence and trust in his Father.

Supplication (*Hiketeria*), Weep Silently (*Dakruo*), and Shout (*Krauge*)

Phoneo, boao, and *anaboao* all clearly show that prayer includes the communication of strong emotion. Prayer need not only be silent or whispered, it can also be loud and a shout. The author of Hebrews hearkens back to Jesus' cries of anguish. The author wants to show in what ways the new covenant is superior to the old covenant in order that the readers not succomb again to the ways of the old covenant (13:9). One way in which the new covenant is superior is that Jesus as high priest has no sin (4:15). Since the high priest is chosen *from* humans (*ex anthropon*), the high priest can therefore act *in behalf of* humans (*huper anthropon*; 5:1). God believes in representative government! Only a human can represent a human. Such a high priest will be able to have empathy for the ignorant and misled, since also the high priest is beset with weaknesses (5:2). Since Jesus has no sin, he did not have to offer sacrifices for his own sins. However, being human, Jesus can have empathy with humans. Jesus is God's Son and also a priest forever. When the Messiah took on human flesh, he became subject to human limitations. Apparently, he had actively to maintain unity with the Father and he had to learn obedience.

The high priest offers gifts and sacrifices for sins (5:1):

---

[28] Liddell and Scott, p. 99.

[29] Matt. 27:50; Mark 15:37; Luke 23:46 *phoneo phone megale.*

> [The Christ] in the days of his flesh having offered prayers and also requests to the one being able to save him from death with strong shouts and tears and having been heard for his reverence, though being Son he learned obedience from what he suffered; and being made perfect he became to all those who obey him a source of eternal salvation, being designated by God a high priest according to the order of Melchizedek (Heb. 5:7-10).

This long sentence has only two main thoughts captured in the finite main verbs: the Messiah *learned* obedience and *became* a source of salvation. Jesus learned in a gradual way obedience or subjection *even though* he was God's Son. The Letter to the Hebrews makes a strong case for Jesus' full divinity (e.g. ch. 1). Yet, being human, Jesus had to learn. As the writer explains, the learning takes place "in the days of his flesh." Learning might not be necessary in heaven. How did Jesus learn obedience? Jesus learned in two ways: "*having offered* also prayers and requests to the one being able to save him from death with strong shouts and tears" and *having been heard* because of his godly fear. The same word, "having offered" (*prosphero*), which is used to describe Jesus' prayers, is also used in Hebrews for the high priest (Heb. 5:1; 8:3-4; 9:7). Jesus' prayers are gifts and sacrifices to God. How can a prayer be a gift?

Jesus offers two kinds of prayers (*deesis* and *hiketeria*). The first type of prayer is *deesis* which is the noun form of *deomai*. *Deesis* is forceful petition in regard to some need. We have seen how Jesus prayed for the need of others and, at the end of his life, for his own need. *Hiketeria*, which occurs only here in the New Testament, is also a request or plea. This noun comes from the adjective signifying "pertaining to a suppliant." *Hiketeria* was used for an olive-branch. It also signified "supplication" because suppliants approached the person whose aid they wanted holding an olive-branch entwined with white wool.[30] It is used of hypocritical prayer to God in Malachi 3:14 and Psalm 73:23 (74:23). Jesus, the son of Sirach, describes *hiketes*, the person who seeks aid or protection, as "afflicted," synonymous with "poor" (Ecclus. 4:4). According to the writer of 2 Maccabees, Antiochus Epiphanes wrote a letter of supplication ("as a kind of olive branch" 9:18 *NEB*) to the Jews in Judah at the end of his life because of a painful disease he had. In this letter he entreats and requests the Jews to maintain goodwill

---

[30] Trench, pp. 191-192.

toward himself and his son (9:26). *Hiketeria* refers to formal request for help which can be done in genuine or hypocritical submission.

Consequently, *deesis* and *hiketeria* are a pleonasm in Hebrews 5:7 since the two words have similar meanings. Both indicate and emphasize Jesus' request. While in the flesh Jesus was aware of the needs of others and of himself and Jesus was also aware of who alone could help him: "the one being able to save him from death" -- God. Therefore, he prayed forcefully and he prayed formally.

His pleas were not done lukewarmly, but "with strong shouts and tears." *Krauge* is "shout." It can simply be a loud announcement (Matt. 25:6) or it can be a shout of vengeance as the shout of the crowd in Jerusalem which drowned out Paul's words yelling, "Take away from the earth such a person, for he ought not to live!" (Acts 22:22-23). A *krauge* can be something which a person should try to replace with kindness and forgiveness when it is a shout flowing from blasphemy, anger, or bitterness (Eph. 4:31-32). A shout can also be a loud shout of joy and proclamation which is most pleasing to God, as Elizabeth proclaimed when she was filled with the Holy Spirit (Luke 1:41-42). Jesus not only shouted, but he *strongly* (or loudly) shouted!

Combined with these strong shouts of prayer was silent weeping. *Dakruo* is "weep," but especially "shed tears silently." *Dakruo* contrasts with many other Greek words for weeping. *Alalazo* and *ololuzo* are onomatopoetic words. These words sound like what they describe, loud wailing in oriental style. *Alalazo* is to repeat *alalai*, a war-cry or a "howl in a consecrated, semi-liturgical fashion" as was done at the death of Jairus' daughter (Mark 5:38). Speaking in tongues without love, is as it were, a "*howling* cymbal" (1 Cor. 13:1). *Ololugon* was the croaking of the male frog. *Ololuzo* was to cry with a loud voice with joy or grief, used mostly of women crying aloud to the gods in prayer. An *ololuktria* was a professional crier at sacrifices. Consequently, when James tells the rich to weep (*klaio*) in a "cry with a loud voice" (*ololuzo*), he implies that their cry might as well be this repeating *o-lo-lu-zo* which the pagans cried out to false gods, because they will not be able to avoid the miseries coming upon them (5:1).

Threneo also refers to the formal expression of grief, to sing a dirge or lament (*threnos*), as the women sang for Jesus on the way to the Skull (Luke 23:27). Jesus describes John the Baptist's ministry as a funeral lament (*threneo*) to which no one audibly wept (*klaio*) (Luke

7:32; cf. Matt. 11:17). *Oduromai* is to give verbal expression to grief as Rachel did for her children and the Corinthians did when they repented (Matt. 2:18; 2 Cor. 7:7). *Klaio* is "weep audibly." It occurs frequently in the New Testament, often in combination with other words.[31] Jesus wept audibly over Jerusalem (Luke 19:41). But the tears which were associated with Jesus' prayers were not audible tears, tears of mourning. They were silent tears. Silent tears are not done to show to others one's sorrow (although they might do that). Silent tears are an external sign of internal sorrow. When Jesus saw Mary and others with her weeping audibly (*klaio*) over Lazarus' death, Jesus in sympathy wept silently (*dakruo*; John 11:31-35).[32]

Jesus' prayers were done with both strong shouts and silent tears. Why were they gifts and sacrifices? Probably they were Jesus' gifts to the Father because they reflected the suffering Jesus had to undergo in his humanity: his shouts of anguish and tears of sympathy. Even his whole life is a sacrifice offered to the Father, concluding with his death (Heb. 9:14).

Jesus' learning of obedience came from these prayer offerings and from the fact that God heard him. If someone offers that one's life to another without any response, what is learned? Nothing. However, because Jesus sent up pleas *and* was heard, Jesus learned obedience. He received positive reinforcement. Why was the Messiah heard? Jesus was heard because of his "reverence" (*eulabeia*). Noah, Simeon, and Ananias are examples of people who are described as "reverent" (Heb. 11:7; Luke 2:25; Acts 22:12). *Eulabeia* is the character and conduct of people of "discretion" and "caution" or "reverence" and "piety." Unlike others', Jesus' shouts and cries did not come from blasphemy or anger. Jesus was able to communicate his feelings of emotion to God in heaven without expressing any lack of reverence toward the Parent. Consequently, he was heard.

Seeing how Jesus prayed with loud cries, shouts, and silent tears, we should never hesitate to express emotion before God and even before other loved ones. If necessary, we should learn to do so. Our goal should be, however, to express our emotion in the midst of

---

31 *Oduromai* Matt. 2:18; *alalazo* Mark 5:38; *pentheo* "experience sorrow" Luke 6:25; James 4:9; *threneo* Luke 7:32; *threneo, lupeo* "be saddened" John 16:20; *ololuzo* James 5:1; *kopto* "beat one's breast for grief" Luke 8:52; Rev. 18:9. Thayer, p. 347. Liddell and Scott, pp. 1217-1218.

32 Paul ministers, as well, with silent and audible weeping: *dakruo* Acts 20:19; 2 Cor. 2:4; *klaio* Phil. 3:18.

reverence toward God. Jesus is clearly our model. The Letter to the Hebrews ends with an exhortation for worship to be pleasing to God "with reverance (*eulabeia*) and awe; for also our God is a consuming fire" (Heb. 12:28-29).

The mystery of Jesus is that Jesus *is* sovereign over all and *becomes* sovereign over all. Because Jesus learned obedience, he became a source of salvation to everyone who obeys him. Because Jesus learned obedience, he was made perfect and was designated a high priest in Melchizedek's order. Without Jesus' prayers, we could never have a perfect high priest in heaven who sympathizes with our weaknesses.

Summary

The Greek words of prayer used by and for Jesus paint for us a full and colorful landscape clarifying what is prayer, who is Jesus, and how to pray. The many words of prayer stretch out the canvas of possible aspects of prayer and also shrink it. Jesus' recorded communication to God in heaven can be limited to request or appreciation or expression of emotion. Requests can be forceful requests for needs, asking something of someone or challenging someone, reverent prayer, or formal supplication. Appreciation can be extreme rejoicing, public praise, giving thanks, singing in praise, blessing, or calling down blessings. Expression of emotion can be by a look, an inarticulate sigh, silent weeping or loud talking, crying aloud, crying up, or shouting. In effect, prayer, as all communication, includes the genuine expression of emotion and the balancing of request with appreciation.

Jesus' prayer life tells us not only about prayer, but also about Jesus. Jesus' prayer flows from who he is. Jesus' deep concern for people's spiritual and physical needs impels him to pray for and to command us to pray for more workers, the means toward completing God's reign on earth, and commands us to undergird our alertness and readiness for Jesus' return to earth by praying for strength. Jesus himself worked with a team, prays for a team, and intercedes for the team. His interest was united with the interest of the Lord of the harvest. Anyone who asks for needs which are God's needs will be affirmed. Furthermore, God, as the One to whom we aspire, will send out to us strength to reach God if we only ask.

Jesus is also an intermediary in behalf of the Godhead and in behalf of the needs of others. Consequently, he prays for Simon as well as for his other disciples. He asks of the Father that we be united and we be kept from the evil one. He asks the Father to send the Holy Spirit. He is the perfect high priest, sympathetic with our weaknesses. However, Jesus as intermediary can be not only our Defense Attorney but also our Prosecutor. As Judge he evaluates our love, belief, and obedience. He can challenge our requests. Jesus could have summoned help from the angels to stop the unjust malevolent evil which took over his own court case, but he chose not to appeal to his Father.

Jesus is also one who expresses praise and thanksgiving. Jesus wants us to rejoice exceedingly because our salvation is secure in heaven, not because we may have power over evil. Jesus' own expression of praise flows out into public praise of the Father because only the powerless, the lowly, like Jesus, receive God's revelation. Jesus' thankfulness for bread received results in the multiplication of bread. Thanksgiving is close to confession. At times, Jesus' prayers become a testimony for the Father and an education to listeners.

Jesus in prayer shows both actual communication within the Godhead and potential human communication with God. Jesus was in intimate communication with God in heaven. Since God perceives in secret, Jesus often prays in private. His prayers are a frequent and a regular part of his life. Jesus regularly prayed at a time and a place where distractions were unlikely to occur. Even as Jesus' preaching and teaching revealed Jesus' divinity, so did Jesus' prayer life reveal Jesus as God. His prayer showed that he was sent by the Parent. As he prayed, Jesus would again take on the pre-incarnate glory. Prayer became communication within the one God. For instance, the Spirit caused joy in the Son to the Father.

Jesus' expression of strong emotion also can liberate our definition of prayer. Although Jesus is always reverent in communication with the Father, he is expressive. He expresses not only extreme joy but also cries of anguish. His communication ranges from a look and a deep sigh to loud shouts, exclamations of loneliness, pain, despair, and affirmation. He weeps in sympathy with others. His prayers become themselves gifts and sacrifices to God as part of Jesus' living in suffering. He is the Heir who deserves the crown. He is Lord and becomes Lord.

Jesus' prayer is an indispensable part of his life because he constantly speaks to the Father who alone loved and knew him. His prayer helped him make decisions because his special calling became clear in prayer. Prayer was also necessary for Jesus to endure the overwhelming demands of his work. Finally, prayer was a time when the Father spoke back to the Son, showing approval and good pleasure.

Study of Jesus' prayer life shows us that our prayers need not be eloquent or lengthy. They may be brief but they should be genuine. We should be free to express our own emotions in prayer, asking that we be given always a reverent spirit. Although we may choose to pray all through the night at times, the goal of our prayer should not be imitating Jesus' or anyone else's schedule of prayer times. Rather, we should imitate the principles undergirding Jesus' prayer. We should plan times for prayer in our schedule when we can be undisturbed or where we can pray with a sympathetic group. However, prayer should also be done in public. The goal is the active, extended, and regular communication to God from a loving heart and an obedient life. The means vary.

We too like Jesus need to express our needs, gratitude, and emotions. Jesus is unique in that he rarely expressed personal need and he never confessed personal sin. Paul several times in his exhortations to the church challenged them to include the various dimensions of prayer in their conversations with God. He exhorts Timothy to ask forcefully for needs (*deesis*), to speak reverently to God (*proseuche*), to draw close to God (*enteuxis*), to give thanks (*eucharistia*) in behalf of all people (1 Tim. 2:1). And again, he commands the Philippians not to be anxious unduly. Rather, when they found themselves anxious they should instead in everything by reverent prayer to God (*proseuche*) and by forceful expression of needs (*deesis*) with thanksgiving (*eucharistia*) let their needs be known to God (Phil. 4:6). Our prayer life should maintain a balance of request and appreciation. Then like our Lord Jesus the Messiah, our calling will become clearer, our work for God will become more powerful, our relationship to God will become more genuine, and, possibly, we will hear God communicate back to us to commend us, even as God commended the First-born: "With you I am well pleased!"

6

Jesus' Postures of Prayer

When we think of Jesus in a posture of prayer, we first think of Heinrich Hofmann's painting "Christ in the Garden of Gethsemane." In this portrayal Jesus is on his knees, hands clasped and outstretched on a mound, looking up to heaven, looking doubtful. The night is dark but one cloud is lighted as is Jesus' halo. Behind thorns lies the garden, a barren brown desert. Heinrich Hofmann's portrayal of Jesus at prayer has appealed to the imagination of thousands of people who have seen his painting reproduced in print, although they may have never gone to see it at The Riverside Church in New York. Why is his painting significant? Although the Garden of Gethsemane is in reality green woods, the pictured desert, the colors, the expression, the posture in the portrait all interpret symbolically Jesus' communication with God in heaven. Looking at Jesus' postures of prayer is one specific way to look at symbolic action in order to understand a concept, prayer. What postures did Jesus take when he prayed? What significance can we draw for today from them? The New Testament records Jesus' physical movements at prayer only a few times: when he prays before his arrest in the Garden of Gethsemane and when he blesses his disciples.

Jesus Prays in the Garden

Three synonomous verbs occur in the gospels to describe descent from a standing position in prayer: *pipto*, "fall," (and its combination *prospipto*, "fall towards"); *proskuneo*, "kneel," and "worship"; and *gonupeteo*, "kneel," (or simply *gonu*, "knee," with a verb such as *tithemi*, "place"). When Jesus was in the Garden of Gethsemane he became deeply distressed. Jesus shows this internal distress by stepping away from Peter, James, and John and kneeling (*tithemi gonu*; Luke 22:41) until he falls (*pipto*) on his face (Matt. 26:39) on the earth (Mark 14:35) and from this position he prays to his heavenly Parent. Since Luke records that Jesus kneels, while Mark and Matthew record that Jesus falls on the ground, a reader might at a superficial glance suppose that the two versions are contradictory. However, the verb which Matthew and Mark use (*pipto*) means not only "fall" or "fall down" but also "fall to one's knees."[1] *Pipto* basically indicates the descent from a higher place to a lower place or the descent from an erect position to a prostrate one.[2] What did going to one's knees or from there to place one's face on the ground signify to an ancient person? Many in the New Testament fall down at Jesus' feet in request, petition, fear, adoration, or distress.

Gonupeteo, which occurs four times in the New Testament, combines *pipto*, "fall," and *gonu*, "knee," to signify "fall to the knee" or "kneel." The father of the epileptic (Matt. 17:14) and the leper (Mark 1:40) kneel down (*gonupeteo*) to petition Jesus for healing. Kneeling was also a position taken to greet a sovereign, which the soldiers did in mockery before Jesus "King of the Jews"(Matt. 27:29). The rich man who kneels asking how to inherit eternal life may have been kneeling to request enlightment or kneeling to greet Jesus as he would a ruler (Mark 10:17). In the New Testament, consequently, *gonupeteo* appears to signify the external expression of positive internal motivations, request for healing, or respect for sovereignty. Even if the soldiers mocked Jesus by kneeling they were mimicking what would normally have been positive, the greeting of a ruler. Origen also explains that while having the hands "outstretched" and the "eyes lifted up is to be preferred before all others," kneeling "is necessary when someone is going to speak against his own sins before God, since he is making supplication for their healing and their forgiveness. We must understand that it symbolizes someone who has fallen down and become obedient" (*On Prayer* XXXI, 2, 3)

---

[1] Barclay M. Newman, Jr., *A Concise Greek-English Dictionary of the New Testament* (London: United Bible Societies, 1971), p. 143.

[2] Joseph Henry Thayer, *Thayer's Greek-English Lexicon of the New Testament*, p. 510; Bauer, p. 665.

Pipto, by itself, can similarly signify the act of petitioning. *Pipto*, like *gonupeteo*, can simply indicate a posture of entreaty, such as that of Jairus or of the Syrophoenicean woman (Mark 5:22; Luke 8:41). However, by falling a person can express positive or negative emotions: thanksgiving, pity, fear, or grief. For instance, the deeply thankful Samaritan leper thanks Jesus by falling at his feet (Luke 17:16). The two slaves in the parable on forgiveness fall on their knees in order to request of someone else pity and patience (Matt. 18:26, 29). When Peter, James, and John hear God's voice after Jesus is transfigured into his preexistent glory, they fall on their faces with fear (Matt. 17:5-7). Similarly, when Jesus calls out to the crowd, "Who touched my garments?", the woman who had been bleeding (and was therefore ritually "unclean") came "in fear and trembling" and fell down facing Jesus (*prospipto*; Mark 5:33 and Luke 8:47). Mary falls at Jesus' feet to say, "Lord, if you had been here my brother would not have died" (John 11:32). Since Mary is weeping her posture seems to indicate deep distress. *Pipto*, thus, signifies a simple request or a request out of fear or it can be an expression of gratitude, fear, or grief. It can also signify "worship" especially when in combination with *proskuneo,* as did the Eastern wise men who "falling down (*pipto*) worshipped (*proskuneo*)" Jesus (Matt. 2:11).[3] Jesus, then, like his contemporaries expresses in the Garden his deep distress or grief and his earnest request by falling to his knees and to his face.

If Jesus expressed his grief and request by falling prostrate, we can make several applications to today. For those of us in a Western culture where we may hesitate to kneel or fall on the ground in prayer we can see that to do so is certainly right if Jesus, our Lord, did so. We can never be too civilized to symbolize externally our internal feelings. Although the New Testament records only once when Jesus did fall to the ground, in addition, it records many instances of other people kneeling in request. However, does this mean we must all kneel when we ask favors of others or of God? What if we physically can not kneel? I would imagine that Jesus would be dismayed if we made rules on posture by which to pray because these postures if genuine are simply symbols of genuine internal emotions. Jesus taught, "When you pray, *say*," not "When you pray, *do*." Nevertheless, as human beings whose faculties of reason, emotion, and movement should coincide, we may need to learn to reintroduce what for us is an appropriate external symbol of our internal desires. Sometimes behavioral change may need to

---

[3] Cf. in Matt. 18:26,27 *pipto* followed by *proskuneo* functions as a pleonasm to accentuate the extreme extent of petition, but not worship.

precede emotional change. In other words, by praying in a kneeling or prostrate position (or an alternative if these positions are not physically possible), we can evoke within us the appropriate feelings of respect to our Sovereign God Almighty.

Incidentally, what is remarkable about these words of kneeling not only is that Jesus expressed his grief and petition by falling (*pipto*, *tithemi*, *gonu*), but also that Jesus' kneeling down is never described in the New Testament by a third word, *proskuneo*.[4] *Proskuneo* comes from *kuneo* ("I kiss," a verb rare in prose and therefore not found in the New Testament) and *pros* ("facing"). Properly *proskuneo* means "to kiss the hand towards one" in token of reverence. Hence among the Orientals it means to fall upon the knees and touch the ground with the forehead to express profound homage before rulers.[5] Hence *proskuneo* can frequently signify "worship" as it does for the wise men, the healed blind man (John 9:38), and the disciples of Jesus at his ascension into heaven (Luke 24:52).[6] Like *pipto* and *gonupeteo*, *proskuneo* can signify requests for healing or for patience (Matt. 8:2; 9:18; 15:25), requests for the special favor of a ruler (Matt. 20:20), or it can express fear.[7] When Mark describes how the soldiers mock Jesus as King of the Jews, he recounts that "kneeling" (*gonu* and *tithemi*, "placing the knees") they showed him "profound homage" (*proskuneo*; Mark 15:19). In the Old Testament, the potential contender for the throne, Mephibosheth, falls (*pipto*) to his face and pays homage (*proskuneo*) to King David in fear for his life (2 Sam. 9:6-8).

Nevertheless, *proskuneo* is never used of Jesus. Possibly the New Testament writers by not using *proskuneo* for Jesus are indirectly communicating that Jesus does not "worship" God the Father as we do because Jesus is God. Jesus, having taken on full humanity, does experience and express deep distress or grief and

---

[4] The only time Jesus uses *proskuneo* about God is in John 4:20-24 where he specifies that in contrast to the Samaritans, "we" implying "we Jews" "*worship* what we know, that salvation is from the Jews."

[5] Thayer, p. 548; Liddell and Scott, p. 1518.

[6] The better quality and older manuscripts support the original reading which includes "worship" such as in the NIV. See also Heb. 1:6, God's angels worshipped Jesus; Rev. 7:11; 14:7; 5:14; 19:4; 19:10; John 12:20; Acts 8:27; Matt. 14:33, disciples after Jesus caused wind to cease; 1 Cor. 14:25, a convicted unbeliever will fall (*pipto*) on his/her face to worship (*proskuneo*) God declaring that truly God is among these prophesying Christians. Cf. Rev. 19:10; 14:9.

[7] Matt. 28:9; Mark 5:6; Luke employs *prospipto* to describe the man at Gerasa (8:28).

does make earnest request to God the Sovereign. Our prayer should include as well worship.

Jesus Blesses Disciples

The second posture of prayer which the gospel writers describe in Jesus' practice occurs when he blesses people by placing his hands on them or by lifting his hands over them. Matthew, Mark, and Luke recount that children were being brought to Jesus so that he might touch them and pray for them by blessing them (Matt. 19:13-15; Mark 10:13-16; Luke 18:15-17). What every child is delighted to find in the gospels is that those disciples who were commanding the children to stop were in turn stopped by Jesus: "Let the children come to me and do not hinder them for to such belongs God's reign!" Mark and Matthew use the verbs *tithemi* and *epitithemi*, "I lay" or "I put on," with the noun *cheir*, "hand," to signify "I place my hands on." Jesus prays for the children while he touches them by placing his hands on them.

If anyone should envision placing hands for blessing to be a somewhat impersonal act, Mark adds the endearing detail that before Jesus blessed the children by placing his hands on them, Jesus embraces the infants. Mark uses *enagkalizomai* which means "embrace" or "hug." *Agkale*, the noun, is "the curve or inner angle of the arm." Thus *enagkalizomai* signifies to "take someone *in* one's arms."[8] In effect, Jesus hugged the children! Then he prayed for them. What Jesus teaches ("God's reign belongs to children") he demonstrates by embracing the children. When Jesus embraced those children, he expressed affection for them. He did not make his prayer an alien ritualistic formal affair but a natural intimate aspect of life. Although the church often is at the forefront of national committees for "The Family," nevertheless often we have been imitating not Jesus but the disciples. Like the disciples we have made children often feel unwelcome to adult affairs. In contrast Jesus loves children, embraces them, and prays for them. However experienced we adults may be we need to learn from children what can make us huggable before God.

Touch is an important aspect of Jesus' ministry. Luke tells us that people sought to touch Jesus because power came forth from him (Luke 6:19; 8:46). Before Jesus healed several sick persons he

---

[8] Bauer, p. 261; Thayer, p. 7.

touched them. The same phrase ("lay hands on"; *epitithemi* and *cheir*) is used several times. Jesus appears to heal by command and by touch.[9] Should anyone conclude that Jesus *had to* touch someone in order to heal them, Luke and Matthew record the incident with the Gentile centurion. His faith was so great that he did not believe that Jesus had to touch his slave to heal him. And, returning home, "they found the slave in good health" (Luke 7:10).

Jesus places his hands on people to bless them or to heal them. He also stretches out his hand (*ekteino*) before touching and healing a person (e.g. Mark 1:41; 3:5; Luke 5:13). When the Bible speaks of people "laying hands on" someone in order to arrest them, it uses the verb *epiballo* as in Matthew 26:50; Mark 14:46; Luke 20:19; 21:12; John 7:30,44. We are also told that before (and even while) Jesus ascended into heaven, he blessed his disciples (Luke 24:50-51). Jesus had been giving his disciples different sets of teachings in Galilee and in Jerusalem. Outside of Jerusalem in Bethany he gave them a final blessing after lifting up his hands (*espairo cheir*).

Often the Old Testament references to "lifting up hands" refer to "hand" in the singular wherein someone, usually a subordinate, tries to destroy the position of a person in power, as did Sheba who "lifted up his hand against" David (2 Samuel 20:21).[10] Moses also lifted the rod to indicate God's actions against the Egyptians (Exod. 14:16). The Old Testament does include at least three clear references to the use of lifting the hands ("hands" is in the plural) as part of a blessing. In the brief "Song of Ascents" the servants of the Lord are exhorted, "in the night lift up your hands in the sanctuary and bless the Lord" (Ps. 133:2). When the service to consecrate the priests was completed, Aaron lifted up his hands upon (*exairo*) the worshippers and blessed them. The Greek takes the preposition *epi* ("upon," "towards") to indicate that Aaron used his hands to point toward the persons he was blessing after he had lifted his hands up (Lev. 9:22). The priestly blessing seems to be a symbolic attempt to represent placing one's two hands on another person. The Lord later gives Aaron and his children the words they should use to bless the people of Israel:

---

[9] For example, Luke 13:13; Mark 5:41; 7:32; [Mark 6:5 and Luke 4:40 do not mention any details].

[10] See also 2 Sam. 18:28; 1 Kings 11:27. Yet Job says he has not "raised his hand against the *orphan*" (31:21).

> The Lord bless you and keep you.
> The Lord make his face to shine upon you,
> and be gracious to you:
> The Lord lift up his countenance upon you,
> and give you peace (Num. 6:24-26 RSV).

Herbert Chanan Brichto mentions that the Aaronic benediction describes God with the metaphor of a king at court who shows his favor by giving the subjects audience, access to "the light of his face," by smiling, "lifting up his countenance," and by friendship, "peace."[11]

The third reference to lifting hands in prayer occurs in Nehemiah 8:6 when Ezra the priest blesses the Lord before he begins to teach the people from the law of Moses. The people stand when he opens the scroll. After Ezra blesses the people they affirm his blessing with an "Amen," lifting up their hands and bowing their heads and placing their faces to the ground in worship (*proskuneo*). Interestingly, in this instance the congregation responds to the priest's blessing by lifting up each member's own hands (presumably toward God).

The tradition of the priest lifting up his hands in benediction continues throughout the years. Ecclesiasticus, written two centuries before Christ, describes Simon the high priest concluding the temple service by lifting up his hands over (*epi*) the whole congregation (50:20). Even in the first century Aaron's priestly benediction continued to be a regular part of the synagogue and the Temple services. The services would end with a priest reciting the benediction in Numbers 6:24-26 in Hebrew. *The Mishnah* even specifies the height to which the priest must lift up his hands:

> in the provinces the priests raised their hands as high as their shoulders, but in the Temple above their heads, excepting the High Priest who raised his hand only as high as the frontlet. R. Judah says: The High Priest also raised his hand above the frontlet, for it is written, *And Aaron lifted up his hands toward the people and blessed them.*[12]

---

[11] "Priestly Blessing," *Encyclopaedia Judaica* (1971), XIII, 1062.

[12] *m. Sota* 7:6, Danby, p. 301 n.2. See also *m. Sota* 7:2 and *m. Tamid* 7:2. The priestly blessing is also mentioned in *m. Ber.* 5:4, *Ta'an.* 4:1, *Tamid* 5:1, and *Meg.* 4:3.

In the provinces the people would respond with three Amens, one to each verse in the Aaronic benediction. The Temple congregation would respond with one final Amen. Moreover, the High Priest would pronounce eight Benedictions:

> for the Law, for the Temple-Service,
> the Thanksgiving, on the Forgiveness of Sin,
> and for the Temple and for the Israelites,
> and for the priests and for Jerusalem,
> and, for the rest, a [general prayer] (*m. Sota* 7:7; cf. *Yoma* 7:1).

The King could also pronounce these eight benedictions except that he would bless the Feasts rather than ask for Forgiveness of Sin (*m. Sota* 7:8).

Consequently, the lifting up of hands in a blessing was a common Jewish expression for the priestly blessing. Lifting up of hands, apart from the act of blessing, could simply refer to prayer. One part of the regular synagogue service was "The Prayers" or "the lifting of the hands." Paul was referring to this custom in prayer when he exhorted the men to lift "holy hands without anger and quarreling" (1 Tim. 2:8). What Paul wanted was not that the men lift their hands in prayer (this practice was customary) but rather that the men not quarrel with each other while in prayer. Jesus, in contrast, at his ascension at Bethany symbolically performs the priestly blessing. As Aaron he lifts up his hands directing them toward his disciples. If he were to follow the Rabbinic oral teachings, while reciting Number 6:24-26, his hands would have been raised as high as his shoulders (since he was not in the Temple at Jerusalem). If he had chosen symbolically to take the place of the High Priest, his hands would have been raised as high as the frontlet.

The writer of Hebrews explains that Jesus was appointed high priest by God, analogous to Aaron's appointment, after the new "order of Melchizedek" because the old Levitical order was insufficient for salvation (Heb. 5:4-10; 7:11-16). Thus, when Jesus lifts up his hands to bless his disciples at Bethany, his hands remain in a position of priestly blessing while he ascends because he ascends to the throne of heaven where he continues until the end of the earth to function as high priest (Heb. 8:1).

These three postures of prayer exhibit almost contrasting significances. Jesus at the Garden of Gethsemane falls to his knees and to his face in deep grief and in earnest request. Jesus, when with the children, embraces them, affirms them as members of God's reign, and prays for them. Jesus at Bethany lifts his hands to bless his disciples using his prerogative as God's appointed high priest. The postures of prayer express internal feelings, internal desires, and response to the needs of others. Albeit even Jesus' distress at Gethsemane was caused by our evil.

To some extent we should imitate Jesus in all these postures of prayer. We too experience grief and deeply felt petitions. We too can show our love by touch and we can affirm children and the child-like in our lives. Although only ordained ministers usually give the closing benediction to a service, according to Peter all believers in God through Jesus Christ are now a "holy priesthood" (1 Peter 2:5). Jesus might be the only High Priest, but now all believers can grant God's blessing to other believers.

Did Jesus Pray Standing?

Jesus knelt and fell on his face, embraced and touched, and lifted up his hands. However, the New Testament never describes Jesus as standing in prayer! Most ancient Jews would stand when praying. Numerous times *The Mishnah* refers to men and women who "stood up in prayer"[13]

Jews would stand to read the Scriptures during the synagogue service, as did Jesus in Luke 4:16. Ancient people would also stand for sentence before a judge, even as modern people stand to receive sentencing today. Matthew records how Jesus stood before the procurator Pontius Pilate (Matt. 27:11). Jesus warns his followers that they too "will stand before governors and sovereigns for my sake in order to bear testimony before them" (Mark 13:9). Similarly, all people symbolically (or literally?) will stand before Jesus when he returns to the earth as judge (Luke 21:36). The judge, in contrast, sits (Luke 22:30). Gabriel announces that he "stands" in God's presence. Probably, when the ancients would stand to pray, they symbolized in their standing that they were communicating to the Judge of judges. Humans would be in the position of sentenced persons, persons whose life or death rests in another's hands.

---

[13] *m. Ta'an.* 2:2; *m. Ber.* 3:5; 4:5; 1:3.

Jesus presupposes the posture of standing in prayer when he tells his disciples, "And whenever you stand praying, forgive, if you have anything against someone, so that your Father, the one in the heavens, may forgive you your wrongdoings" (Mark 11:25). In the parable, the Pharisee and the tax collector are both standing (Luke 18:11, 13). Jesus does not ever specify a more or less acceptable posture for prayer, but he does denounce choosing a place for prayer in order that other believers can esteem your piety.

Jesus is never described as standing in prayer. However, the New Testament authors probably did not mention that Jesus stood to pray because standing was such a common prayer posture.

Summary

The posture we take with our body communicates as do the words we articulate with our mouths. If we stand, we proclaim God as Judge of judges. If we kneel or fall to our face, we proclaim God King of kings. If we lift our hands towards another, we proclaim God Priest of priests. As Rabbi Eliezer told his disciples when he fell ill, "When you pray know before whom you are standing and in this way you will win the future world" (*b. Ber.* 28b). Jesus models for us that deep distress and earnest entreaty need not be locked within us but they can be freely given to God in prayer. If we embrace, touch, and lift up our hands to bless others, we can do so also in imitation of our High Priest, Jesus, the Lover of all lovers, Physician of physicians.

Prayer postures were employed in the New Testament to symbolize grief, fear, request, thanksgiving, adoration, worship, blessing. Similarly we need to demonstrate our genuine feelings before God. And as we create and see new postures of prayer we do well to analyze what truth we are stating in a symbolic way. Our postures tell us about ourselves and about our God. Are we sentenced persons standing before a Judge? Are we kneeling for mercy or request before a Sovereign? Are we funnels of God's blessings? Are we priests representing the one pure God?

7

Passover Prayer of the Paschal Lamb (John 17:1-12)

Jesus' Passover prayer for his disciples comes at the end of a poignant series of interactions between Jesus and his followers. The long journey to Jerusalem has ended. Jesus has entered the metropolis to a roaring welcome that has thrown his adversaries into dismay.

The Setting

The same crowd that stood astonished as Jesus called the dead forth to life mingled with the mobs already milling about Jerusalem, waiting for the Passover festivities to begin, telling everyone who would listen that this great and unique newsmaker was coming. Eyewitness John records in his gospel in 12:17 that his fellow eyewitnesses, the crowds at Bethany, were buzzing the news about, and further in 12:18 that the crowds gathered because of the greatest of all signs. The man born blind had challenged his accusers, "From forever (out of the ages) it has not been heard that anyone opened the eyes of a person born blind" (9:32). Who beside the greatest of all the prophets, Elijah, had ever brought a dead person back to life? So the crowds tore off palm branches in their exuberance, shouting,

"Hosanna! Blessed is the one coming in the name of the Lord, the Ruler of Israel!" (12:13).

No wonder the Pharisee leaders who gathered with the chief priests in council when the first reports of Lazarus' raising had reached Jerusalem were frustrated. This upstart Jesus had already stirred up their precarious situation enough. Rome under that mercurial prima donna Pontius Pilate had threatened Israel's security already and Pilate's loathing for the Jews was painfully obvious. John in 11:48 tells us the leaders were worried that everyone would believe in Jesus and Rome would in retaliation destroy "our place" (probably meaning the holy place in the temple) and the nation. The leaders were right to be worried.

So Jesus entered Jerusalem to a roaring, tumultuous welcome, but one with sinister undertones. His own actions reveal the tension he was sensing outside and feeling within himself. No sooner had he made his grand entrance to the acclaim of the crowds and was so sought out that even foreigners were clammering to see him (12:20-21), than, revealing his troubled thoughts to his disciples, he hid himself (12:36).

Jesus' sudden absence left a power vacuum that the Pharisees were quick to fill. For them the problem of Jesus' popularity had proved to be as deadly serious as they had reckoned. Even many of the authorities were believing in Jesus, John reports in 12:42. The term he uses, *archon*, means ruler, official, authority, judge, and when used in John 3:1 in the phrase "ruler of the Jews" means a member of the Sanhedrin itself. And did Jesus not also associate with publicans and prostitutes here in Israel? And what of that disgraceful performance at the house of the distinguished Pharisee who had out of sheer common courtesy lowered himself to invite this uncouth ruffian to his own table -- only to be crudely insulted (Luke 11:37ff)? No doubt the power vacuum left by Jesus was swiftly and skillfully filled, for it was filled so effectively that scant days later the same crowds who were screaming to crown and acclaim him were shrieking to kill him.

In this context of anxiety and the mercurial unrest of the populace, Jesus and his followers prepare to observe the Passover. Traditionally Jesus and his disciples are pictured as being alone when they celebrate that Passover feast that becomes the last supper. But were they indeed alone? In the three accounts in Matthew 26:17-20, Mark 14:12-17, Luke 22:7-14 Jesus sends his disciples ahead to prepare the feast, and we are told he sat at table with the twelve. A review of the Passover service employed in Jesus' time reveals that the celebration was a familial event. A key part of the ceremony was the asking by children what the event was all about. Did Jesus omit this part because he had no children? Did the youngest disciple take the part of the child? Or was Jesus' mother and some of the faithful women with small children or perhaps the householder and his family sharing the first part of the meal with Jesus and his followers? Alfred Edersheim in a fascinating argument suggests that the unnamed house was in reality the home of John Mark, later writer of the gospel. Edersheim argues that Mark is the unnamed youth who slips on an inner garment and steals after Jesus and his followers when they go to Gethsemane. We recall that a soldier tries to seize him and he tears out of his under garment and races off naked into the night (Mark 14:51-52). We understand that Mark's home was large because Acts 12:12 tells us many were gathered there praying when Peter was released by the angel from prison and brought the astonishing message of his miraculous release to the astounded housemaid Rhoda. The house must have been a strong, well built one since Epiphanius tells us Hadrian found the building with the upper room still standing in A.D. 135. Cyril of Jerusalem in the 300s also identified it as did several other ancient pilgrims to Jerusalem. Today the mosque En Neby Daud claims to have the upper room, called the Cenacle, enshrined on its first floor.[1]

Josephus in *The Wars of the Jews* 6.9.3 tells us that from ten to twenty gathered for the Passover meal (so that all might have a portion of the lamb and none might feast singly). Jesus, Edersheim notes, only asked for the *katalyma*, the hall or hostelry, traditionally the word was used for a place where troops were billeted. Edersheim notes the other place the term is used is for the barn where Mary bore Jesus, so that he who was born in a *katalyma* asked only for his last supper to be in one. But the householder gave him the *aliyah*, the prized and furnished roof room, the best meeting room in the house, where a group could come and go privately by stairs to the roof.[2] Perhaps Mark's family joined them, and young Mark or a younger brother was the child who asked the traditional question, "Why is this night different from other nights? For on other nights we eat seasoned food once, but this night twice; on other nights we eat

---

[1] O. R. Sellers, "Upper Room," *The Interpreter's Dictionary of the Bible* (1962), IV, 735.

[2] Alfred Edersheim, *The Life and Times of Jesus the Messiah*, II (Grand Rapids: Eerdmans, 1947) 483-484.

leavened or unleavened bread, but this night all is unleavened; on other nights we eat flesh roast, stewed, or cooked, but this night all is roast?" Perhaps Mary and the family of Mark and the mother of James and John, or perhaps as many as seven other faithful followers or family, enjoyed Jesus' company in the last supper. The average large dining room was about fifteen feet square. The text, however, does not mention any of these people being present. Perhaps instead Jesus, he who attended and celebrated so many weddings and feasts with family and friends that he was slandered as a drunkard and carouser, chose this one night not to celebrate a family feast. Perhaps he did not do so for this one year of the Passover he was called to modify the celebratory Passover with the sober and meager feast of the bread and wine of the Lord's Supper. He was acknowledging that now at last God was not going to spare the first born of Israel. God was not going to spear the Egyptian and spare the Israelite. The first born of Israel was going to die. Jesus would have no passing-over to celebrate this year. He was to prepare himself and his disciples for his becoming the sacrificial lamb, his blood spread with hyssop on the door posts of the world.

The recording of that Passover meal, what we now call the Last Supper, begins at John 13 and continues on until it ends at Jesus and his disciples quitting the upper room after the hymn that followed Jesus' prayer for his disciples at the end of John 17. The Greek text of John allots five chapters for the events in the upper room. That is slightly more space than it allots for Jesus' entire arrest, imprisonment, death, resurrection, and final words, 2783 or 2770 words (depending on one's reading of which words comprise the true text). We Christians hinge our faith on these latter events, and yet John invests as much space or even slightly more in recounting the words Jesus shares with our spiritual ancestors in the upper room. Certainly such a fact supports Jesus' insistence that his words are as significant as the works for which he was being celebrated. These works are our precious heritage. They are the tools we have been given to interpret and understand the startling events to come. As heirs, we need to understand them intimately.

We have already seen the tumultuous events that surrounded Jesus' arrival at the upper room. Now the prayer Jesus gives comes at the end of another tumultuous series of events between Jesus and his disciples. If he has already rocked the crowd with his teachings, his works, and his presence, now he initiates a series of poignant teaching devices that leave the disciples dumbfounded, and dismayed.

The disciples had prepared in an upper room to which Jesus, in the synoptic accounts, had given them detailed directions, a Passover feast that proved to be a most unusual meal. During that meal Jesus rose, took off his outer clothes, tied a towel around his waist, poured water into a basin and began to wash his disciples' feet -- to Peter's manifest protests. When Jesus explains his action, the disciples are even more chagrined, for Jesus identifies his betrayer. That identity escapes many of them as they clamor to know if -- grievous of all catastrophes! -- each himself might be the one to betray the chosen one who brings the words of the Father.

Now while Jesus has them all in dismay, he speaks words to comfort them. He asks them to trust him as they trust God (14:1). He tells them of the homes he is going to prepare for them in the great mansion of his Father, a place from which he will come again personally in order to bring them. He promises that they themselves will do greater works than even he has done -- an astonishing statement in itself, coming from one who has fed masses from a boy's lunch, made vintage stock out of washing water, given the gift of sight to the blind, leaping to the lame, cleansing to the leper -- and life to the dead! To his astonished disciples during the course of one earthly meal Jesus has entrusted the blueprint for his church on earth, an edifice that has spanned the centuries and spans the earth today. Following these memorable events Jesus gives his disciples their last instruction before he is to undergo his great passion, his suffering and death on the cross.

In this bewildering context he tells them not to be troubled. Then he gives them all his teaching in one last great metaphor. The Jesus who performed his first earthly debut miracle by enlivening a party and besting the host with a vintage of rare finesse dips again into the language of the winery, to the very first stage of production, the growing of the vines. I am the true vine, he says, my Father is the vinedresser, and you are the branches. Through verbal pictures he paints for them what will happen if they stay trusting in him -- and what will happen if they do not. He warns them that they will face severe opposition from the world. Like the man born blind they will be put out of synagogues, shunned, even killed (16:2). And their murderers, like the later Saul of Tarsus, will think they are doing a favor to God when they kill them! But Jesus assures the disciples that the Holy Spirit will bolster and comfort them. Finally he predicts his resurrection. What a meal!

The Lord's Prayer in John 17:1-12

At this point Jesus lifts his eyes to heaven and prays the prayer recorded in John 17.

"Father, the Hour Has Come; Glorify your Son, in order that the Son May Glorify You, just as You Gave Him Authority over All Flesh, in order that All Whom You Have Given to Him He Might Give to Them Eternal Life" (17:1-2).

The Hour Has Come. We have been studying the instructions about prayer Jesus gave to his disciples, the parables about prayer with which he illustrated these teachings, two renditions of a model prayer he gave at their request, and even several brief snatches of the prayers he himself prayed, but now we have recorded for us an extensive, passionate prayer of Jesus on behalf of his disciples. If we have yearned to know what Jesus' prayers themselves were like when Jesus earnestly entreated his Parent, we now have recorded for us a most extensive and passionate example. Jesus lifts his eyes and says, "Father, the hour has come." The emphasis in his opening sentence is on the One addressed and the particular moment in which he addresses that One. Literally he prays, "Father, has come the hour." Greek, in which the prayer is recorded, does not depend on word order as does English but relies rather on the endings of words to indicate to us what part of speech they are and in what tense or case. Therefore, word order can be used for emphasis. Whatever word begins the sentence indicates what is being emphasized. Jesus engages the Father in conversation and cries, "has come the hour." Naturally, we translate the sentence into proper English word order as "the hour has come," but in doing so, as English word order demands, we lose what is being emphasized in the Greek. All through the gospel of John Jesus has been awaiting his "time."

As far back as the early halcyon days of his first public appearance at the marriage feast at Cana, Jesus was already noting the nature and passing of the hours, awaiting the appropriate time. At that first great marriage feast, framing like a bookend the story of Jesus, awaiting to have set against it in eventual closure of the episodes of Jesus' work that last great eternal marriage supper of the Lamb, the heavenly party which will never exhaust its wine or its joy, Jesus notes, "My hour has not yet come" (John 2:4). His life's blood is still his own, not yet poured out for the redemption of many. So, he takes common water and makes it into the finest wine the guests have yet tasted. This indeed is a convivial foretaste of glory divine. But the bitter sweet wine crushed out from the life's blood of the grape is only a type of the bitter sweet draught of salvation that the thirsty will drink at the expense of the first fruit of humanity. The vinegar that Jesus will taste on the cross tells the true tale. Bitter, bitter is the portion of the cupbearing slave who drinks the poisoned cup so that another may live. Thus, with his time not at hand, his hour not having come, Jesus increases the joy of his family and friends, the gracious bridegroom who turns common earth to the splendor of heaven, washing water to the fullest bodied wine.

His coming out party literally having been affected, Jesus launches into a whirlwind ministry of astounding teachings and astonishing miracles. His name is on so many lips that his skeptical brothers, annoyed and uncomfortable with their familial upstart, scoff, "If you are doing these things, show yourself to the world" (John 7:4). Jesus retorts, literally, "The time of mine is not yet come, but the time of yours always is ready (or at hand)" (7.6). Immediately afterwards he does go up to the Feast of Tabernacles but in secret, without fanfare, not in public appearance. And when he begins his astonishing teachings and some of the crowd from Jerusalem seek to arrest him, the text tells us they fail "because *not yet* had come his hour" (John 7:30). While the emphasis is on the "not yet," the word used for "had come" is the one we will find again in John 17:1 when Jesus' hour has at last come. Further in 8:20 when he inflames the crowd while speaking in the treasury of the temple, no one arrests him "because *not yet* had come his hour" (John 8:20). The phrases in 7:30 and 8:20 are exactly the same to a word. Emphasis is on the "not yet," and the words employed are the ones Jesus will utter as he opens his prayer. No doubt this is a phrase Jesus himself must be using over and over again as he marks the passing of the hours, while working on his task, fulfilling his commission, accomplishing miracles and preaching and teaching poignantly as he watches for his time.

It comes, as we have seen, when Jesus finally does make his great public entry, the triumphant Palm Sunday march into Jerusalem. Immediately after his arrival when he is the talk of the festival, some Greeks seek him out and astonishingly Jesus replies to the news, literally, "*Has come* the hour in order that the Son of Humanity may be glorified" (12:23). We see by this word order that the verb at last has shifted to the front of the sentence. Finally it stands before "the not yet" of Cana and his near arrests or "the time" of the mockery of his brothers. The hour *has come* and Jesus is troubled (John 12:27). Now he speaks of his death and conducts his disciples carefully through all the lessons and warnings of the upper room. With this final casting of his repeated sentence he opens the last great prayer he will deliver on behalf of those in his caretaking, "Father, has come the hour."

The Glory of Jesus. As the disciples crowd uncertainly around him, no doubt bewildered and troubled by the confusion of his accusations and the increasingly troubling talk of a place he will go where they cannot, they hear him restate the reply he gave to Andrew and Philip when the Greeks begged to see him in 12:23. There he replied enigmatically, "The hour has come that the Son of Humanity may be glorified." Now he prays, "Father, the hour has come; glorify your Son, that the Son may glorify you ...." What can Jesus mean? How can "the Son" be glorified, when all the prospect of coming events does for him is trouble his soul? What can be the fulfillment of this non-sinister-appearing phrase, since it will wrest him away from his disciples? What is this hour that has come to him? What is this glorification that will occur that Jesus has been awaiting, indeed for which he has been searching each moment? The opening of the prayer is a plea for glory for the Son, a reminder that Jesus glorified God and a request that God should glorify him. What can he mean?

The word *doxa*, as we saw when we examined the doxological ending the early church set on the model prayers Jesus gave, is a word that runs throughout the narrative of John. In the prologue that precedes the story of Jesus, wherein John sets a theological hermeneutic or interpreting device by which to understand the strange and marvelous biography to come as the advent of the "Word of God," John includes in his early description the information that when this Word that pitched his tent of flesh among us was scrutinized carefully by those around him, what people beheld was glory. This specific glory was a glory as of one only begotten from the Father; a shekinah glory like that which used to descend on the tabernacle during the wanderings of Israel's ancestors in the wilderness. This was a glory filled up to the brim with the attributes of God, grace, that is steadfast love, and truth (John 1:14). Then at Cana in John 2:11, when John's explanatory introduction has given way to the chronicling of events, Jesus' first sign of the changing of water to wine manifests his glory and the disciples stand amazed, and for the moment they are convinced and believe in him.

In John 5:41 Jesus affirms, "Glory from people I do not receive." How significant this affirmation is becomes painfully evident when the acclaim of the crowds turns to howls for Jesus' blood. The parallel is pointedly made by Jesus in 5:44, "How can you believe, who receive glory from one another and the glory that comes from the only God you do not seek?" As Jesus explains further in John 7:18, seeking one's own glory by speaking on one's own authority yields only lies. But speaking on God's authority and getting glory from God yields truth. The text explains in 7:39 that Jesus' teachings about the Spirit had not yet been fulfilled. The Spirit was not yet given to those who believed, because Jesus had not yet been glorified. Here we see in this paralleling of the "not yet" with Jesus' glorification the understanding that when the hour comes the glory would come too, and then the Spirit would be bestowed on believers. Continually Jesus explains, as he does in 8:50, he is not seeking his own glory. The Father, he explains in 8:54, glorifies him. Ironically, the Pharisees use *doxa* in the expression with which they charge the man born blind to be truthful, "Give glory to God; we know that this man is a sinner!" (John 9:24). But the irony *is* that the man born blind *is* giving glory to God. He is telling the truth.

As Jesus draws into the final acts of what is rapidly appearing to be a tragedy but will astoundingly reveal itself to be the great comedy, the most joyful tale that humans will ever tell, his preoccupation with the concept -- really the weight of his coming glory -- fills his mind and his speech. When he hears Lazarus has fallen ill, Jesus approaches the event in which, while restoring life to a beloved friend, he will seal his own doom, for this resuscitation will confirm the Pharisees' desire to kill him. As this lifegiving becomes a type of the greater lifegiving he will give to us all, Jesus observes, "This sickness is not to death but in behalf of the glory of God, in order that the Son of God may be glorified through it" (11:4). We see here he has thrown off his phrase Son or Heir of Humanity and replaced it now with the other fully true description of who he actually is, the Son or Heir of God. When in 11:39 Martha for practical reasons protests that if the stone is rolled away from Lazarus' tomb there will be an odor (think how she must have recalled the irony of these words when she finds to her astonished delight the stone eventually rolled away from Jesus' own tomb with equally wonderful, exhilerating results), Jesus replies in verse 40, "Did not I tell you that if you might believe you would see the glory of God?" And see it they all did, for he then prays, "Father, I thank you that you heard me. But I myself had known that always you hear me; but on account of the crowd standing around I spoke, in order that they may believe that you yourself sent me" (John 11:41-42). And he bids Lazarus come forth.

One wonders if the Father replies to Jesus' call to belief by ironically causing Caiaphas to speak beyond his will in 11:49-52, prophesying from God that the leaders understand nothing, that expediency demands that one should die for many. 11:51 tells us that Caiaphas was empowered beyond his own inclinations because of his office as high priest that year. In any event, Jesus' fate is sealed. The human machinery that will produce his divine glorification is now in motion.

If John in his prologue has given us a theological understanding with which to interpret the coming events, now in the beginning of chapter 12 he gives us a prophetic framework in which to set this glorification to come. 12:15-16 tells us when Jesus was glorified, his disciples connected the prophecy in Zechariah 9:9 with Jesus' triumphal entry into Jerusalem at the Passover. When Jesus is troubled by the coming of his hour yet refuses to demand the "cup," or what is in store for him, be taken from him, God's voice thunders out a reply to Jesus' request to " glorify your name" (12:28): "And I glorified and again I will glorify." Then John adds a further piece to the prophetic frame, citations from Isaiah. Why does John tell us he included them? Because the prophet "saw his glory" (12:41). Sadly, some of the authorities who, as the prophet Isaiah, also recognized Jesus' glory abandoned their new faith because they were afraid of being put out of the synagogue, loving or valuing the glory of people over that of God (12:42-43). What quenches their initial fervor is a calamity Jesus will later promise his disciples will befall them too. They will be put out of the synagogues and even killed as a service to God by the misguided! (16:2).

Despite what the disciples may have been anticipating in the past, all that this present talk of glory seemed to mean for them was that they would soon be sorely troubled. They might have realized this if they had understood exactly why Judas slunk away and if they had noted that, when Judas left, Jesus exclaimed, "Now has the Heir of Humanity been glorified, and God has been glorified in him" (13:31). What can this mean? When the traitor leaves to destroy his master, the master interprets the act as one which brings him glory? To Jesus Judas' act commences the process wherein both the Father and Son will be glorified. But how can Jesus be glorified by an act of rank betrayal?

Interesting to note is that though Jesus himself is troubled by the future prospect of the glorifying process, he worries about his disciples and comforts them. "Let not your hearts be troubled," he encourages them in both 14:1 and 27. He promises they will be doing greater works than even he does. Whatever they ask in his name, he will do it. Why? That the Father may be glorified in the Son. He pleads with them to believe his works if they doubt him himself. The works prove that the Son is in the Father and the Father in the Son (14:11). And "my Father" will eventually be glorified by the disciples bearing much fruit thereby proving themselves to be Jesus' disciples (15:8). Finally, he prophesies the coming Spirit of truth (16:13) will glorify Jesus by taking all truth which is Jesus' and thereby the Father's and declaring it to the disciples (16:14-15).

All of this talk of glory culminates in the prayer in the upper room when Jesus speaks of glorifying the Father and of being glorified. What can it all mean? What is this glory that is thundering down upon Jesus in his imminent hour? What kind of impending weight of glory is about to fall upon him --perhaps crushing him?

Looking forward beyond the prayer to the other side of the frame, we discover the last mention of *doxa* in the verb form is in 21:19 when Jesus gives to Peter what might be considered a terrifying prophecy, particularly if Jesus happened to be delivering it to us personally. He foreshadows by what death Peter will "glorify God." Another way to read this foretelling, of course, is as Jesus' comforting of mercurial, emotional Peter, abashed and brooding before his risen Lord about his own failure to carry out his pledge back in 13:37, "My life on behalf of you I will lay down." We see Peter's bold emphasis comes back to accuse him. Jesus prophesies a second and successful privilege for Peter of the ultimate service. What then in this light, we wonder, is the glory that Jesus seeks to have the Father give him when he enters into his great prayer for his disciples? Let us examine specifically what he asks.

In verse one Jesus prays, "Father, the hour has come; glorify your Son, in order that the Son may glorify you . . . ." He follows this request in verse two by explaining as he finishes the sentence, "just as you gave him authority over all flesh, in order that all whom you have given to him he might give to them eternal life."

If people have continually wondered and queried humbly or challenged boldly by what power Jesus has healed and forgiven sins and expulsed demons and proclaimed such wonderful and intimate and authoritative truths about the great God of the universe (this God whom Jesus claims uniquely to know as Abba, intimate Father), Jesus has continually replied that his authority has not been derived from people but comes directly from God. The ramification of this fact is that Jesus has now come as the reigning monarch on earth. He is the one who has been given by God "authority over all flesh." Jesus' authority as a result figures everywhere, both in his dealings with what are to be his subjects (if God's intentions are indeed for him to be ruler) and also within those potential subjects' expectations of Jesus. Jesus comes proclaiming the rule of God. The Devil tempts him with the lure of authority over all the kingdoms of this world. The people at his triumphal entry threaten to take him by force and make him king. Even Pilate will mock him with the question of his authority, emblazoned over the instrument of his death, proclaiming boldly above this Christ's dying head in the three languages of Israel, Hebrew, Greek, and Latin, "Jesus of Nazareth, the King of the Jews" (John 19:19-22). Jesus himself will argue, "My reign is not of this world," and will point out that, if it were, he would have allowed his servants to fight for him (John 18:36) and not stop them as he does at his arrest in Gethsemane after his final prayers. There he proves dramatically that his rule is not to be fought for in earthly terms when he heals the sword wound that Peter inflicts when Peter lobs off the ear of a servant of those rulers of this world's ecclesiastical institutions who challenge and ultimately destroy this unworldly ruler Jesus. Jesus will argue again in this very prayer that those disciples over whom he has been given authority are themselves no longer of this world. Therefore, when we seek to understand his glory, we must perceive his glory as something not of this world. Its source is from another world. Its full expression will be in another world. We may glimpse it here. But it will dazzle us elsewhere, when the ruler returns to the throne.

Still, the authority given to Jesus over all flesh has an earthly purpose with a heavenly end. The disciples are those whom the Father has entrusted to Jesus, so that Jesus might give them eternal life. Jesus' gift, we might infer, is a condition necessary for the disciples to be able to witness Jesus' full glorification in eternity. Eternal life is also necessary for the disciples to have time enough to know the Father and the Son. So Jesus now continues in his prayer with an explanation of exactly what eternal life means. And he provides another piece in completing the puzzle of what exactly his present glorification is. So, we must first understand what eternal life means for Jesus and second understand what the completion of

Jesus' work means for Jesus, for us, and for Jesus' Father before we are able to comprehend the paradoxical enigmatic glory of this unearthly monarch.

"And This Is Eternal Life, that They May Know You, the Only True God, and the One You Sent, Jesus Christ" (17:3).

Those who say that the concept of living eternally sounds boring do not fully understand what eternal life is in Jesus' vision. We often struggle to explain, when telling others of our exciting faith, that Christianity is not a religion but a relationship with God. All the trappings of candles and choirs and sermons and psalms mean nothing if they are not aids in deepening our love affair with the great creator God who stoops to embrace us and raise us back up from our stumbling. Here Jesus supplies the foundation for that claim. For him eternal life is getting to know God more and more deeply, and, since God is infinite and infinitely deep, that loving prospect will take an endless eternity. But wait. Watch those same challengers of the attractiveness of the prospect of life eternal when their own lives are threatened by sobering news at the doctor's office. How most of us moan at the prospect of dying and go to whatever measures we can, more and more desperate, to remain alive and in company with the ones we love. Now we speak no more about the loathesomeness of the prospect of living eternally! Well, heaven is the best of our warmest, sweetest relationships on earth intensified in all their love and warmth and affirmation and virtue to the infinite power. Eternal life is the span of time it takes to get to know the source of love and joy and beauty -- what a wonderful task! Jesus, we see, craves to be in the Father's presence. The disciples love to be in Jesus' presence and are deeply disturbed at the prospect that he goes where they cannot go and leaves them behind, abandoned. No one wants to be separated for any great length from someone they love. Heaven is the end of the pain of separation from love.

Interesting to note, too, is that eternal life in Jesus' definition is not only the time it takes to fall more and more deeply in love with the great Lover, but with Jesus Christ as well. His definition states, "that they may know you, the only true God, and the one you sent, Jesus Christ." If Jesus were only a messenger, simply someone pointing the way to God, as John the Baptist pointed the way to Jesus, then his role as herald would soon be fulfilled, his importance would diminish, and as a well trained butler who announces the card of the great personage arriving and steps deftly, discretely aside, he would shimmer off into the nether regions as the great P. G. Wodehouse had his incomparable Jeeves do. After all, we do not stop the mail carrier for a few hours' desultory chat. If we do, we delay the mail. We cannot invite the pizza deliverer in for dinner and a game of checkers. It will cost that deliverer a job. The messenger's importance lies in delivering the message and then the messenger is off with either a return message, a completely different delivery, or free time to pursue his or her own interests. But eternity as getting to know God also involves getting to know God's messenger. While normally we do not have to know the messenger to understand the message sent, here we do! For in seeing Jesus, we have seen the Father.

Having set out this context as the opening of his prayer, Jesus continues to explain the nature of his most unusual glorification in verse four.

"I Myself Glorified You upon the Earth, the Work Having Finished that You Gave Me that I Might Do" (17:4);

We can clearly see in this literal rendition of verse four what Jesus has chosen to emphasize. Jesus begins by stressing "I, myself." The redundancy drives the point home: I, the one who is speaking, through my actions glorified you upon the earth. The verb is cast in the past tense. This is something I, myself, did and it was done on earth. Now, instead of ending the sentence and beginning a new one, which could be easily done by constructing these two thoughts into two main clauses, Jesus instead employs a participle, making the second part of the sentence after the comma dependent on the first. Rather than a main clause which can stand by itself, the latter statement is now appositional, that is, it becomes an explanation of what has just preceded. So, Jesus is saying, I myself glorified you upon the earth. What do I mean by this? Or, how did I do it? Literally, "The work having finished that you gave to me that I might do." As his explanation Jesus stresses that God was glorified through the completion of the work that God gave him to do. We can see in the literal rendering that the emphasis is upon the work. God was the one who commissioned the work to Jesus with the understanding that Jesus would do it. In doing it Jesus glorified God. So if we are to understand what glorifying God meant to Jesus and therefore what he expected when he wished himself to be glorified, we can understand by discovering exactly what this work of

Jesus was that God gave him to do and how in being done it gave glory to God.

In Jesus' first public debut at the marriage of Cana we saw that the elements and themes that culminated in this last great prayer and in the ensuing act on behalf of his disciples were already present. Jesus spoke of his hour, did a sign, and manifested his glory by the great work of turning water to wine. His disciples, we were told in verse 2:11, believed in him. By the time of chapter 4:46-54 he is demonstrating the potency of his power by healing while a long distance away from those being healed. In the same chapter just prior to this remarkable act which has him returning again to Cana and healing at Capernaum, he has extended the definition of his mission to the Jews by including a two day sojourn among the Samaritans.

At the Samaritan well he explains to his disciples, "He who reaps receives wages and gathers fruit for eternal life, so that sower and reaper may rejoice together" (John 4:36). The obedience he speaks of, we will soon lcarn, is linked to a Jewish kind of hearing, the hearing that precipitates acting, "The one hearing my word and believing him who sent me has eternal life" (John 5:24). This relationship of hearing and believing and having eternal life, we see, he will explain again in John 17 during the course of his prayer. To hear for Jesus is to believe the life-giving word. To believe the life-giving word is to do the work of God. To do the work of God is to glorify God and to be glorified by God. All of these concepts are tied intrinsically, inseparably together. The work of God ties up Jesus' identity with God's and authenticates the words he preaches.

Thus, Jesus' work is identified with his Father's work and implied in its identification is a claim of divinity. The Pharisees realized this and were scandalized. As John 5:17-18 notes, when Jesus explained, "My Father is working still, and I myself am working," "This was why the Jews sought all the more to kill him, because he not only broke the Sabbath but also called God his own Father, making himself equal with God." According to Jesus, the "works which the Father has granted me to accomplish, these very works which I am doing, bear me witness that the Father has sent me" (John 5:36). Here we see that the works testify to his relationship to God and certify his claim that God sent him. Such a claim and such mighty acts naturally evoke a reaction. When the people after the feeding of the five thousand ask, "What must we do to be doing the works of God?" (John 6:28), Jesus replies, "This is the work of God, that you might believe in him whom he has sent." We see by this explanation that the first great act for would-be followers in Jesus' schema is to believe in Jesus. In a Hebrew understanding to think is to do, to believe in Jesus is to act under his rulership. That work then flows out in words to produce belief in others and in good works that bring God's reign to this rebellious earth. All this good work is opposed to the world's works which Jesus identifies as being evil (John 7:7). As Jesus summarizes his position, "The works that I do in my Father's name, they bear witness to me" (John 10:25). Therefore, as 10:38 indicates, if the Pharisees refuse to believe the words of Jesus, they ought to believe the works which prove Jesus and the great Parent are in unity. Even to his disciples Jesus charges in 14:11, "Believe me that I am in the Father and the Father in me; or if not, on account of the works themselves believe." And this capacity to do Jesus' works Jesus is going to pass on to his disciples. "Greater works," he tells them in 14:12, they will do.

What essentially we have set up for us here in John is a schema that unites words and actions in the person and activity of Jesus and the diagram of a relationship that Jesus initiates with us with a resulting response from us of preaching and actions because of that relationship. The end result is that God is glorified, Jesus is glorified, and even we are raised to a higher place as citizens of the great reign of God, heirs with Christ of the endless riches of God's grace. In the prologue that begins his theological biography of Jesus, John tells us that Jesus is the word of God come to earth. Jesus' words give life to us so that, if his words remain in us, we can bear much fruit (John 15). Fruit includes one's words having effect (15:7).

We can see such an example of powerful words bearing the good fruit of performing good works that give glory to God in the example of Peter and John himself which Luke records in Acts 3:4. Accosted by a lame beggar on their way into the temple, they fix their gaze on him and Peter commands on behalf of them both, "Look at us!" Peter's and John's words command the beggar's full attention, just as once John tells us in his prologue and again in the opening of his first epistle that John himself once fixed his attention on Jesus, scrutinized him, handled and examined him (I John 1:1-3). "Focus your attention on us!" Peter commands the lame beggar. "Gold and silver are not at my disposal." The beggar we are told in 3:5 is expecting to receive something from John and Peter. Peter immediately deals with his expectations and disposes of them. He is not about to give him a fish, as the old proverb goes. He is about to give the beggar the means to fish for himself, "that which I have, this to you I give; in the name of Jesus Christ of Nazareth be walking" (Acts 3:6). The beggar immediately leaps up, pulled by Peter's strong hand, and begins himself leaping about unaided now, walking, jumping, and praising God.

Years later aged John, who, Eusebius tells us, has reviewed the other three gospels by Matthew, Mark, and Luke and confirmed their accuracy and who wants to add more details and explanation about the marvelous early work of Jesus, writes up the incredible experiences he had with Jesus in the retrospect of seeing Jesus' words and works actualized in his own ministry (*History of the Church* 3:24). The John who preached mighty words of his own in the temple, who helped restore the lame man, who saw Ananias and Sapphira struck dead, who felt the power of the Holy Spirit come thundering down upon him, who Clement told us once charged on horseback into the center of a robbers' band to restore their leader to a saving and sanctified life in Christ (*History of the Church* 3:23), this same John from the vantage point of seeing Jesus' words fulfilled is the one who is explaining. Thus, through Jesus' mighty words in John that caused John's mighty acts, Jesus was glorified, the Father was glorified, and the people who saw the lame man healed stood astounded before Peter and John as these disciples shared with them Jesus' words of life. And as the leaping lame man praised God, many believed in Jesus (Acts 4:4). Words, works, glorification all melded together because Jesus the One Great Word of Life was faithful to his commission, sharing the words of life with his disciples and after doing many good works finally doing the great work of salvation so that in the disciples' deliverance God, who entrusted them to Jesus, would be praised and the Parent in turn would praise the Child, first-born of the new family of God, Heir to God's kingdom.

And Now Glorify Me, You, Father, with You with the Glory which I Was Having with (in the Presence of) You before the World Existed (17:5).

Jesus' Glorious Finale Invoked. This prayed sentence begins with the time statement "*now* glorify me. Again, this prayer, unique in Jesus' recorded ministry, takes place *now* that the hour has come. Everything preceding the visit of the Greeks in John has been done in expectation of Jesus' time coming. We have already seen by the announcement opening the prayer in John 17 that the time *has finally come* and this prayer is prayed in this fullness of time. The bulk of Biblical scholars who study the gospels today talk in terms of the eschatological or end times expectation of Jesus and his disciples. Rudolf Bultmann even thinks "the glorifying" of Jesus means Jesus has himself become the "eschatological event," all of the future being defined in terms of people's response to Jesus, a future now beginning to come to pass as the disciples respond.[3] While Jesus' ministry does look forward to the great marriage supper of the Lamb when he will sit in his rightful place with his enemies as his footstool, an eschatological realization is also found in the here and now.

Earlier we noted that the full glorification of Jesus will happen in another time in another place in a reign not of this world. Yet now we find that there is also a glorification that will happen *now* in this time in this place. The Father is asked by Jesus to do it. Note Jesus' specific addressing of the Father. Redundant in Greek where neither specific personal address is needed (the verb, as we mentioned, indicating which person is speaking or being addressed), Jesus intentionally underscores twice who he is requesting to give him glory: *you, Father*. "And now glorify me -- you, Father -- with you with the glory which I was having with you before the world existed."

Jesus' Glorious Existence Recalled. If Jesus makes insistently clear whom he is asking for glorification in the latter part of verse 5, he also makes insistently clear who he is who is doing the asking -- the one who has already been in the Father's presence. Look at the second time statement in the verse: "With you I was having (that glory I am asking for now) when I was in your presence *before the world existed.*" Jesus wants *now* what he had *before*. Before what? We ask. Before this very world existed!

Jesus has made his preexistence clear and forthright throughout his ministry. In John's gospel we see Jesus continually identifying himself as the extra-terrestrial who has come down from heaven, from the very presence of the Father. As early as the night visit of Nicodemus in John 3:13, Jesus identifies himself as one who has descended from heaven. When John the Baptist's disciples come to John, as recorded in 3:25-36, with the report (complaint?) that "all are going to [Jesus]," that preacher that John himself baptized, John replies first that no one can receive anything except what is given him from heaven (3:27) and second, he who comes from heaven is

---

[3] Rudolph Bultmann, *The Gospel of John: A Commentary* (Philadelphia: Westminster, 1971), p. 492.

above all (3:31). Jesus himself says in 6:38, after depicting himself as the bread of life, who, like the water of life he depicted as himself by the well in Samaria, gives eternal sustenance, "For I have come down from heaven . . . ."

These days since such books as Eric Von Daeniken's *Chariots of the Gods*, Gerhard R. Steinhaeuser's *Jesus Christ: Heir to the Astronauts* and a heavenly host of theological science fiction potboilers which have dazzled the bestseller list, contemporary readers might be tempted to conclude Jesus stepped off a starship, orbiting our earth from the dog-star Sirius. But Jesus was communicating to the faithful of Israel and they knew exactly what he meant when he claimed to have come down from above. They began to murmur and then dispute among themselves. He amplifies in 6:38, "For I have come down from heaven not to do my will but the will of the one having sent me." And that will he tells us in 6:39 is "that I should lose nothing of all that he has given me but raise it up at the last day." What does Jesus mean by this extravagant claim? He will demonstrate his meaning poignantly when he raises the dead Lazarus back to life. Then his claims about being the bread of life, fallen like manna from above, the breaking of his flesh as a life source to all who partake of its sacrifice, may not sound so hard a saying as it did back in the synagogue at Capernaum in John 6:60.

Where Will Jesus Be Glorified? We have seen Jesus specifically identify who he is and who is the one who will glorify him, but where exactly will this glorification of Jesus take place? We have seen established *when* it will take place --now, immediately. But *where* exactly is Jesus asking to have it done? In other words, does the passage emphasize Jesus' glorification *here* or does it emphasize his glorification *in God's presence in heaven*? The second option would put Jesus' glorification fully into the eschaton, the coming glorious future. But such a reading would ignore the significance of the word *now*. This is not, as we have seen, a glorification that is only going to take place in the future. This is one that is going to take place now. But, perhaps Jesus is saying, glorify me up in heaven so I can get through the pain I am about to confront and endure on earth. But if the Father does that how will such a long-distance glorification help Jesus? Even if we recall Jesus' long-distance curing by a word that heals across the miles, the effect is felt at the word's destination. The miracle is effected where the sick person is. That is where the healing is manifested. Here, then, the effect would in the same way have to be evident on earth, where Jesus is. What makes the most sense is for Jesus to be saying, show some of that glory that I was having before I came here, in fact before there even was a here. And this is not some secondary, alien glory for which I am asking. This is your glory and I had it with you. The shekinah glory of God is what I shone with. And truly that is the glory that flashes out when Jesus is doing God's works.

So, in that sense, verse 17:5 is the inverse of Philippians 2:6-7. In Philippians 2 the external form (*morphe*) reflects an internal identity. Being emptied of glory, Jesus took the form of a slave. Now he asks to have that glory he gave up restored. Does God honor his request? If so, where is it done? The Father did glorify Jesus at the transfiguration. But the transfiguration was already a past action. In context what was about to happen was the great work of the crucifixion and the resurrection.

Now we see the point of Jesus' tying in the doing of his work with the concepts of glorifying God and being glorified by God. And we must make no mistake about it. Jesus is doing God's work when he submits to the crucifixion. When the gospel writers, in persecution themselves, recall in writing the last tumultuous days of Jesus' work on earth, they do not recall a poor carpenter preaching love who was misunderstood by the religious and political leaders of his day, dragged off, and murdered in another of history's great catastrophes. They recall instead Jesus saying, "On account of this the Father loves me because I myself lay down my life, in order that again I may take it up. Nobody takes it from me, but I myself put it from me. Authority I have to put it down, and authority I have again to take it up; this commandment I received from my Father" (John 10:17-18).

That is a reason why Jesus told Peter to put up his sword and why he healed the first person struck in his own defense. That is why he does not call on angels or Elijah or the Father to rescue him from the cross, despite the jeers of the crowd and of the thief who dies beside him. Dying is his final great work. And then God glorifies him because of it, because the Father is the one who raises him from the dead (cf. Paul's confession in Romans 10:9-10).

If we are looking for a spectacular glorification of Jesus after the request of 17:5 (which apparently the disciples in the havoc following the great calamity of Jesus' death were not), we certainly discover it exploding out of the tomb on Easter morning. Jesus' resurrection is the most dazzling display of God's glory the world has ever seen. Theologians these days may quibble over whether one does right to read the story of Jesus as a theology of the cross or a theology of glory, but the actual events of Jesus' story wrap up all these meanings in one earth-shaking cumulative finale. Starkly fulfilling the prophecies of the curse of the first sinful humans, Jesus is crushed by the forces of evil only to in turn crush them himself under his heel, his enemies cast down to be his footstool. Bound by death, Jesus explodes the bonds of death. Cast into the pit, Jesus is raised by God. Covered with shame and spittal and blood and disgrace, Jesus is covered with glory and praise. Disciples scattered, he lives again to see his disciples emboldened and empowered so that they go forth to turn the world upside down for their victorious conqueror. The prayer is indeed fulfilled after Jesus' most shattering moment of defeat. Shattering triumph. Victorious glory!

I Made Known Your Name to the People Whom You Gave to Me out of the World. Yours They Were, and to Me You Gave Them, and Your Word They Have Kept (17:6).

Making the Father Known. If Jesus has identified himself as the one who came from outside the world, the one who had glory with the great Parent before the world even existed, the one coming down from above with a message from his great Parent above, now Jesus identifies his followers also as ones who are being lifted out of the world. Speaking of his prior work, Jesus says, "I made known your name to the people whom you gave me out of the world." How could Jesus have made God's name known? Had not the Jews known God's name since the great unveiling of God's identity to Moses in the wilderness? But what exactly did God reveal to Moses? A statement about God's existence. I am. If DeCartes' great maxim was "I think therefore I am, " God's statement goes one claim further. God has no former conditional clause. God simply states, "I am." And all the ways scholars seek to render that statement, "I will be that I will be," "I am existing," "I am that I am" and so forth, simply establish God's claim to existence -- more than that -- God's revelation of existence. When God is pressed further as Jacob pressed, begging his celestial grappler's name, or as Moses pressed, begging to see the face of God, God withdraws into the cloud of our unknowing. What name did Jesus reveal to the people God gave him? Abba! Daddy! Is not this the intimate understanding of God? What is the significance for a Jew to know a name? A name for an ancient Hebrew told a deep truth about a person's nature, a person's character. So Esau, the red and hairy man, is a beast of simple, passionate, animal desires. He wants food, he eats. No birthright matters when his belly shouts out it is starving. Jacob, supplanter, supplants his brother. Moses, out of the rushes, takes his people out of the land of rushes. Jesus, whose name means salvation comes from God, comes from God with salvation. Therefore, what Jesus reveals in his person and in his teaching is that the name and therefore the nature of this God on whom all Jews call is Jesus' Abba, the loving Parent of humans. Those who have seen Jesus have seen their Parent. When Philip asks, show us the Father, Jesus replies, do you not know me? Jesus has come so that the Father the disciples call upon can be known to them. They know the Father through the Son.

God's Prior Claim. But Jesus' passage of prayer has something even more enigmatic to claim about his disciple's relationship to God than even the stupendous, staggering contention that they now know more fully than even their high priests and rabbis knew the God of the universe because of their relationship with God's child Jesus. Jesus' prayer identifies his disciples as people already a priori belonging to God, people whom God gave to Jesus, "Yours they were, and to me you gave them."

What Jesus is claiming to have done is to have shared God's words with God's chosen people. He has done God's mighty works, the mighty works of the God they have already known as conqueror and deliverer in order to demonstrate and validate his own teachings. So far has God condescended to the chosen people that Jesus has continually pleaded that his disciples may believe the words or believe the works. Jesus spends years working with the frail belief of the disciples, tending and nurturing it so that it will grow again into the lovely, atavistic edenic blossom of true belief. Such is not to say that the words of Jesus in themselves do not have power. Because of the words of the Sermon on the Mount the people gasped and gaped in amazement as if they had seen a theophany, an appearance of God.

Much scholarly paralleling has been done between the twelve apostles and the twelve tribes of Israel and the point of all that speculation is found herein. These disciples, Jesus assumes in his prayer, are already God's. They belong to God and God entrusted them to Jesus. Now in one sense Jesus is introducing his disciples more directly to God, but in another sense he is giving these disciples, who are already God's and were entrusted to Jesus, back to God. Jesus has already pointed out that no one can come to himself unless the Father draws that person. These, then, are the Lazaruses he will raise again on the last day (6:44). The great Shepherd knows the sheep and the sheep know the Shepherd's voice. These are the ones for whom eternal life is intended, those who believe (6:47). These are those who eat living bread and will not die (6:50). We can see why the great early theologians of the church wanted the Lord's prayer petition for bread to be understood as the living bread, for the disciples at the last supper are symbolically supping on the living bread and therefore are destined to live forever. They are the final guests driven in by the host to the banquet and ultimately to the glorious marriage supper of the Lamb, Jesus' Cana forever.

So, in one sense Jesus is introducing his disciples to the Father. As they have requested, he is showing them the Father by giving them over to the protective Parent. But in another sense they are already that Parent's, for God gave them to him.

Keeping God's Word -- Becoming Disciples. In the final phrase of John 17:6 Jesus concludes, "and your word they have kept." "Yours they were," he points out, "and to me you gave them, and your word they have kept." In our comparisons of John 14:13-14, 15:7-8, 16:23-24 we have seen how keeping the word is akin to doing the works is akin to bearing the fruits is akin, and all ends, in being disciples. Believers become disciples of God in doing all this. They *are* disciples *when* doing all this.

The living word which Jesus has entrusted to them from God is going to become infinitely more difficult to keep than the disciples suspect. Hounded away from their arrested leader, they will cower around meager fires in the stark cold semi-desert night, huddled and shivering with the greater chill of despair within them. Peter will curse and deny Jesus in his misery. All will flee, as naked of hope as the young man whose cloth is torn off by the guards, running naked and shamefaced into the biting night (Mark 14:51-52). If ever anyone has been stripped of hope -- literally -- these poor Galileans have been, watching their lord stripped and beaten and degraded and killed.

But the words live on within them. Those words that they have received from God pulse on, keeping in the disciples' innermost identity, their natures, their spiritual genetic structures, the reality of whom they have become in God's sight. Even while fallen, disgraced, hopeless, denying, they are still disciples. And their own hopes and boldness will rise together with their risen lord to triumph.

Now They Know that All Which You Have Given to Me Is from You (17:7);

This conclusion by Jesus must be proleptic. He must be looking into the future at an event certain enough to be considered a present reality. As late as the conversation recorded in 14:8-11 which occurs after the triumphal entry into Jerusalem, the disciples themselves are still questioning Jesus to the point where he must plead with them that if they do not believe him that he is in the Father and the Father is in him at least they should believe his works. And that interchange occurs, according to John's record, in this very upper room in the time between the defection of Judas and Jesus' promise to his disciples of greater works. What is to come? Peter's denial. The scattering of the flock. The slaughter of the shepherd. How can Jesus say that they *know* that all that Jesus said and did is from God? They will look to all appearances like that is the very last thing that they *know*!

John apparently puzzled over this bit of irony for the years between the time that Jesus said these words and the time John, teacher, caretaker, and shepherd himself, wrote his pastoral letters while riding circuit between his various churches. We are told continually in the gospel of Luke that Mary treasured the various words and events surrounding her remarkable son in her heart. Perhaps John, Jesus' beloved disciple, did too,[4] for in the conclusion of the first letter attributed to him he writes to another set of timid and worried disciples who wonder about the depth of their faith in Jesus, "These things I write to you, those believing in the name of the Son of God, that you may know that you have life eternal" (I John 5:13). The knowledge John claims is an assurance given to those who believe. The human responsibility is to be believing. Belief implies doubt. But if we are believing even with all our doubts (and we recall believing for a Hebrew means acting on what we believe), the promise is we can *know* we have eternal life. On God's side, the side of God's new-covenant promise, are no doubts. As far as God is committed, if we come with our doubts and our wishes and our hopes, wanting to be true to God's covenant and acting as covenant people, we can rest assured, we can know as fact from the secure eternal rock of all truth, that we have eternal life.

The knowledge of which Jesus speaks, then, John has apparently concluded from the advice he gives in I John 5:13, is a

---

[4] Perhaps, John and Mary, who lived with John since Jesus' charge, "Woman, behold your son! . . . Behold, your mother!" (John 19:26-27), shared these treasured memories, insights, and questions together.

knowledge not destroyed by Peter's denial, not lost when the disciples scattered, not choked to death by doubts and the mockery and opposition of the world. The disciples know because God has put that knowledge in their hearts. The word of Jesus has been given to them and that word is living inside them. It may slumber in the winter of their passion but it will spring to life in the warm spring of the resurrection of Jesus, their boldness resurrecting with their Lord. It will blossom and flourish for the words are words of truth, words of life, living words from the source of life which are life-giving words themselves. Like a glowing, pulsing heartbeat they stir the blood of faith, a gift itself from the great and loving God, and they will pump this faith through the veins of resolve. Out of the healthy, glowing witness comes new words of life to quicken others. And the truth grows on, ever fresh, ever new, eternal life.

Because the Words Which You Gave to Me I Have Given to Them, and They Themselves Received and Knew Truly that from You I Came out, and They Believed that You Yourself Sent Me (17:8).

Here we see explicitly stated that the words which have given the disciples life have come from God. Verse 8 is an amplification of the latter part of verse 7, "all which you have given to me is from you." On whose authority does Jesus speak? Where does Jesus get his message? The parallel between the source of Jesus' message and the source of Jesus' disciples is striking. Jesus has pointed out that the disciples already belonged to his Parent in verse 6 and they were entrusted to Jesus by the Father. Now he states that his message, his words of power, were also the property of God entrusted to him. Jesus gave God's words to God's people. Verse 6 tells us he also made known God's name to God's people. What God has given to him, Jesus has given to his disciples. And trusting in the power of God's words to quicken God's people, to live and cause life within them, he cries again that the disciples knew that Jesus came from the Father, indeed that Jesus was sent by the Father. No wonder Peter experiences such agony when he denies Jesus, weeping bitter tears of shame. No wonder Judas suffers such gnashing frustration, such despair and guilt and self-destruction. No wonder we know shame, and guilt, and biting disappointment when we deny Jesus before others. The living words that have been shared with us are stirring within us. They are strong young shoots bursting through the concrete of sin and cowardice. For as he planted them in his first disciples, Jesus has put the words of life into us. And they rise and pound to break out of us and enliven others.

We note the emphasis by Jesus on the fact that the disciples themselves have been the ones to receive and believe. Again, as we have noted, the verb with its case endings already indicates who is doing the action. It does not need, as English does, a pronoun to tell us who is acting. But Jesus uses the pronoun, asserts that they *themselves* are the ones who received. The disciples have participated in this endeavor. They are acting on their desires and becoming true disciples, as John 15:7-8 notes.

I Myself Ask concerning Them; Not concerning the World Do I Ask but concerning The Ones Whom You Have Given to Me, because They Are Yours, and All that Is Mine Is Yours and Yours Is Mine, and I Have Been Glorified in Them (17:9-10).

If we have seen Jesus emphasize the "they, themselves" who were receiving God's words of life, now he re-emphasizes the "I, myself" who is asking. He has returned his plea back to the foundational emphasis of verse 4. Over and over again Jesus has stressed that answers to prayer, while based on God's powerful and loving nature, also depend upon the faith of the asker. Thus Jesus lectures the disciples on the power that they would have if their faith were only tiny mustard seed size (Luke 17:6; Matt. 17:20). He encourages the father of the tormented son that all things are able to be done by the one who believes (Mark 9:23). He reprimands the people of Nazareth that miracles are *not* taking place because of their miniscule belief (Luke 4:23ff; Mark 6:4-6). As James, Jesus' earthly brother, so well encapsules the teaching, "A working prayer of a righteous person can do much" (James 5:16b). And Jesus is the ultimate righteous person whose working prayer *does* do much.

Thus Jesus highlights the significance of the persons involved: the "I, myself" who is asking and the "them" for whom the asking is done. This is why Jesus is certain the Father will answer his prayer. He specifies that at this point he is *not* asking concerning the world. This fact he makes specifically clear in these verses and in the verses immediately following. He is, he specifies, asking on behalf of those who were God's because being God's they are Jesus' and what is Jesus' is God's. Jesus is glorified, we remember, by God, and he identifies the vehicle in which that glorification comes: he is glorified in the disciples.

Emphasized thoroughly and poignantly is the relationship linking Jesus and people. This connection has been transferred from a prior relationship between God and people. Literally he prays, "I myself concerning them ask . . . because yours they are." Beginning one clause with "I" and the second with "yours" emphasizes possession and action within the Godhead. This relationship develops into the soteriological plan, the passing of God's people to Jesus' custody so that now the Savior can ask for God's people to pass back to his and their Parent's custody.

Royce Gordon Gruenler in his superb and sensitive study *The Trinity in the Gospel of John* has read the authority statements of Jesus as expressions of "reciprocal equality and sovereignty." To him "the mutual glorification, oneness, and equality of Father and Son are expressed in terms of mutual generosity." The "hospitality" of the "divine Family," as he describes the triune relationship, now "extends to the family of believers." He sees in John 17:8 Jesus claiming equality of possession and glorification with the Father. Yet, "Father and Son (and Spirit) are eternally and consummately hospitable to one another in perfect unity." This, then, is what the soteriological plan that Jesus models as perfect servant describes for humanity.[5]

Out of this mutual sharing in the Godhead comes mutual glorification, Jesus glorifying his Parent, the Parent glorifying the sent Son, the disciples glorifying them both. So Jesus in giving life to his disciples receives glory for his activity, that glory, of course, in verses 5 and 24 that Jesus had before the world was made. If in verse 4 Jesus said, I glorified you by doing your work, the disciples now glorify Jesus by doing God's works. If Lazarus' raising is a physical work of resurrection, in parallel the disciples too are quickened spiritually to life. They were dead in sins, now they are alive to God's works. Resurrection both literal and spiritual, we see, is one type of God's work. In chapter 12:20-36, we recall, the seed that falls into the ground brings new life. Crucifixion, then, is glory because it produces the resurrection of Jesus and of us, we Lazaruses whose hope is in the great day when Jesus calls us forth. Jesus' use of *doxa*, glory, ties promise and action together. Jesus has said, "If you love me, you would keep my commandments" (John 14:15). Here praising God accompanies doing God's works. So Jesus is faithful in doing God's works, even to the death on the cross (Phil. 2:8).

---

[5] Royce G. Gruenler, *The Trinity in the Gospel of John* (Grand Rapids: Baker, 1986), pp. 123, 125, 130.

Thus if crucifixion and resurrection are tied together, if unless a seed falls into the ground it cannot bring life, then the work Jesus does must culminate in his crucifixion. It must culminate in God raising him from the dead. That is why Jesus prays that he be given the glory which he had within the Godhead before he came. That is the glory of resurrection, of death-defying life. The glory Jesus had in the presence of the Father will now be restored to him in the glory of resurrection. Jesus will now become again the eternally living sovereign of Glory. "Lift up, gates, your heads, and be lifted up, everlasting doors and the Ruler of glory will come in. Who is this Ruler of glory? The Lord, strong and mighty, the Lord mighty in battle! (Psalm 24:7-8). Out of ignorance says Paul in I Corinthians 2:8 the rulers of this world killed the Lord of glory. Thus, in Philippians 2 we are told Jesus emptied himself, and here we see he does all the works the Father assigns, culminating in the final act of service, the crucifixion. Therefore, he asks for the glory of Philippians 2 to be restored to him. The Father does give that back to him after the final act of work is completed, the crucifixion, and that giving back of Jesus' glory to him is the resurrection.

So, perhaps, from this realization we can conclude that Jesus' *doxa* is tied up with his immortality. Perhaps the emptying was of his immortality so that God might die at the crucifixion. And when Jesus' glory is returned he is resurrected, for he has been given his immortality back. Thus God in Jesus has become mortal. We see here no dualism. The teaching is not that the mortal Jesus dies while the divine logos remains alive. God is emptied of a characteristic, glory, and by it, in this argumentation, immortality. So God dies and then God is resurrected by God. "Lilting dualistic goop," Reverend Randollph, the late Reverend Charles Merrill Smith's character, calls it in the novel *Reverend Randollph and the Wages of Sin*.[6] But the "hope of the glory of God" the apostle Paul calls it (Rom. 5:2). This is why when Judas leaves to betray him, Jesus announces, "Now was the Son of Humanity glorified" (John 13:31)." The crucifixion is the seed planting of the resurrection.

And No Longer I Am in the World, and They Themselves Are in the World, and I to You Am Coming. Holy Father, Keep Them in Your

---

[6] Charles Merrill Smith, *Reverend Randollph and the Wages of Sin* (New York: G.P. Putnam's Sons, 1974), p. 137.

Name Which You Have Given Me, in order that They May Be One just as We (Are) (17:11).

Again we see the emphasis on time and persons in the way Jesus has ordered this declaration. "And no longer," he begins literally, "I am in the world, and they themselves in the world are." He ends the second phrase with the continuing verb of being. "No longer," a terminal time statement, an adverb, begins his observation while "are," a verb in the present tense of continuing action, completes it. My existence here, he is saying, is complete, theirs is continuing (and in reality for the long-lived John, just beginning). Both in the opening and closing sentences of the verse Jesus is speaking proleptically. Obviously, he is still very much "in the world." That will become painfully obvious when he is taken by force, struck, spat upon, cursed, mocked, staked on the cross, and hung up to die of pain and exposure. But by using proleptic language he is establishing that what he is saying is so certain to occur that he is treating it as if it has already occurred. As Hamlet's famous gasp at the end of his tragedy, "I am dead, Horatio" (V, II: 344), Jesus' own death and removal from the world are so sealed that he may speak of them as present. Thus, by his speech and by God's seal on Jesus' earthly death, he is, as he says, for all purposes "no longer of this world," no longer of the things of this world or of the duties of this world. No longer may he be shepherd of his flock, physician of hearts to the publicans and sinners, honored guest at the weddings and festivals, vigorous challenger of the Pharisees. When he was in the world, his followers in the Parent's name were given to him, but now proleptically he says he is no longer in the world. He has turned his face to Golgotha. His disciples are now turned back over to God, to become one with God even as the Son and the Father are one.

While I Was with Them I Myself Was Keeping Them in Your Name Which You Have Given Me, and I Guarded (or Protected), and No One out of Them Was Destroyed except the Son of Destruction, in order that the Scripture Might Be Fulfilled (17:12).

That Jesus guarded the disciples must have come as rather shocking news to this burly band of laborers, who included several fishermen, at least one militant zealot, the turn of that century's version of a Zionist, and several former followers of that bold prophet of the desert John the Baptist. No doubt they felt, as they well demonstrated on several occasions, that their job was to protect Jesus. So they tried to turn away the sick clammering to be healed when they saw Jesus was exhausted. The disciples tried to shoo away the children from Jesus and would no doubt have driven away the woman at the well had they been there, for, as she herself noted, a Jewish male addressing a Samaritan woman in public was a social impropriety. To defend their Sovereigns' honor James and John were even ready to call fire down on a Samaritan village which would not receive him (Luke 9:54). Finally, Peter would seek to defend Jesus by the sword, slashing away at the first of the arresting officers as if Jesus' kingdom had been of this world and his disciples an emperor's inner guard, sworn to protect him with their lives. But Jesus' reign was not of this world and his battles were not fought with the human dupes of earthly principalities and powers. His war was declared against the great reign of evil, the war in heaven which had invaded earth. Against these supra-natural monsters, swords were as potent as toothpicks. How Jesus must have grimaced when, while preparing his disciples for his departure, he reminded them that earlier when he had sent them out they took no money pouch or bag or sandals and they lacked nothing, but now they had better take all these things and a sword too, for Jesus was about to be taken away. "Lord, look," they cried eagerly, "here are two swords" (Luke 22:38), and Jesus must have shook his head at their pathetic naivete when he said simply, "It is enough." Hardly would two swords be enough to wage earthly war. But Jesus the commander was protecting his guards! Now, when that fortress was removed, they would feel the ringing blows of their real adversary. And yet the words of life were alive in them. And these precious powerful words and the transferred guardianship back to the Father would deliver Jesus' ragged and frightened little expeditionary force through the D-day of spiritual warfare and muster them into a vast and willing army of powerful spiritual warriors that would rock the world.[7]

All of them would be guarded and delivered. All, that is, except one. How tormenting this qualification of Jesus has been for people to accept! "No one out of them was destroyed except the son of destruction, in order that the Scripture might be fulfilled." Again Jesus was speaking proleptically. Judas was not yet destroyed. But he had fled the upper room and was even then conferring with the authorities who were amassing the force that would arrest Jesus.

---

[7] Jesus gives another indication of the protective spiritual blockade he has set around his disciples when he tells Peter that Satan has demanded to have him but Jesus has prayed that Peter's faith will not fail so that after the invasion of evil has oppressed him Peter will recover and strengthen the others (Luke 22:31-32).

Jesus' prayer tells us the "son of destruction" was exempted "in order that the Scripture might be fulfilled." If our contemporary age knows any gospel, it knows the gospel of Judas. Famous rock musicals like *Jesus Christ, Superstar* and to a lesser degree *Godspell* create a defense for Judas. From the very first modern motion picture about Jesus, Cecil B. DeMille's wonderful masterpiece the original silent "The King of Kings," in which we believe H. B. Warner gives one of the best portrayals of Jesus brought to the screen, Judas is already moving in character from the greedy thief presented in the Scriptures to a disappointed political revolutionary, dismayed at the apparent collapse of Jesus' political movement to establish an earthly reign and in terror of the wrath of the conquering constituted authorities. As screenplay writer Jeanie MacPherson, joined by Henry MacMahon in authoring the 1927 novelization, depicted Judas' motivations:

> The tragedy to Judas lay in the ruin of Messianic plans and the dread menace of the High Priest's vengeance . . . ."Mary, -- art thou blind?" cried Judas. "Canst thou not see the folly of following this Pretender? His Kingdom is a myth -- and Caiaphas will destroy the followers of this crownless King!"[8]

Since that time movies about Jesus have been regularly portraying Judas as a political revolutionary either disenchanted or desperate to force Jesus' hand and thereby precipitate the establishment of his political rule on earth.

The wealth of scholarly literature over the years has presented Judas in a variety of ways. Roman Catholic Biblical scholar Donatus Haugg in his 1930 doctoral dissertation classifies four main schools of thought about Judas: greedy sinner, devil incarnate, a hero who brought Jesus to fulfill his work, legend. When Jesus' historicity was questioned, so was Judas'. Numerous other theories are added by the editor's introduction to Bertil Gaertner's monograph "Iscariot." Among these are Jewish scholar Joseph Klausner's theory that the educated Judas saw through Jesus as a false prophet, a fraud unable to work miracles among those who knew him or in Jerusalem, so that, loyal to the law, Judas turned him in. Others have presented Judas as diversely as the brother of Mary, Martha and Lazarus of Bethany, a faithful disciple who in the spirit of Jim Jones' followers

---

[8] Henry MacMahon and Jeanie MacPherson, *The King of Kings: A Novel* (New York: Grosset and Dunlap, 1927), pp. 130-131.

commits suicide to be with his master, a bumbling political wheeler/dealer whose attempts to reconcile Jesus and the temple authorities ends in disaster,[9] or a dupe of Jesus' or God's. This last perspective has increasingly been the recent presentation of Judas on stage, in song, in book -- the scapegoat for Jesus' messianic delusions or God's thirst for blood. This stance reacts to the historical presentation of Judas, the son of perdition, as ending "damned for all eternity." But was Judas' fate against his will?

Interestingly, contrary to what one might expect from the ways theological conservatives and liberals are usually portrayed in the stereotypes of the popular mindset, those who have been probably inaptly named "liberal" in their Scriptural outlook seem much more likely to take a literal reading of this passage, imputing a severe and ferocious determinism to God in the case of Judas than those who take a conservatively high view of the authority of Scripture. The results of reading through the commentary literature on the passage are certainly surprising. For example, Archbishop J. H. Bernard, writing in the second volume of the standard classic commentary on John in The International Critical Commentary series writes:

> It had often been discussed by theologians whether Judas had really been predestined to destruction, or whether his fall from faithfulness was of his free choice. Such questions are foreign to the philosophy of the first century. For Jn., all that happened to Judas was, indeed, predestined, but that this involves any difficulty as to his guilt does not suggest itself to the evangelist.[10]

Rudolf Bultmann speaks of "the fact that only the one for whom it was decreed was actually lost,"[11] while J.N. Sanders and B.A. Mastin also take a hard line, commenting that the formula "son of perdition," a term also used for the Anti-Christ in II Thessalonians 2:3, was placed on Jesus' lips by the early church and signifies "man destined for perdition." They conclude, "There seems to be an

---

[9] Bertil Gaertner, *Iscariot*, trans. Victor I. Gruhn (Philadelphia: Fortress, 1971).

[10] J.H. Bernard, *A Critical and Exegetical Commentary on the Gospel according to St. John,* II, ICC (Edinburgh: T. & T. Clark, 1928), pp. 570-571.

[11] Bultmann, p. 504.

undoubted predestinarian overtone in this passage, where *is lost* may well mean 'lost eternally'."[12]

John Calvin, on the other hand, who is universally seen as a source of the theory of double-predestination in popular thought, that is, the idea that some are created to be saved and some to be damned, comments:

> But that no one might think that eternal election of God was overturned by the damnation of Judas, he immediately added, that he was *the son of perdition*. By these words Christ means that his ruin, which took place suddenly before the eyes of men, had been known to God long before; for *the son of perdition*, according to the Hebrew idiom, denotes a man who is ruined, or devoted to destruction.

Calvin's concern, we soon discover herein, is not double but single predestination, that is, the preservation by God of his saints. In fact, Calvin goes on to address the seemingly damning notation of Jesus' that Judas' destruction occurred "in order that the Scripture might be fulfilled," by qualifying:

> Judas fell, *that the Scripture might be fulfilled*. But it would be a most unfounded argument, if any one were to infer from this, that the revolt of Judas ought to be ascribed to God rather than to himself, because the prediction laid him under a necessity. For the course of events ought not to be ascribed to prophecies, because it was predicted in them, and, indeed, the prophets threaten nothing but what would have happened, though they had not spoken of it.[13]

---

[12] J. N. Sanders and B. A. Mastin, *A Commentary on the Gospel according to St. John* (New York: Harper and Row, 1968), p. 374. F. Godet and Rudolf Schnackenburg call the phrase "a justification on Jesus' part." John Marsh suggests that "lost" is financial. Judas as the "loss" or "lost" man is a play on his complaint of the "loss" of ointment. F. Godet, *Commentary on the Gospel of St. John*, III (Edinburgh: T. and T. Clark, 1900), p. 209; Rudolph Schnackenburg, *The Gospel according to St. John, Commentary on Chapters 13-21*, III (New York: Crossroad, 1982), p. 182; John Marsh, *Saint John*, Westminster Pelican Commentaries (Philadelphia: Westminster, 1968), p. 566.

[13] John Calvin, *Calvin's Commentaries: John-Acts* (Wilmington, Delaware: Associated Publishers and Authors, n.d.), pp. 879-880. See also Leon Morris, *The Gospel according to John,* The New International Commentary on

For Calvin, God is the God of Jesus who knows every sparrow that falls (Matt. 10:29).

F.F. Bruce agrees, commenting:

> Despite the predestinarian flavour of the language, Judas was not lost against his will but with his consent. He might have responded to Jesus' last appeal to him in his gesture of fellowship at the supper table, but he chose to respond instead to the great adversary. Jesus has no responsibility for Judas' fatal decision.[14]

According to Dionysius, bishop of Alexandria (A. D. 200-265), Judas "proved careless" but Jesus never gave up on him, still seeking to dissuade him in the garden, and so, he concludes, neither should we ever give up on those who fall away (*Gospel according to Saint Luke, Exegetical Fragments*, 2).

God, we infer, could have brought about God's purposes without the sacrifice of Judas. Judas, Caiaphas, Pilate, the crowds, and we, no doubt, if we had been there, however, lent willing hands.

---

the New Testament (Grand Rapids: Eerdmans, 1971), p. 728 who writes "God used [Judas'] evil act to bring about His purpose."

[14] F. F. Bruce, *The Gospel of John* (Grand Rapids: Eerdmans, 1983), p. 332. See also Lyman Abbott, *An Illustrated Commentary on the Gospel According to St. John* (New York: A. S. Barnes, 1879), p. 207.

8

Passover Prayer of the Paschal Lamb (John 17:13-26)

The Lord's Prayer in John 17:13-26

If Jesus has been speaking proleptically in John 17, he now shifts into the present tense for a most pastoral reason. First, he states a summary of all that he has been saying lest anyone among his disciples be confused. His prayer, of course, is addressed to God, but, as we shall see when we analyze the prayer in its entirety, it is as well a pastoral prayer, in fact the quintessential pastoral prayer. As the disciples at his farewell exulted to Jesus, "Look, now you are speaking plainly!" (John 16:29).

And Now to You I Come, and These Things I Speak in the World in order that They May Have My Joy Fulfilled in Them (17:13).

Lest anyone miss the point of what he has been saying to the Father, he encapsules that point in one plain, pithy summary statement: "And now to you I come . . . ." Jesus' hour has come. The time has been fulfilled. Now he is going back to his great Parent. But the sentence does not stop there. Jesus adds an explanation. We may have been wondering why he has been developing at length a theme that was crystal clear to the Father, who as a member of the triune God-head planned these events. "These things I say" (these things, Father, he is implying, that you already know so well) "in the world . . . ." Jesus' specific point of locating where these words are spoken, where these assurances are given, becomes of primary importance when we discover the nuances of the use of the phrase "in the world" or its close and significant variants across the whole sweep of this last great prayer of Jesus for his disciples.

Jesus makes no less than eighteen references to the world in a prayer of only twenty-six verses. Fourteen of the references are in prepositional phrases. The remaining four present the world as the subject of verbs, two in the perfect tense and two in the subjunctive mood. The prepositional phrases are set throughout the prayer from as early as the third sentence in Greek, the fifth verse in English, to as late as the twenty-fourth verse. The nominative, as opposed to the objective, use of the "world" begins late, just after the middle of the prayer, and increases in frequency in the closing verses. Verse 14 explains that the world has hated the disciples because they are not of the world. Verse 6 has already told us that God gave Jesus the disciples out of the world so that they no longer belong to the world. Thus verse 14 confirms that the world as a result hates these expatriots, these estranged ones, these refugees and rebels, because they are no longer the world's own. Jesus, he himself makes perfectly clear in verse 9, is not praying for the world or on behalf of the world. And yet Jesus does not hate the world in return for its hatred, nor does he teach his disciples to hate the world. In fact, verses 21, 23, and 25 explain that the unity and love expressed through the disciples' unity together and with Jesus and through Jesus with the Father will demonstrate to the world that the Father has indeed sent Jesus, as Jesus has claimed and soon the disciples will claim, according to verse 21. Verse 23 reiterates this point and adds another, that the world will also know that the Father has loved them even as the Father has loved Jesus, a pathetic note when one takes it in the context that these active references to the world began with the painful point that the world has hated Jesus and his disciples. On an equally pathetic note the references to the world end, "Righteous Father, the world has also not known you . . . (v. 25). So we see the world hates. Christian unity is prayed for so that the world may believe. And the final observation is made that the world has not known the Father. How can Jesus know that for certain? The world has not known Jesus or his disciples, and, as Jesus has stated, the one who has seen him has seen the Father (John 14:9). Failing to recognize Jesus, the world fails to find the Father.

The "world" in these senses appears to be the societies of human beings who reject Jesus and in similar ways have always rejected God's attempts to deal with sin and forge a reconciliation with them.

On the other hand, the temporal or time references in verses 5 and 24 speak of the period before the world was created and its societies came about. That is the time when Jesus had his glory which he emptied out of himself in order to come here, the glory which he would like back so that his disciples might believe. In this sense he appears to be using the term "world" to talk about the creation of the earth and the organizing of its subsequent fallen societies.

The double sense of the world as earth and the world as fallen and rejecting human societies is maintained in the various verbal plays Jesus proceeds to make with the prepositional phrases. He is not of the human societies and he is going out of the earth. The disciples were of these societies but are no longer a part of them, yet these disciples are remaining on the earth.

While his disciples remain on the earth and in its human societies, while no longer of its societies since they have become citizens of heaven, their task is to display unity and love so that the world may believe the Father sent Jesus. Jesus himself does not do anything else on behalf of the world in this prayer. Verse 9 specifically states that he is *not* praying for the world. He is praying for those, verse 6 tells us, that God has given him out of the world, meaning out from among the rebellious societies, but verse 15 states Jesus is not praying that these believers come "out of the world" in the sense that God withdraws them from the earth. No, as verse 11 specifies, they will remain on the earth when Jesus is no longer on the earth. So Jesus speaks of his disciples' part in the soteriological plan, their sanctification through their witness to the truth of Jesus' commission from the Father, while he is still in the world's societies on the earth, for it is a commission that his disciples must fulfill while they are still in the world.

When in verses 14 and 16 Jesus specifies carefully to the Father and to his disciples that these disciples are not of this world in the same way that he is not of this world, he does not say that they came down as he did from heaven but that they have been chosen out from among the world. They have been set apart even as Jesus was set apart by God and as a result the world hates them. They have nowhere to turn now for love but to the Father and to each other. The band is knitted together by the love of this Jesus who must now leave them. So verse 18 summarizes the facts. As you, Father, sent me into the world, now I send them back into the world from which you drew them out, not to be of it, but to bear witness to it by their unity and their love for one another that what they are saying about me is true. You did indeed send me. You always loved me and you love them. And they will show this truth by loving one another. The world will see their unity, and, though it has not known you, it may know and may believe you sent me.

All of this Jesus says "in order that they may have my joy fulfilled in them." Paul will talk about completing the sufferings of Christ in his body on behalf of the bodies that comprise the body of the church (Col. 1:24). This is crucifixion. Jesus speaks of having joy fulfilled in the actions and unities of the resurrected disciples, that scared little band which is now risen by God into a great army of love. This is indeed resurrection. Jesus' commission from God lives on in earth and its societies in Jesus' disciples. Thus, Jesus' work on earth is completed and it is not completed. What he has been sent to do, die for human sin, he will now do. Yet greater works than he has previously done on earth his disciples will then be empowered to do. God's commission transferred to Jesus is now transferred to the disciples. They and we, if we follow them, continue and complete God's commission to Jesus through Jesus' commission to us. And in their actions melting into our actions, Jesus our Lord's joy is fulfilled.

I Myself Have Given Them Your Word, and the World Hated Them, because They Are Not out of the World just as I Myself Am Not out of the World (17:14).

Here Jesus uses "world" both as subject and object. We have taken an overall survey of the variety of uses of "world" in the entire prayer. Now we see how these uses function together in the individual thought units that build throughout the prayer. Jesus says, he, the one sent, gave to his disciples God's life-giving word. As a result, human societies hated the disciples as an active response. Why? Because, while the disciples may have belonged to God already, they became different from other humans. When Jesus gave them his Parent's word, they became like Jesus, who came from heaven not from rebellious human society. Jesus was himself the logos, the living word of God. Thus, Jesus gave the disciples himself when he gave them the living word. And as a result, the disciples began to become Christ-like.

What was the world's response? It transferred some of its hatred of this alien Jesus to a hatred of the disciples. Christians often pray to become more Christ-like. Do we really know what we are asking? In becoming more Christ-like we become more like the one who came down from above, this alien presence, this stranger in a hostile land, this sojourner, this wanderer who, when foxes have holes and birds have nests, has nowhere to lay his head. When like Peter we ask to follow Christ, we do not know the ramifications of what we ask. In taking up our cross we become more like the one despised, the one spat upon and rejected, the one crucified on that cross. We become strangers to what was familiar before. We talk of being citizens of heaven. But Jesus says here that that means we are denouncing citizenship on earth. In effect, we have become expatriots of the world and those formerly our compatriots turn away from us as traitors. The disciples were to glimpse the full effect of this new alienation for a couple of horrible days when their rebel lord was executed like a common insurrectionist. But the sense of anomia remains. Our moorings here are cut by the sharp two-edged sword of the words of Jesus. Like Joseph T. Bayly's Herb Gooley in his classic short story "I saw Gooley fly" we are afloat with a new supra-natural source of power that confounds and terrifies the world. And in societies' confusion with the non-familiar comes alienation and hostility. They no longer know us. They fear us. They soon can hate us for our differences as they hated Jesus.

I Do Not Ask that You Might Lift Them out of the World but that You Might Keep Them out of Evil (or from the Evil One) (17:15).

If all that Jesus said in the previous verse is true, why do the disciples not take to the air like Gooley and float away to heaven in a few private raptures? The old gospel hymn cries out that the angels are beckoning to us from heaven's golden shore so that we don't feel at home in this world anymore. Does our lord not expect us to emigrate? Jesus understands that normal response. The answer he gives has been used as the foundational basis for the theology and practice of Christian social action, Christian political action in civic and world affairs, and for the healing ministry of the earthly church. Jesus specifically tells the Father he is not asking that the disciples be lifted out of the world. They are to remain in the world, active witnesses. He is asking for protection.

The similarity of this petition for his disciples' protection to the petition for protection in his model prayer begs to be observed, and we will do this thoroughly when after our exegesis of the text is completed we reevaluate the entire prayer structurally in the light of the model prayer the Lord taught us.

One other observation we might make of the prayer as a whole is that, in the manner in which Jesus has presented his cumulative concerns so far, one might complain that Jesus appears on the surface to be as much preaching to his disciples as praying to his Parent! Homiletics professors in seminaries and Bible schools warn their students against the practice of using the pastoral prayer, for example, to preach a mini-sermon and drive home a few particularly unpopular points the minister would like the people to accept. The practice is often called "preaching from the shoulders of God." Yet Jesus does not share this general information with the Father and with his disciples like those obnoxious preachers who lecture us when we have our heads bowed, our eyes closed, and our mouths shut. He is more like a parent praying with a child. He lays all his concerns out in simple language so that his children, here his disciples, will understand just what is happening. They will understand in their context for what specifically on their behalf their lord and protector is beseeching the great heavenly Parent. He does not simply tell his disciples what will happen to them. Rather, he mentions his prophecy in the context of prayer so that while transferring the disciples' custody to the Father he is assuring the disciples that the same conditions made with him still persist. Carefully in his prayer, while Jesus is enlisting the protective aid of the great power of heaven, he is detailing exactly what the present situation is and the future one will be and exactly what are his requests to meet the coming problems so that in remembrance his disciples will have both something to which to cling during the catastrophe to come and afterwards something to build a church upon. We recall that in chapter 16, which records the events just prior to the prayer, at least three times Jesus has spoken about going away. Here again he deals with his disciples' fears at the disturbing news of his leaving.

Out of the World They Are Not just as I Myself Am Not out of the World) (17:16).

Verse 16 drives the point of verse 6 home again. Verse 6 told us God drew the disciples out of the world and gave them to Jesus. The subsequent verses told God and the disciples what exactly that has come to mean for the disciples, how as a result they were alienated just as Jesus was alienated and how they incurred the world's wrath just as Jesus did. Now verse 16 concludes they are, therefore, alienated from human societies just as Jesus is alien from the aims and approval of human societies. Jesus' phrasing here is full of puns. He states that they are out of the world (in other words not from human society anymore) because Jesus is not out of the world (does not have his origin in the world), yet Jesus does not want them lifted up out of the world, off the earth, physically! One set of phrases, then, is metaphorical while the next is literal! The point of the puns is to preserve a tension -- the tension of anomia in the disciples' consciousness and in their relationship with the world.

Anomia is a condition people might feel when they have changed cultures for too long a time. Missionaries might enter another culture for a number of years. Great Britain or Hong Kong or North America or Africa or Korea or Australia or South America or Europe might be their real home. But when after ten years the Korean missionary returns from the streets of North America or the French physician comes back from the forests of the Amazon or the Australian teacher goes home from the coasts of Malaya, everything is changed. Home is a strange land. The missionary no matter how assimilated has never felt as truly at home in the adopted culture as back in the beautiful land of her or his childhood. But wait! Now that the missionary has stepped back off the plane or the ship or the barge onto home soil he or she steps into another foreign country. Home is different. It has become a strange land. New idioms are in the language, new styles are in the streets. Ten years of trends and developments and cumulative mindsets and national moods have swept the country and been gathered up in the great storage house of the national memory. None of this the missionary shared. The television programs are strange. The children act differently. The schools are radically changed. Even the churches look different. The missionary or the oil company executive or the second language teacher has no home now. Every land has become a strange land. The feeling is anomia. Foxes have holes, birds have nests . . . . Such is the state of the called-out disciples. Born in the human condition originally, they are now out of the prevailing sinful human mindset, in perspective, in loyalty. They are out of this world because the One who called them out of this world has come from outside the earth and is now going physically back out of the earth. But that one does not want them literally leaving the earth and its societies. They are to remain *in* while *out of* this world. No wonder the Christian church does -- or should! -- have adjustment problems to the mores of the world.

Sanctify Them in the Truth. Your Word is Truth (17:17).

What, then, are the disciples to do in this world where their master wants them to remain? Verse 17 gives the disciples the first hint of what program God has in mind for them. The first step happens to them.

Hagiazo is the word for sanctification used by Jesus in this verse. We still have cognates of that word in the English language. "Hagiology" is the study of the saints, in other words, those who have been sanctified. What does "being sanctified" mean? What exactly is going to happen to the disciples when God the Parent answers Jesus the Child's prayer and sanctifies those disciples God gave into Jesus' safekeeping and whom Jesus is now giving back? The Gospel of John uses one of the forms of "sanctify" in four different places.

In John 10:36 the Pharisees' tension has mounted to breaking point. Infuriated at what they consider blasphemies against the holy God of Abraham, the Jews have snatched up stones to stone Jesus to death because of his radical claims that he and the Father are one, that he gives eternal life, and that no one can pry his followers out of his hand. Accosted in the portico of Solomon, Jesus is obviously backed out or swept out of the temple in the heat of the argument to a place where stones are available and where he can be slain without profaning the temple. But Jesus appeals to all the good works he has done. The Jews, unlike some who consider themselves Christian theologians today, had gotten the full ramification of what Jesus was saying, and they protest, "Concerning a good work we do not stone you but concerning blasphemy, even because you being a human are making yourself God!"(10:33) Then Jesus answers with a Scripture and challenges: "(Of) the one the Father sanctified and sent into the world are you saying that you are blaspheming, because I said, "I am the Son of God?"(10:36)

The predicate nominative "Son" of God is listed here first, followed by the first person active singular form of the verb "to be," which in Greek contains both the subject and verb. Thus the emphasis is on the predicate nominative, literally, "Son of God I am."

Jesus is emphasizing the point of scandal, his outrageous claim. Through the Scripture quoted he reveals the potentiality of that claim extends to the Jews themselves. He demonstrates the same thing to the disciples who have been drawn out of the world, called out as a new kind of covenant people, just as God first called the original covenant people out in Genesis. They become "gods" to God because they have become "sons of God" to the Son of God (cf. Psalm 82:6). But what can God sanctifying Jesus mean here? It cannot mean cleansing Jesus from his sin because we know that Jesus is the perfect sinless Son of God, the unblemished sacrifice for human sins (Heb. 4:15). He as God was perfect and through suffering was confirmed as perfect (Heb. 2:10), though suffering and tempted in every way as we are (Heb. 2:17-18). We are told the Father sanctified, or in many translations consecrated, Jesus and sent him into the world. The implication seems to be that the Father called Jesus and set him apart for a task, then sent him into the world.

The next three instances of "sanctify" are here in John 17. The adjective form is used in verse 11 as an address for God, "Holy Father." By this we usually understand "pure, apart from human sin and untouched by it." The final instances in John's gospel are in our present verse and in verse 19. Verse 19, as we shall see, follows the request in verse 17. Jesus is asking that these who have been taken out of the world and no longer belong to the world be not simply drifters but be intentionally set apart by God. As God is already pure from sin, they be made pure from sin by God so that they can become a holy people. God's process of "making people pure" Jesus is about to perform.

Just as You Sent Me into the World, I Also Sent Them into the World (17:18);

Why should the Father do Jesus' last request? Why should God sanctify this motley group of disciples as if they were holy priests of the house of Levi? Jesus firmly establishes the relationship again between himself and the Father and himself and the disciples. Jesus is the intermediary between God and God's disciples, what we have called classically the true mediator between God and humanity. Jesus sets up a logical equation. In the same way as you, Father, sent me here into the world, I in turn also took those ones you had drawn out of the world and sent them back into the world. That is why they are where they are. But they are still the ones you drew out, so please set them apart as holy, purified people. They belonged to

God. They were entrusted to God's Son. Now they are returned to God for safekeeping as they are sent back into the world on both's behalf.

And on behalf of Them I Myself Sanctify, in order that Also They Themselves May Be Sanctified in Truth (17:19).

Verse 17 ended with the simple pithy maxim, "Your word is truth." We recall the two primary characteristics of the description of God given in the Old Testament are grace and truth. Truth is *emeth* in Hebrew, a word used to describe God in such classic declarations as Exodus 34:6, where the great Lord passes by the no doubt terrified Moses, proclaiming from the cloud of unknowing that surrounds God and protects humans from the sheer devastating purity and majesty of the appearance of God, "The Lord, the Lord, a God merciful and gracious, slow to anger, and abounding in steadfast love and faithfulness" (RSV). That word translated "faithfulness" is the word for truth, *emeth*. It means, according to the Brown, Driver, Briggs lexicon, "reliability," "sureness," "stability," "continuance," "faithfulness," "truth."[1] Jesus has requested in verse 17, "Sanctify them in the truth." He is calling the disciples apart from others to be set in the boundaries of the great reliable, stable, faithfulness of God. Small wonder, then, that when they will be buffeted about by the devil who wishes to sift them like wheat they will not be lost. They will be moored securely now in the great truth of God. They will be fastened to the mighty rock.

Jesus then adds, "Your word is truth." John has described Jesus as the word of God, the *logos* that came to earth. In verse 8 Jesus has talked of giving the disciples the words which God had given Jesus. God's living, incarnate Word of truth has given the words of truth. The disciples are moored in his promises and soon will be secured by his great sacrificial act. We note that Jesus says, "Your word is *truth*," that he does not use the adjective which would have made a perfectly logical conclusion to the sentence: "Your word is *true*." In fact, the predicate adjective might seem to be a more logical choice than the predicate nominative: "Your word is truth." But Jesus is not describing something which simply has a quality. The dog is brown, the house is big, your word is true. He is claiming something spectacular, something foundational. Your word is

---

[1] Francis Brown, S.R. Driver, and Charles A. Briggs, *A Hebrew and English Lexicon of the Old Testament* (Oxford: Oxford University, 1953), p. 54.

equated with truth. The phrase can be turned around. Truth is your word. What is true is God's word. Jesus is truth, therefore Jesus' words are true. When God speaks, things are created. The true word of God is the word that gives life. Jesus is the giver of true life and he comes to give that abundantly. Peter exclaimed when all others were turning away, to whom can we go? You have the words of eternal life (John 6:68). That is because Jesus is the word of life. Jesus is the truth.

Therefore, verse 19 concludes the argument, "And on behalf of them," that is, for the sake of these ones you have called and I have sent, "I myself set myself apart or I myself sanctify myself, so that they may also be set apart or sanctified in truth." Since they are in Jesus just as Jesus is in the Father, as a result they are in truth. What Jesus the new Adam does is done for his disciples. In John 10:36 we saw the Father sanctified Jesus, and now in a flash of insight into the coordination of purpose and action within the trinity we see Jesus also sanctifies himself. He acts inversely to the old Adam who rebelled and made himself unholy. Jesus obeys and makes himself holy, as he was made holy and sent into the world. Therefore, if, as Paul argues, in the old Adam sin entered the world, then in the new Adam the world is reconciled (Romans 5:12ff). What Jesus is about to do he does not do for himself. Consecrated, sanctified, set apart, sinless, he does not need to be reconciled with God. But what he does when he is set apart and sent by God into the world he does in order that his disciples may be consecrated in him through his action. They partake of this great quality of God and through God's acting truth are sanctified or set apart in a great sure, reliable, steadfast, continuing for all eternity truth. As body of Christ, they are the body of truth, for truth is God's word and that living Word's words.

But Not concerning These Only Do I Ask, but Also concerning the Ones Believing on account of Their Word in Regard to Me (17:20),

Now Jesus widens out his concern. Up to this point, beginning in verses 1 through 5, he has been concentrating his concern upon his own status and relationship with his Parent, reporting, or in effect confirming, that he has accomplished the work on earth the Father gave him to do. He has claimed that by doing this work he has glorified the Father and asks that he himself be in turn glorified. One way we might understand this request is that Jesus is asking for a reward for his good, hard work. But another way to understand it is within the context that Jesus has laid aside his glory to do that good, hard work on earth, and now he wants what is his by right returned to him, the glory that he has had in God's presence.

From verse 6 to 19 he widens his focus to embrace the new children of his Parent, the disciples God gave him to protect. We have seen in detail that he solicits protection and sanctification for them.

Now in verse 20 he widens his concern even further. He prays not only for the original ones the Father gave him, but also for all the ones who will believe in Jesus because of these disciples' witness. Jesus is praying for us who take up the same cross the disciples did and follow Jesus.

One might interpret verse 20 as developing verse 9. In verse 9, we recall, Jesus states specifically that he is not praying on behalf of the world, or, we might infer, on behalf of those of the world, but he is praying on behalf of those God has given him, his contemporary disciples. Now he is specifically praying beyond his contemporary disciples to their disciples, the next generations which continue on to us and extend beyond us to all those who will believe on account of the good news these first disciples and their disciples spread in the name of Jesus.

In order that All May Be One, just as You, Father, (Are) in Me and I in You, in order that Also They May Be in Us, in order that the World May Believe that You Sent Me (17:21).

The logical precision and progression of 17:21 is extremely interesting. In the literal rendering of the way the Greek has placed the words Jesus has spoken we find an argument being constructed. Verses 20 and 21 actually comprise one sentence. We have divided them in order to examine each part. Verse 20 we could view as the prologue or setting of the argument, I am praying beyond these I have around me to the ones they will make into disciples . . . . Why am I doing this? Now proceeds the reason or the explanation of his action. The phrase "in order that" repeats three times, linking three of the four clauses that will follow.

First, he says, he acts in order that all may be one, all contextually here being all the disciples to follow along with the contemporary disciples who are gathered around Jesus. In essence he means here the entire church that will be built on the rock of his words entrusted to his first disciples. How shall all of these be one? Just as the Father and Jesus are unified in purpose and love. Oneness, unity, then, with Jesus and the first disciples is the mark of the true church. So Jesus asks for oneness for the present and future disciples, a oneness that will reflect the oneness within the perfectly unified triune Godhead.

Why does he ask for this? He continues "in order that also they may be in us." Now the oneness becomes more than a mere reflection of God's oneness. It becomes actual unity with God and with Christ, that is, unity with the Godhead. We saw earlier how eternal life was comprised of not only knowing God but also of knowing the one whom God sent, Jesus Christ (verse 3). Now we see this theme restated firmly. Unity of all the disciples melts into unity with the Father and Jesus Christ. Here we see a unity that might make us think of the Hindu view of oneness in the universe, the individual blending with the eternal all. But the distinct difference is that that human blending that might transmogrify in classic Hinduism as it spins out of the wheel of life into the form of a snake, or snail, or cow, or prince, and in contemporary liberal Hinduism represents the blending of the atoms of the dead with the atoms of creation, does not in Christianity describe such a complete blending. Oneness between the Parent and the Child does not eradicate distinctions, just as unity between the contemporary and future disciples does not eradicate distinctions. We retain our individuality just as the separate persons of the trinity retain their personhood. And yet we have a unity that gives a corporate identity stronger than our individual identities. Thus love makes us lay down our individual safety for our friends, in the same way as Jesus will soon do this for his friends. Why will he do this? To effect the sanctification that will be the first step to produce this oneness. And what will the oneness that will result between the Father, Jesus, the contemporary disciples and the future disciples do? It will bear witness to Jesus and the One who sent him. Why is that done? Again, "in order that" the world may believe.

But, how can the world be Jesus' concern? Has he not specified in verse 9 he is *not* praying for the world? And does he not shortly thereafter carefully separate his disciples from the world which they are not "of"? Such is clearly the case. And yet now he shows he does have a concern for the fallen human society itself. This is why John, Jesus' beloved disciple, has told us in his first epistle that Jesus died not only to pay for our sins but also for the sins of the world (I John

2:2). Here we see again poignantly expressed Jesus' concern for the world.

Some may argue that the world here merely means the future Gentiles who will believe in Jesus. Or perhaps Jesus simply wants to be vindicated before his detractors. But let us examine what his concerns are. Verse 20 opens with a prayer for all Christians into future times, all "those who believe in me through their word." This category would include future Gentile believers. But now Jesus expands his ministry to be concerned that even "the world may believe that you have sent me." As we move along to the restatement of verse 21 in verse 23, perhaps we might feel a pull to interpret negatively verse 23, "that the world may know that you sent me and loved them (the disciples) even as you loved me." We might feel constrained to read this as a final realization, a last grudging, damning admission by rebellious human society that Jesus and his disciples were, after all, in the right, that God did authentically send Jesus. Certainly this is a possible reading, the world seen as bludgeoned into grudging acknowledgement by the bestowal of God's love on Jesus and his followers, those whom the world itself would not love.

On the other hand, why cannot this passage as easily express Jesus' great love? After all, Paul tells us in Jesus God was reconciling the world to himself (II Cor. 5:19). Why, then, cannot Jesus' great concern be that none be lost? After all, the words of I John 2:2 cannot be denied. Jesus did indeed die not for us only but also for the sins of the world. Why cannot Jesus long to reconcile the entire world? O Jerusalem, he cries, how many times like a mother hen I have longed to take you under my wings . . . (Matt. 23:37-39). We were like children, he laments, we played happy music but you would not dance. We wailed laments but you would not mourn (Matt. 11:16-17).

Jesus' intention for his disciples' oneness is evangelism. In his prayer is the next foreshadowing, after the missions of the twelve and the seventy-two, of the great commission to go into all the world preaching the good news about Jesus to every nation, baptizing in the triune name of God, making disciples, teaching them all these words of salvation, all the commandments Jesus gave those who believe in him and who come to love him (Matt. 28:18-20).

And the Glory Which You Have Given to Me I Have Given to Them, in order that They May Be One just as We Are One (17:22),

What glory can Jesus mean here? What glory can this timid little band expect, huddled as they are uncertainly around a leader who in a few moments will be ripped away from them? What glory will they evidence as they run frightened into the darkness, scattered by the wolves who have swept down upon their shepherd? What will be glorious about Peter weeping bitterly in the night, about a naked young man cowering shaken and ashamed and exhausted in the scanty shadow of some cold wall, Thomas devastated at last with the worst of his fears befallen, the depths of doubt crashing through the flimsy dyke walls of his fledgling faith?

Earlier, when we did our study of verses 1 and 2, we examined the request of Jesus against these same circumstances when he asked for himself to be glorified. We noted that Jesus' glorification was tied into Jesus' completing the work the Father gave Jesus to do. Therefore, we can infer that the disciples' glorification would be tied into the disciples' completing the work that Jesus gives them to do. Jesus' teachings and healings are reflected in Acts by the disciples' teachings and healings, Jesus' proclamation and miracles by their proclamations and miracles. We noted in our exegesis of verse 5 that full glorification, of course, occurs in another time in another place in another dimension of the reign not of this world, yet we noted there and we note here that the language of Jesus' declaration, in this case the perfect tense, that past action affecting the present time, indicates there is a glory already given now in this place in this time. Jesus, we noted, was glorified in the Father's presence before coming here and has asked that that glorification again be brought here in God's presence. The disciples, of course, have seen the transfiguration and have caught a glimpse of that pre-incarnate glory, yet we concluded that something more was being requested.

The seed of the crucifixion bursting into the magnificent bloom of the resurrection provides the full expression of Jesus' glory here. We recall, as the disciples recalled (for it was what John recorded about the event [John 11:4]) that Lazarus' resuscitation brought glory to Jesus. Even more did Jesus' own resurrection shower shekinah glory upon him. Now, for the disciples, he observes that the glory which God gave to him he has given to them, in order that they may be one as Jesus and his Parent are one. We recall Jesus was glorified in God's presence. The disciples, as we shall see in the next verse, are themselves about to be glorified in God's presence. We shall see after the resurrection they will do greater works than even Jesus did and preach the words of power demonstrated by their mighty miracles.

But before they can do these things they too will do a great work. In a sense they will be crucified with Jesus. Crushed and scattered, they will feel their hope has died only to have it resurrected gloriously along with their risen Lord. Perhaps, then, the language may be seen as proleptic, that is of speaking of a future reality as if it has already taken place. We see that they are not yet one. Jesus has given them glory already so that this oneness might take place. But the point is that the glory has already been given and it will bring about unity. Baffled, scattered, the disciples endure the chill of the nights of the tomb and huddle together in a closed room, thrown upon each other by a common grief. But within them the words of life live, to them the promise of greater works has been given, on them the protective prayer of their shepherd has been laid. And suddenly in their midst is their risen Lord, stirring them to life with the great breaths of hope and joy and eternal affirmation. And further, what is even more glorious, perhaps, about this promise of glory is that the claim by Jesus is made in this last section when the disciples addressed include, the whole church of future disciples.

I in Them and You in Me, in order that They May Be Perfected in Unity, in order that the World May Know that You Sent Me and Loved Them just as You Loved Me (17:23).

We noted in the preceding verse that Jesus has given the disciples glory for a purpose, that they might have unity. He continues and expands that unity to include not only unity with each of the other disciples, but also unity with Jesus and his Parent as well. A perfect unity is what Jesus is calling for. Therefore, as Jesus is defeated and then made triumphant, gaining glory in the sight of God, so are the disciples about to be defeated and then made triumphant, granted a similar glorification in the presence of God as they are united to God by union with God's Son. As Jesus asks for and receives glorification in God's presence, so are the disciples in a sense glorified, as they are united to God, brought into God's presence, and then stirred to mighty acts and powerful proclamations that glorify Christ and by that glorify God. The perfect unity is an astounding thing to examine. Everybody wins. And everybody serves everybody else. God glorifies Jesus, Jesus glorifies the disciples, the disciples glorify Jesus and the Father.

What is the result? As we have seen before, the world watches and discovers that, yes, God did indeed send Jesus and God does indeed love the disciples as God loved Jesus. And astounding too is the fact that this plea for unity is placed in the part of the prayer that has been expanded to include the disciples to come. Thus, the point is made as poignantly relevant to contemporary Christians as it was to the first disciples. The watching world watches Christ's followers. What does it see? Does it see by lives, by works, by words that God sent Jesus? Does it see that God loves Christians? Does it see that God loves Jesus? Does it see unity? Does it see a love for each other? What does it see when it looks at the church?

Perhaps the greatest criticism fired at the church of Jesus Christ today is that it is characterized by in-fighting among its various divisions and it has created discord and misery throughout the centuries. Critics cite the church's opposition to Galileo, the Spanish Inquisition, the burning of John Hus, the Salem witch trials, the war in Ireland, even the murder of John Lennon. Christian periodicals are filled with controversy over the interpretation of the Bible, the leadership of women, the movement by practicing homosexuals to gain recognized leadership and affirmation in the church, the bombing of abortion clinics, the just-war stance of the New Right, the funding of Communist organizations that kill missionaries by the ecclesiastical left. Denominations regularly split. Publicized power struggles rage in the Southern Baptist Convention, the Missouri Synod Lutheran Church and schools, in the World Council of Churches. Jesus Christ prayed that his disciples be perfect in unity or completely one so that the watching world may know that, yes, the great Parent who wants unity for all the human family sent Jesus and loves Jesus' disciples dearly even as the great heavenly Parent loves the divine Child Jesus. But what happened? Did the prayer of Jesus fail? Is it yet to be fulfilled? Since the petition occurs in the final section of the prayer, perhaps its intention is to be fulfilled as the church matures from milk to meat, as it develops into the full grown body of Christ. But do we honestly see such a thing happening? Does the church today evidence more unity than did the early church? Do we see around us signs that the church is maturing into perfect unity, that it is becoming completely one with the sweetness of obedience and the familial spirit that marks the relationship of Jesus with his Father?

We who are Christians need to take a hard, searching look at our church and decide whether we have loved Jesus by keeping his commandments.

Normally, we counter accusations such as those cited by distinguishing between the acts of true Christians and acts done in Jesus' name which are not synonymous with Jesus' commandments and are not done by those we would recognize as truly Christian. The question of disunity begins even deeper and has a more primal place in the body of Christ than even in the distinguishing of the true church from all those claiming to act in Jesus' name. Against these latter Jesus already warned in his frightening depiction of the final judgment recorded in Matthew 7:21-23. In that passage Jesus paints a terrifying picture of active religious workers clammering before him that they have prophesied in his name, done miraculous works in his name, even exorcised demons in his name, only to hear the heavenly Lord of glory declare, "Never did I know you; go away from me the ones working lawlessness." Normally translators have been content to follow the King James' Version's "ye that work iniquity," or the Confraternity's "you workers of iniquity." We would do better, however, in this case as the New American Standard has done in translating more literally, "*you who practice lawlessness*" for the Greek reads literally *anomia* workers. More sinister than its cognate form in English with which we dealt earlier, the "a" privative appended to the word *nomos*, law, gives a negative force, no-law or lawless. We stress this point for the Jesus who has declared that if we love him we are to keep his commandments now declares to those who claim to have acted in his name, "Go away from me (you) ones working lawlessness." No matter how many mighty works these have done in his name they have apparently not acted because of his commandments.

A dramatic example of this distinction between acting in Christ's name but not because of Christ's commands was given by Irish rebel leader Bernadette Devlin McAliskey, the popularly acclaimed "Saint Bernadette" who, as a 21-year-old Queen's University, Belfast psychology student, was the youngest member to be seated in the British House of Commons since the 18th Century and who today carries the scars of eight bullets in her back, having been gunned down in her home on January 16, 1981 by members of a Protestant paramilitary group. She commented:

> The media persist in painting the struggle in Northern Ireland as some peculiar religious war, as if

> the Catholics and Protestants had nothing better than to go at each others' throats over the question of papal infallibility or the immaculate conception. . . . We are struggling for the same things the people in Central America are struggling for --political freedom and economic justice.[2]

In another frightening passage, recorded in Matthew 25:31-46, the great Jesus as judge assigns to eternal abandonment all those not extending acts of mercy to the least of his followers who suffer physical want, illness, or imprisonment. An act for the least of his family is an act for Christ.

As near as the immediate moments preceding Jesus' great prayer for the unity of his followers, we see the disciples falling out in verbal battle over who among them will be greatest (Luke 22:24). In the inner circle we see Judas betraying Jesus. At the gathering of the disciples before the ascension we see Thomas falling out with the others about whether Jesus has truly resurrected or not. In the early church we see disputes between these same apostles, those "reputed to be pillars" (Gal. 2:9) and Paul, the former persecutor of the Christians. As well, we see Paul battling the Judaizers, Ananias and Sapphira struck down for dishonesty, Paul and Barnabas falling out over the desertion of John Mark. Clearly in these examples some of those at fault are not members of the true church, as Jesus declares of Judas when he calls him the "son of perdition." But in other cases, such as the dispute between Paul and the other apostles or Paul and Barnabas or the disciples among themselves, we have clear examples of Christians fighting Christians. What can we make of it?

Surprisingly, the New Testament is filled with advice about how to dispute correctly. In the Sermon on the Mount Jesus assumes we will have difficulties with each other but warns we must clean them up quickly before daring to approach God in worship (Matt. 5:23-24). We have already seen his strong charge to forgive before we can expect to be forgiven in the Lord's prayer, a prayer which will follow closely upon this teaching in Matthew's gospel. Paul, who as a strong contender for the faith figures in a number of our examples, advises the Ephesians, "Be angry (the word even allows "be furious!") and do not sin. . ." (Eph 4:26). How can we be angry without sinning? By not letting the sun go down on our unresolved anger, not letting a

---

[2] Colin Nickerson, "Bernadette Devlin McAliskey on War, Peace and Justice," *The Boston Globe*, November 9, 1982, p. 2, cols. 2-3.

day pass while we nurture a grudge, and not letting the evil one seize our anger and use it as an opportunity to corrupt us. How can the evil one make us do evil? Through letting our anger grow into hatred for one another. Jesus warns against hating one another in the verses immediately preceding his command to be reconciled before daring to approach God's worship. The evil one also plants in our anger what the writer of Hebrews has called a "root of bitterness" (Heb. 12:15), an evil growth that secretly increases until it has poisoned us and our actions.

Given these realizations, what should Christian unity look like? God has obviously created Christians in a multitude of different ways. We are, after all, a body full of many contributing parts. No matter how intellectually, creatively, emotionally we have been put together or experience has shaped each of us, some expression of orthodox Christian worship will appeal to us. The point to look for Christian unity is not in the individual churches or denominations but in the great single church of Jesus, the church Universal. We do not have to regiment all Christians into one earthly church to achieve Christian unity. Many black and Latin-American Protestant Christians see worship as celebration. Most white Christians, and nearly all mainline white Christians, see worship as contemplation. The styles of service are mutually exclusive. Must we all worship in the same style to be unified? Reformed Christians affirming covenant theology bank on infant baptism as a sign of the new covenant being bestowed on the children of the new Israel. The majority of Baptists recognize only adult believer's baptism as being a valid fulfillment of Jesus' command. Must all Christians baptize the same way? Must all share the same view of communion to be unified? Must all agree on whether Christian contemporary music, the tasteful pseudonym for Christian rock and roll, is an appropriate form for spreading the good news of Jesus, or can Christians agree to disagree as did Paul and Barnabas? We believe that God allows styles of interpretation within the multifaceted body of Christ. Therefore the point is whether we baptize, not when we baptize, if we also make sure the baptized person is or is brought up to be affirmed a Christian. The responsibility is on the baptizer, a-priori or a-posteriori. Who knows for certain what happens during the Lord's Supper? Nobody but the Lord. The point is whether we share in the Lord's Supper -- and that in a righteous manner, reconciled with each other and with our Lord. What we do not want to change is the content, not the practice, of the faith first given to the saints.

The point is this: Christians love Jesus by following Jesus' commandments. What are Jesus' commandments? The New Testament is filled with them. When challenged to choose which is the greatest commandment, Jesus himself cited two, "You shall love the Lord your God in all your heart and in all your self (or life) and in all your mind (or understanding or attitude or purpose); this is the great and first commandment. And a second like it, Love your neighbor (literally, the one who is near) as yourself. In these two commandments all the law hangs (or depends) and the prophets" (Matt. 22:34-40). With this guide in mind we Christians should examine all our actions, and specifically all the actions we claim we do in Jesus' name.

Therefore, being different parts of the body, Christians do not all have to look alike. Christians do not have to worship in the same style to contribute a voice to the united praise of the church Universal. They are not required to be Presbyterians, Baptists, Methodists, Nazarenes, Charismatics, Brethren, Roman Catholics, Disciples of Christ, or a member of any of the other truly Christian denominations who recognize that the fully divine God and human walked among us and did for us what we could not do for ourselves, provided a means of salvation from our rebellion. They do have to love God with all their being and their attitude and their action. And they do have to treat those who have been created with them with the solicitude with which they treat themselves.

The great passage in the magnificent prayer we are studying teaches that Christians show unity with each other by revealing through actions toward one another that God loves them as God loves Jesus. Christians must speak and act towards one another in a manner that conveys the love of God to the watching world. In this, despite the variety and perhaps because of it, Christians show their essential unity. Like the great God they worship, Christians are plural, but they, too, are one.

Another way to approach this curious phrase, literally "in order that they may be perfected (a participle) into one" is through the verb from which that participle is built, *teleioo*. Literally the word means to bring to completeness, wholeness. Epictetus uses it to describe completing a work of art. Philo uses it to refer to finishing the building of a tower. The New Testament employs it when describing Jesus' fulfilling his commission from God.[3] Therefore, perhaps Jesus is saying that as he fulfills God's commission and becomes perfectly, completely united in God's will through his glorifying and being glorified by God, so does he anticipate completing the work of unifying the disciples with God and with each other. Jesus, to whom the disciples have been entrusted, becomes completely one with God in order that the disciples may become completely one together. Jesus' present action sets into motion the machinery to produce an equal oneness among the disciples.

John himself as an old man returns to the concept when writing the epistle which we call First John. For example, in I John 4:7 he urges his readers, let us love one another, for love is of God. He explains that the one loving is born of God and knows God, in other words, has a unity with God. Then he refers to Jesus' commission from God; manifesting God's love among us. In verse 12 he brings his words to a point, if we love one another, God's love is perfected in us. The word John employs for "perfected" or "completed" is the precise word, *teleioo*, that Jesus used in the prayer he gave on behalf of John and the other disciples. John now knows that the work of the Holy Spirit is to bind the disciples together with God. Thus in I John 4:17 he tells us what the end, the result of the completion of that love is, that Christians may have confidence for the day of judgment. This love casts out fear. Fear anticipates punishment. Anybody who fears, John writes in 4:18, is not perfected in love. We love, he tells us, because God loved us. So, anyone hating his brother or sister neither loves people nor God. The person claiming to love God must love the brother God has given her, the neighbor God has set down near him, the people God has created with whom to share the world. In verse 17 John explains that Christians need to have this love perfected in them, this confidence before the final judgment, because as Jesus is, so are Christians *in this world*. Here in this phrase we hear the prayer in John 17 echoing. And the world in which the disciples remain, the world that watches them, will see the work of Christ completed in the disciples because the disciples are unified in not fearing the judgment to come. They are one in loving each other as brothers and sisters should. They are one in manifesting through action and attitude the perfect love of God which casts out the fear of future decline, divine reprisal, of death, of final judgment.

---

[3] Gerhard Delling, "*Teleioo*," *Theological Dictionary of the New Testament* (1972), VIII, 80-81.

Father, What you Have Given to Me, I Wish that Where I Am Myself Those May Be with Me, in order that They May Perceive My Glory Which You Have Given Me, because You Loved Me before the Creation of the World (17:24).

Verse 24 contains an enigmatic petition from Jesus to the Father. "Father, what (or that or which) you have given to me" reads the best manuscripts, the papyrus p^{60}, the two authoritative early codices Sinaiticus and Vaticanus, even the freely eclectic and often divergent codex Bezae. Later manuscripts change the phrase to "*those* you have given to me" but Jesus is already using the singular to refer to the disciples for whom he has prayed for unity. The one, he is saying, those made one in completed work, in perfected love, Father, the one you have given me, I wish this body could be where I am. We have noticed back in verse 11 Jesus has already identified himself proleptically as being no longer in the world. Now he prays, I wish they could be with me and see my glory, that full glory that the Father gave before the world was ever created. So much of the full story of Jesus is unknown to the disciples. So much of the full picture of life is unseen by us. Here on earth we all look at heavenly things through the hazy images of a badly tarnished mirror. The transfiguration may be over but still Jesus longs for his timid, wanting-to-believe-but-doubting disciples to see the full burst of glory, the thunderous radiance of the full glorification of a person of the trinity. Addressing his Parent further, he continues:

Righteous Father, Also the World Did Not Know You, but I Myself Knew You, and They Themselves Knew that You Sent Me (17:25),

So much, we have noted, is unknown and unseen by the disciples about the true glory and the true nature of Jesus. And so much is unknown by the world about the true nature of God. God sent Jesus to reveal the nature of God and God's love to people. The disciples have seen the Father through looking at Jesus, but the world has not known God. They have not recognized Jesus as God's Son, as the one sent from God. Only the disciples, the "they themselves" in verse 25, have known God through Jesus. Only they have recognized that Jesus was sent down from the God who made heaven and earth.

Verses 24 and 25 in their two addressings of the Father work together to describe the situations of the two various parties into which humanity has been split by the advent of Jesus. Verse 24 discusses those who believe, and Jesus' longing for these to have vindication for their belief and for Jesus himself to have vindication for his claims, though not perhaps in the entire world's eyes. This world, he declares in verse 25, has never known the Father anyway. Small wonder it rejects Jesus so preemptorily. Only Jesus, the one who has come from the God-head, really, intimately, authentically knows another person of the God-head. And now the disciples know that God has sent Jesus. We see here spread throughout the prayer the distinctions from the past between the ones being lost and the ones being saved. From the opening of the prayer, as far back as verse 2, in the initial mention of the disciples, we see Jesus identifying them as the ones God has given to him. In some apriori manner they already belonged to God, even though they were not to meet God in deeper measure until they met Jesus. But these are the true covenant people, the true children of Abraham. These are the faithful remnant, the disciples since the dawn of humanity. From these simple, faithful people, trying to do the will of the One who created them, comes the chosen nation of priests.

In contrast stands a metaphorical unity - the world. Jesus prays his disciples be one. Well, the world is one. All the scoffers, the superiority-complexed, the haughty and greedy and hypocritical are united in their rejection of Jesus. The great mouth of the babbler of Babylon roars, "Crucify him!" The many voices blend into one shrill ululation, "Kill! Kill! Kill! Kill!" Into that din will stumble the frightened little flock, scattered and wailing. That they might have unity, but not as the world unites, a unity of love, of loving Jesus and the Father and one another, Jesus prays. The world does not know this kind of unity. "Righteous Father," Jesus identifies his Parent when praying about the world's ignorance. The fact that God is completely righteous is the reason why no one knows God except those who see God in Jesus. No one has known the truly righteous God but Jesus, the one united with that God. Only those who are made righteous can come to a knowledge of the "Righteous Father."

The world has not known God. We remember Jesus specifies in verse 9 he is not praying for the world. The world has not seen God in Jesus. Now it must watch the disciples to see Jesus in his disciples and though that means, through one step now removed, to see God in Jesus. It can see God's love through Jesus' love in the love of the disciples. But as Jesus ends his prayer he centers his concern and his petitions back on the disciples, those who unlike the world know that God has sent Jesus.

And I Made Known to Them Your Name and I Will Make Known, in order that the Love with Which You Loved Me May Be in Them and I in Them (17:26).

In his final statements in the conclusion of the prayer that must carry his disciples on into tribulation, temptation, and severe anguish Jesus summarizes what he has done for them, what he will do, and why he has done what he has done.

The prayer he taught them began, "Father of ours, the One in the heavens, let it be hallowed your name . . . ." Thus, the most important initial contact he has taught them to make with God, the way in which they should approach God, is by first hallowing God's name. After all, how does Jesus summarize his work for them? How does he encapsule the point of his ministry among them in his final statements on their behalf before the great catastrophe? I made known to them your name, he prays to the Father. That is what Jesus did. He has focused on making God's hallowed name known and has further glorified God in that process.

When Moses first confronts the strangely bizarre phenomenon of a bush that burns with a consuming fire yet leaves that which it burns intact, and he learns that a great power is calling forth a people to be led out from another people to become heirs of a land of promise, he begs to know that power's name. Who shall I say called me? Who can I say spoke to me and told me to do all this? When Jacob, staggering from his battle, begs to know the name of his wrestling opponent, we see the primacy, the centrality of Israel's concern to know who exactly is this great power who acts for its benefit in its history. The desire of the disciples in asking, "Teach us to pray . . . show us the Father," is the same quest to know God's name. Knowing a name, we recall, for a Hebrew is knowing a person, knowing a nature. What Jesus' ministry to the children of Israel has been is to have made known the name of his Abba, his Father. A name is a synecdoche, a word standing for the whole nature of a person. He has revealed the name, the nature, the character of God. God is love. Loving this Creator with all one's entity, all one's being, all one's attitudes and actions, and loving the human creation that Creator has given to share this beautiful garden world with us fulfills the intention of the great Parent. Those Old Testament characteristics we saw that traditionally described God are brought into focus by Jesus and highlighted to his disciples. Loving kindness characterizes the Parent he has revealed to them.

Mighty truth characterizes the Parent he has revealed to them. He has revealed to them the nature of the One who sent him.

I made known to them your name, he prays, and I will make known. Jesus is not finished! He has made known, he declares, using the indicative active past tense (the aorist), and he will make known, he affirms by using the future indicative active tense. These are strong tenses for a strong verb. He means what he says. He will do his future work. He will make known God's name to them. We must keep this in mind when we follow him into the garden of Gethsemane and try to understand the meaning of his agony there. For now let us simply keep his affirmation in mind. Why does he say he has done this and why will he do this? He acts in order that the love with which God loved him may be in the disciples as Jesus also is in them. Here is a summary statement of the entire prayer and all its intentions for the benefit of the disciples. Here is the sound that will echo in John and he will treasure and repeat as an old man when he writes to his spiritual children, his sermon from the mount of his years. I have made your name known to them and I will make your name known to them in order that that wonderful, life-giving, fully sustaining agape love with which we in the trinity love may be in them (or among them or shared with them and probably all these meanings) that they may know divine love even as they have known me who has lived with them and been examined by them and who fed them and healed them and took care of them with the loving solicitude of a mother her child, a shepherd his sheep, of a hen her chicks.

Fascinating is the fact that if there is a final verb "am," it is in ellipsis, "and I in them." The verb is not specified. While this is a normal enough practice in Greek, this particular prayer does specify a number of instances of the verb "to be" (most recently in the very clause that precedes, "the love . . . may be in them." But in this final wording "am" is not specified. As we have noted the last phrasing reads "in order that the love with which you loved me may be in them and I in them." Jesus identifies himself as having blended completely in them, as being completely, perfectly unified with them. What he prays for the disciples to achieve with each other, what he has revealed he has already achieved and is experiencing with the Father, he identifies as now having himself with the disciples. He is in the church. He is among the believers. Here is the truth of his statement: where two or three are gathered in my name, there I am in the midst of them (Matt. 18:20). As he is at one with the disciples, he asks that the love of God, nothing less than the pure perfect love which he himself has enjoyed, be given to the disciples. Jesus knows no holding back, for Jesus no hoarding what God has given and siphoning off a trickle to the disciples, crumbs from the marriage supper of the Lamb. When the bridegroom comes he wants his friends to feast. The Jesus that made barrels of wine at Cana wants his disciples drunk on the new wine of the Spirit. And Jesus, on his side, will drink a bitter cup to the dregs for them. He will not hold back. He will die for them with the greatest love that one can show, that one lays down one's life for others. This is love unsurpassable. This is no less than God's love, for this is the love God displayed when God walked among us. And this is the love Jesus asks to be among the disciples even as Jesus is among them. This indwelling love is the final petition of Jesus for his friends.

"The Lord's Prayer" in the Lord's Prayer: The Relationship Between the Prayers in Matthew 6 and Luke 11 and Jesus' Prayer in John 17

When we analyzed the two prayers that have come down to us under the name "The Lord's Prayer," we noted that a number of commentators have felt the name "The Disciples' Prayer" a more appropriate title. After all, they argue, Jesus provided the prayers as models in his early addresses (e.g. the Sermon on the Mount) and when his followers asked him specifically for advice on how to pray. Therefore, the prayer model ought to be seen in precisely that light, as a schema Jesus constructed for his disciples.

Those who have carefully progressed through the analysis of Jesus' own prayer as recorded in John 17, however, have no doubt been struck as we have by the proximity between the concerns of this prayer and those listed in Jesus' model prayer. Given these structural similarities, an entirely different way to read the prayer we have just studied is as Jesus' own personal appropriation, adaption, and expansion of the prayer model he provided. We recall that Walter Rauschenbusch was revolted by the practice that we all do (and most of us every Sunday), mumbling the model prayer like some sort of ancient incantation, devoid of meaning or feeling. What the prayer is is a model, an example of the kind of concerns that are appropriate to bring to God, the kind of structural progression one ought to adopt when daring to approach the presence of the great Ruler of the Universe. Therefore, the prayer is exactly that, a blueprint, a model from which to build appropriate prayers. How appropriate, then, if Jesus himself used the structural model to form this prayer. Perhaps the idea sounds like a theory we suddenly thought of and decided to test against the material. As a matter of fact, however, the realization began to grow upon us as we slowly studied the prayer in the manner in which we have just done. As we thought about each section we began to see the same concerns emerging with some striking differences. We recall that Jesus repeated his model prayer from the early exciting days of the Sermon on the Mount to the later bleaker, wearying days of his last great journey to Jerusalem. We saw when comparing the two models he gave that Jesus had already adapted the prayer to the reality that was facing him, the realization that indeed he was condemned to suffer and die. Now that he has entered Jerusalem, sent Judas about his evil business, set the wheels of his last great confrontation and sacrifice into motion, how appropriate for him to structure one last great prayer on the model he gave to the church.

The Place of the Prayer in John 17 in Jesus' Ministry

To understand Jesus' adaption of the prayer, we must take a moment and examine what we have learned about the prayer. We are now at the end of the journey, in fact, we are at the end of all journeys for the earthly Jesus, except the last great exile of execution. Jesus recognizes as he opens the prayer that his hour has come. So Jesus himself sets the time of the prayer into the time-scheme of his ministry. This is the moment toward which he has been working. With the advent of the Greeks in 12:20-23 time for Jesus has changed. Now he is praying on the brink of the fulfillment of his hour and the dawn of a new era. The impact of this statement on John, who recorded this prayer, must have been immense for John will begin his entire gospel record with a statement on time. In the words recorded in John 16:26-27, set just before this last great prayer of Jesus, Jesus informs his disciples that "In that day," that is after the resurrection, Jesus does *not* say he will pray to the Father for the disciples, but the Father will love them directly. And at that time what they ask in Jesus' name the Father will give. Great changes are indeed about to occur.

Having given this setting and statement on time, he now lifts his eyes to heaven and begins by addressing God, "Father." All three prayers begin in precisely this way. John 17 announces that the hour has come and then all three prayers, John 17's, Matthew 6's, Luke 11's, move into a statement about glorifying God. Just a moment ago we cited Jesus' warning that he gave his disciples just before praying this prayer. He said, in that future coming day because the Father loves you, what you ask *in my name* the Father will give. Both the prayers in Matthew and Luke call for our first statement of prayer to be a praising, a hallowing, a blessing, a glorifying of God's name. Jesus in John 17 moves immediately to that petition too but he asks that *he*, the Son of God, be glorified so he may glorify the Father here on earth. Jesus is asking that both his name and the Father's name be jointly glorified. Jesus, the faithful, completely obedient Child, can make the honest statement that he hallows God's name in his actions and in his teachings. And further, when Jesus, who has been given the name above all names, is glorified, the Father's name is glorified.

The prayers in Matthew and Luke now move to the petition that God's kingdom come and God's will be done. To what does Jesus in John 17 move? He gives a report that he has accomplished the work that God gave him to do. Jesus has done the will of the Parent on earth, just as that will is done in heaven. Jesus points out that God gave him power over all flesh, he has come as a ruler, though his reign, as Pilate was never able to understand, was not a rule like Caesar's. As George MacDonald wrote in his beautiful poem "That Holy Thing," "On the road thy wheels are not, Nor on the sea thy sail!" And yet the reign of God had come to earth in Jesus with the true eternal power over all humanity to give everlasting life. Thus, Jesus did God's will by accomplishing God's work.

Then Jesus moves into the other petitions, but he does not ask for himself. He asks on behalf of his disciples. Setting out carefully in the next several verses the ones for whom he is specifically praying, singling out the disciples from the world and the son of destruction, he begins his requests in John 17:11 and 15, asking God to keep them in God's name and protect them from the evil one. We recall that they have all just eaten and received communion, their daily bread risen to a higher plain. Now he prays fervently for the God of sustenance to sustain them. Jesus addresses their greatest need at this point. He wants to emphasize their set-apartness from the world, so they will be delivered from the negative earthly testing about to fall upon them all. He does not emphasize their oneness with the world in basic human physical needs, as the daily bread petition does, but stresses their oneness with himself and with God and asks on behalf for their severe and soon crucial spiritual needs. Their bellies are full. Their spirits will be hungry. They need to be rescued from evil and from the evil one.

We note that the prepositional phrase used in Matthew is *apo tou ponerou*, deliver us from the evil one or from evil. But in John 17 Jesus uses twice the preposition *ek* "out of." He prays, I do not ask that they be lifted out of the world but that they be kept from out of evil, from out of the clutches of the evil one. The disciples are to remain in the world in a way Jesus is no longer in it today, since he is not physically walking among us in our world. But they are not to be so in and of the world that they are ensnared, as so many people are ensnared, by the traps of evil laid down so cunningly by our great adversary, the evil one.

But what about the petition about forgiveness? Is that not here too? That petition is included here in the most poignant fashion possible, by the one who is about to show the greatest forgiving love that can be shown by laying his life down for both his disciples and his murderers. Jesus has already noted that he has given his disciples eternal life by passing to them the words of life, by letting them know him and through him the great Father who sent him. Now Jesus moves to the momentous act of protection he is asking God to do for them. He prays, sanctify, purify them in the truth. In verse 19 he states, for their sake or on behalf of them I purify myself that they may also be purified in truth. Jesus does not need to pray as we need to pray, "Forgive us our debts or sins," for Jesus himself did not sin (Heb. 4:15). No, he does not need to pray for himself the petition for forgiveness in the Lord's Prayers. What he does do is pray it for others and do it for others. In his actions, as seen in this announcement, he fulfills the petition in the Lord's prayers. He does the act that forgives us all our sins forever. Jesus has been forgiving sins all through his ministry, forgiving the sins of individual people as he tells them to get up and walk, see at last, speak, go and sin no more. Mary of Bethany in anointing Jesus (John 12:1-8) has already prepared him to be the sacrificed for us. Mary in priestly function presents the sacrificial lamb. Jesus' heart is troubled because, sinless as he is, he is about to become that sacrificial blood atonement. He is about to take on the sins of the world. At the cross he becomes impure. So God, as we shall see, will have to turn God's face away from this human of sorrows. God must forsake him for God the pure will not embrace sin. Then, how is he able to commend his spirit to God? He is able, because with the shedding of blood he is now purified and he has purified his disciples. Dead, he yet lives and God can accept him.

We can see this specific truth in the Greek word with which Jesus has chosen to express this program of redemption in John 17:

17 and 19. The normal Greek word for making someone holy is *hagizo*. But we note in these verses an extra vowel has been added. We do not have the common *hagizo* but *hagiazo*: to make *very* holy. According to the authoritative lexicon by Liddell and Scott, the normal term *hagizo* means to make sacred, especially by burning a sacrifice.[4] But with the extra vowel we understand Jesus is praying that God make the disciples extremely sacred by burning a gigantic sacrifice. A *hagiasterion* is a holy place, a sanctuary. Jesus' body, we understand, is a sanctuary in which the great sacrifice is made. The sacrifice is made in Jesus' body and of Jesus' body. Like burning down the entire temple as one vast sin offering, the temple of Jesus' body is destroyed on behalf of sinning humans, his disciples, his friends. But as Jesus has warned his opponents in John 2:19, "Destroy this temple and in three days I will raise it up." As John footnotes for us in John 2:21-22, Jesus spoke about the temple of his body, and, John recalls, we disciples remembered that he said this when he was raised from the dead. The veil of the temple was split when Jesus died. His own body, his *naos*, the sanctuary, was the sacrifice. He made a sacrifice in and of the holy and the holy of holies. Imagine what this means. Israel gathers to worship. They are all standing outside waiting for their symbolic act of contrition to be done by their representative when the priest ignites the sanctuary and burns down the temple! This is the one great unique and complete sacrifice. This is why, to symbolize this fact, that the veil between the holy and the most holy place is rent apart. The fire of God's presence bursts out in Pentecost. Out of the holy place God's fire comes roaring in the sacrifice of Jesus and into God's people at Pentecost. God is answering them directly.

What is Added to the Model of the Lord's Prayer in this Prayer?

Most dramatically added is the new information that to know God is to know Jesus, to glorify God is to glorify Jesus, to be united with God is to be united with Jesus. We gain eternal life from both God and the one God sent. Further, as we can see, while Jesus does ask for things for his disciples, that they be kept in God's name (verse 11) from evil (15), *not* be lifted out of this world (15), but to be sanctified in truth (17, 19) (a request that is made for us future disciples too [20]), for oneness together and with God and Jesus (21, 22, 23), yet Jesus does not so much ask for things as he states that he has done them:

---

[4] Henry George Liddell and Robert Scott, *A Greek-English Lexicon* (Oxford: Oxford University, 1940), p. 9.

given us words (8) and word (14), made the Father's name known so we will have the Father's love (26), even given us glory (22), while wanting us to see his glory (24), having the power to give us eternal life (2). And these things he speaks in the world, for he wants his disciples who remain to have his joy fulfilled in them (13). This is a prayer at the accomplishment of one's work.

Jesus has completed his work (verse 4), but, we are not finished in doing our part and requesting God's reign come and God's will be perfected in us and our world. We note Jesus prays, *I* accomplished your work, *I* glorified you. We simply pray, let your kingdom come, let your will be done. With us the agent is not so clear because we may not necessarily deliver what we request or what we promise to do. May your kingdom come, we pray. We hope somebody brings it in. We hope to give it our try, but . . . .The way this is expressed grammatically in the Lord's prayers in Matthew and Luke is that the first three requests are either imperatives of permission or imperatives of command where the agent is unclear. The third person imperative, which is what is employed, leaves the agent who is going to do the action unclear. But later on in the petitions, asking for the giving of bread and the forgiving of sins, the agent is clear. God is going to do it. We may not keep our end of the covenant, God, however, is going to keep God's end. Now, Jesus, on the other hand, in his prayer in John 17:1 uses a direct second person singular aorist, that is the past or punctiliar tense, active imperative, "You glorify your Son," not simply, "Let your name, or in this case *my* name, be hallowed." We see how this contrasts with the third person singular aorist passive imperatives used in both Matthew and Luke. "Let your name be praised, Let your kingdom come . . . ." We are only asking for God's permission for these things to occur. The agent who is going to do them is not specified. But Jesus specifically states what he has done and what he is going to do and asks God directly to make it happen. Jesus asks God to do something and God's answer will be in Jesus' act! Further, Jesus' prayer with his use of that intensified word for purification *hagiazo* is asking in 17:17, "Let us clean up your disciples by using truth." That is what he means by "sanctify them." In Matthew disciples pray in the passive *hagiastheto*, let it be done, let your name be praised. We are praying, essentially, let us have cleaned up our use of God's name. But God will have to do it through us.

So the difference in Jesus' praying in John 17 and our praying by the models of Matthew 6 and Luke 11 is that Jesus prays in the active voice, asking that God act, while we pray in the passive voice, asking that the act be done. We ask that it be done, Jesus asks that God act. Jesus himself is going to do it on God's behalf and has already begun doing it. Do we wish to be more like Jesus? Let us do the greater works he promised us we will do in his name. In his model let us too become the agents that God uses to accomplish God's will on earth.

This gives us in retroactive perspective a whole new way to read these Lord's prayers or Disciples' prayers in Matthew and Luke, especially since Jesus has prayed that we be equipped with all we need, God's protection and our oneness. Looking back at these model prayers through the perspective of John 17, we might actually be praying, "Our Father, let's let your kingdom come instead of hindering it as usual. Let's do your will for a change here on earth as it always is being done already in heaven. Let's just ask for our daily bread, what we physically need now, instead of a bakery full of loaves that we can hoard in case we manage to accomplish a nuclear holocaust. And forgive us for all those sins we do, and while we're asking, let's drop all the grudges we've been nurturing so carefully. And don't let us follow up on our temptations, but rescue us from the ramifications of our actions."

That prayer will begin to take our praying on a road which will end in our becoming more like Jesus. Maybe someday we too can find ourselves able to change around the first three imperatives in the model prayer as Jesus changed them around in his prayer in John 17. Maybe we will be able to change them around because like Jesus we will actually do them.

The Great Pastoral Prayer

As we can see, what Jesus has done in his prayer in John 17 is that Jesus has taken his model and built on it a perfect intercessory prayer on behalf of others. What Jesus has done, essentially, is formally reintroduce his disciples back to the Father. He has constructed for them a prayer of presentation.

Having asked the Father to glorify Jesus himself, having reminded the Father that Jesus has fulfilled his commission, Jesus now asks the Father to accept Jesus' disciples since Jesus will no longer be there to guard them directly. So Jesus asks for unity for them, a unity reflecting the unity of the Trinity. He begs protection for them as they are in the world and he asks the love of God to be given to the disciples. What this is in the fullest sense is a pastoral prayer by Jesus on behalf of his disciples. It is earnest, careful, measured, complete. Jesus fully covers his disciples by his concern and his requests.

Like a pastoral prayer it has all the classic elements we still use in our services. Many ministers these days structure pastoral prayers on the acronym ACTS. We can see the elements in the structure present in John 17. Adoration: the prayer asks for Jesus to be glorified as the Father is glorified. Confession: Jesus does not need to beg forgiveness, but he himself will become the means of that forgiveness. Celebrating God's providential passing over of Israel, he himself will become that sacrificial Paschal lamb for the new Israel. The Passover Lamb gives the Passover prayer, a plea to God for God's continued protection and mercy. So, in his prayer, Jesus, the sacrificial lamb, prays God will keep his disciples from the evil one and sanctify them from their sins. Supplication: In this prayer the predominant petition is for God to take care of the disciples. In that sense instead of a prayer of confession Jesus provides a means of confession and a prayer of supplication.

Thanksgiving: This is the final category we usually include. We note we have listed this letter out of order because thanksgiving is not so apparent here. And yet we must recall that Jesus has just given the Lord's supper and as we see from Mark 14:23, Matthew 26:27, and Luke 22:19, when Jesus broke the bread he gave thanks. In fact, thanksgiving permeates the Passover service. After the initial blessing of God over the first and second cups of wine, the meal proper of unleavened bread, roast lamb, wine, and bitter herbs was brought in. At this point the youngest child asked the parent why this night was different from other nights. Rabbi Gamaliel when recording the reply states, "Therefore are we bound to give thanks, to praise, to glorify, to honour, to exalt, to extol, and to bless him who wrought all these wonders for our fathers and for us" (m. Pes. 10:5)." So the Lord's prayer for his disciples, given as it was in the context of the Passover meal or shortly afterwards, was framed in thanksgiving.

How could Jesus have prayed such an others-oriented prayer, faced as he was with his own impending death? After all, the disciples were only to be scattered, but he was to be murdered. The great Teresa of Avila pondered this same mystery when she was writing about the fifth dwelling place in her remarkable classic *The Interior Castle:*

> Well, then, how is it, Lord, that You weren't thinking of the laborious death You were about to suffer, so painful and frightful? You answer: "No, my great love and the desire I have that souls be saved are incomparably more important than these sufferings, and the very greatest sorrows that I have suffered and do suffer, after being in the world, are not enough to be considered anything at all in comparison with this love and desire to save souls (5th: 2:13).

Marvelous Savior, from the depths of his love for us, Jesus gave us something foundational, indeed, when he gave us the models of the Lord's Prayer. He gave us a basic structure he would use himself when he prayed on our behalf. And after he prays this extensive prayer, all of Jesus' prayers would themselves become extremely basic. For John this great prayer we have studied will be the last of Jesus' recorded prayers until those he gasps on the cross. John's gospel omits the garden prayers and simply presents the resolved Jesus, who, ordering Peter to put up his sword, affirms, "The cup which the Father has given to me, shall I not drink it?" (John 18:11) But the path to this resolution has been a way of sorrows and the other gospels take us down onto it with Jesus, as we go into the garden and into his glory.

9

The Last Prayers of Jesus

Prayers at Gethsemane

The end of all journeys, the end of all prayers. Jesus entering Gethsemane has already prayed for the protection of his disciples and now, at last, he prays for himself. But Jesus' prayer for himself by himself in the garden has none of the careful watch-guarding quality of his pastoral prayer. Rather, what is recorded stands in stark contrast to the prayer in John 17. Now Jesus' prayer is blunt, sporadic, and impassioned. He keeps interrupting it and returning to his disciples, urging them desperately to stay awake and pray too. Then wearily he trudges, even stumbles off a little distance, for he must have been as exhausted as they, and repeats his prayer over and over again. The many words of the Gentiles cannot mean repetition, as we have noted in the appendix, for in his anguish Jesus repeats again and again his plea to his loving Parent. Where Jesus' prayer for his disciples was emphathetic and caring, his prayer for himself is terse and brutal. He states his desire aloud, "Daddy, Father, all is possible to you, bear away this cup from me . . ." (Mark 14:36). We think of Calvin's startling words, which we cited earlier, that even Judas could have escaped being the traitor guilty for all eternity for betraying the innocent blood of Jesus. Can Jesus really have been asking that in God's omnipotence our salvation be effected without his personal sacrifice? In his mind was the terse and firm reply he gave on another occasion, the coming of the Greeks in John 12:27, when with troubled soul he asked, "What shall I say? 'Father, deliver me out of this hour?' Rather, on account of this I came into this hour." No sooner does he ask, "Father, bear away this cup," then he immediately counteracts it with his iron clad resolute obedience, "but not what I myself wish but what you (wish)" (Mark 14:36). If in this garden as in another garden long ago a perfect human is being tempted to avoid doing what God wills, this new Adam will succeed in obedience where the old Adam failed. And on account of his perfect obedience by accepting the verdict of death levied on the failure of the old Adam he will take on himself the judgment of all. Dragged from this garden, he will make Paradise possible to all who will let their sins be paid by his sacrifice. The paschal lamb readies itself to be the blood atonement. Yet while he awaits the advent of his accusors he struggles with the terrifying spectre of the cup he must drink. And what exactly is "this cup" which Jesus wishes could be taken away?

All three synoptic gospels, Mark's, Matthew's, and Luke's, use the same word, *poterion*, to describe what Jesus wants to have taken away from him. The word, while used for a normal drinking-cup or wine-cup, was also used to describe the receptacle employed in giving offerings in temples in the Tebtunis Papyri from 2 B.C.[1] Thus the normal word for a drinking receptacle, one used over and over some thirty-two or so times for a variety of descriptions in the New Testament, also becomes, through Jesus' use of it, the cup of offering that Paul will recall in describing the eucharist to the Christians at Corinth in I Corinthians 11:25. But what exactly is this "cup" that Jesus hesitates to drink in his agonized prayer in Gethsemane? Frankly, we do not know what the cup is. Those Christians who want to stress Jesus' essential humanity say that it is the extreme agony of death on the cross.

The early church, for example, took great comfort in Jesus' experiencing fear of torture and death. The prospect of persecution was uncomfortably near to them and a reading of their literature shows that many were terrified of suffering, just as we would be, but taking heart in Jesus' endurance, they endured. So Justin Martyr in his *Dialogue with Trypho* 103, writes:

> His heart and also His bones trembling; His heart being like wax melting in His belly: in order that we may perceive that the Father wished His Son really to undergo such suffering for our sakes, and may not say

[1] PTeb. 6-27, Liddell and Scott, *A Greek-English Lexicon*, p. 1454.

> that He, being the Son of God, did not feel what was happening to him and inflicted on Him.

Cyprian in drafting his poignant letter for the African synod, urging other church leaders to forgive those who because of fear had offered unholy sacrifices to pagan deities or to the emperor in recent persecutions, parallels the cup of the Lord's Supper with the cup of martyrdom. In his *Treatise on the Lord's Prayer* 14, he says of Jesus' request for that cup to pass from him:

> And further, the Lord, setting forth the infirmity of the humanity which he bore, says, "Father, if it be possible, let this cup pass from me"; and affording an example to His disciples that they should do not their own will, but God's.

The point for the early church was that, while loathing the prospect of torture and death, Jesus still determined to do God's will. The great lawyer Tertullian in *De Fuga in Persecutione* 8 suggests that Jesus wished to have his "cup of suffering" taken away, but instead drained it in accordance with God's will. In the same manner so should Christians when faced with the loathesome prospect of persecution not run away, taking "into your own hands the removal of the cup from you, and instead of doing what your Father wishes, doing what you wish yourself."[2]

Robert Gundry introduces for us the second major interpretation of the cup that Jesus wishes to have pass from him: that Jesus was not primarily disturbed by the prospect of physical torture, though this, of course, was unappealing.[3] Rather, he dreaded the separation from God, the heinousness of becoming the scapegoat, the sacrificial lamb, the human of sorrows who must bear the world's curse and from whom a pure and holy God must turn away.

---

[2] See also John Calvin, *The Gospel according to St. John 11-21 and the First Epistle of John*, Calvin's Commentaries (Grand Rapids: Eerdmans, 1961), p. 157; *A Harmony of the Gospels: Matthew, Mark and Luke, Vol. 3, and the Epistles of James and John*, Calvin's Commentaries (Grand Rapids: Eerdmans, 1972), pp. 149-150; Lyman Abbott, *An Illustrated Commentary on the Gospel according to St. John* (New York: A.S. Barnes, 1879), p. 213; Eduard Schweizer, *The Good News according to Mark* (Richmond: John Knox, 1970), p. 313.

[3] Robert H. Gundry, *Matthew: A Commentary on His Literary and Theological Art* (Grand Rapids: Eerdmans, 1982), p. 533; Hugh Anderson, *The Gospel of Mark*, New Century Bible (London: Oliphants, 1976), p. 320.

So Vincent Taylor, while recognizing the metaphor cup contains "suffering and death" adds to it "the thought of divine judgment on sin," explaining, "It is alien to the spirit of Jesus that He should ask for the cup to be taken away if it is no more than one of personal suffering and death . . . Jesus had to school Himself to the necessity of redemptive suffering which involves the bearing of sin."[4]

The Reverend Paul Bricker, while recognizing fully Jesus' anguish, sees in his passion the deep interplay of Old Testament symbolism. Jeremiah 25:15-31 provides the background of the "cup of wine of wrath" poured out by the roaring God on the nations. This too is the cup to which the book of Revelation alludes (Rev. 14:10; 16:19), and draining that cup of divine wrath terrifies Jesus. When does he drink the cup? He refuses all drinking on the cross until the fulfillment of the key events culminating in John 19:28, when knowing that all is finished, he fulfills the Scripture by crying, "I thirst." With the sour wine on the hyssop branch (hyssop was used to paint the blood of atonement on the doorposts and lintels at the Passover in Exodus 12:22) he drinks the vinegar of God's wrath and cries, "It is finished." What is finished? He has drained the cup of wrath poured out on the nations. His has become the blood atonement on our doorposts. Now he can bow his head and die. He can rest for his work is done. And from this moment through his sacrifice instead of the cup of God's wrath we all can drink the cup of Psalm 116:12-15 which has become a cup of blessing. As Paul warns, we can still drink the cup of wrath and divine judgment if we take communion unworthily (1 Cor. 11:27-32). Or like the Israelites in Exodus, instead we can have our life's door painted with the blood of the sacrificial lamb Jesus and drink a cup of blessing, for Jesus has drunk the punishment for us. This is why Jesus questioned James and John about their foolish offer to drink the cup he drinks (Matt. 20:22). While they and we do indeed drink Jesus' cup of suffering (verse 23), the once for all draught of the sacrifice for sins has been done by Jesus.[5]

As fully human, Jesus took eternally the curse for sin that lay since Eden upon humanity. When the first humans were promised they would die (Gen. 2:16-17; 3:19), the sober punishment was levied. Drawing death from a source of life is accursed in God's sight. So the humans ate of the tree of good and evil and basically only learned evil

---

[4] Vincent Taylor, *The Gospel according to Mark* (London: MacMillan, 1966), p. 554.

[5] Statement by Paul Bricker, pastor, unpublished sermon, 1987.

and death. They had already known goodness. Now they were shut away from the tree of life. Soon to enter Canaan, Israel was warned not to cut down fruit trees (Deut. 20:19-20) and a curse was placed on whomever died on a tree (Deut. 21:22-23), whomever drew death from a source of life. Jesus in his full humanity became the human who died on the tree. Perfect, he did not need to die for his own sins, so he was able to die for others' sins. As a human had sinned so a human died. Cursed now for all eternity, Jesus, who died on a tree for all humanity, must be eternally separated from God. But the beauty of the soteriological plan is that Jesus was also fully divine. As a loving part of the Trinity, Jesus would always be united with God. Therefore, the curse was fixed on the head of Jesus. Jesus would eternally carry humanity's curse, while, as a member of the Godhead, Jesus remains at the same time perfectly united with God. The triumph of complete victory is won, but what a price of complete defeat in complete rending anguish, physical and spiritual, must be paid! No wonder Jesus either in his humanity or in his divinity or in both wonders if another way can be found. And no wonder we who barely glimpse heavenly things can only speculate on what the full meaning of the cup must have been for Jesus.

Finally, when all our speculation is finished, we do not really firmly, completely have revealed to us what Jesus meant. And why not? The disciples were too sleepy to record it all for us. Only disconnected fragments of this prayer were afterwards recalled and recorded by the drowsy disciples, somnolent as they were after such traumatic teaching, a heavy meal and its full preparation, and, at the very least, four cups of wine apiece. But then Jesus' prayer in Gethsemane is not a teaching mechanism for us to learn some great aspect in the mystery of the exact theological out-working of our justification. Instead, it is a glimpse into the true character and great sacrifice of Jesus. We see his agony and his magnificent obedience to God. What we can know from it is that Jesus faced his death or some aspect of it with dread not with relish. He was not some pathological maniac with delusions of grandeur who carefully manipulated the authorities into sacrificing him on the cross in a pathetic, misguided delusion of apotheosis, that is, forcing himself to be made a god in the way in which he is so often painted in literature today. Instead, he dreaded some or all aspects of his crucifixion. But he was determined to do his Parent's will at any cost -- to our lasting benefit. And from then on the prayers of Jesus are gasps out of pain.

Prayers on the Cross

Doubtlessly Jesus prayed continually throughout his trial and imprisonment and his scourging, but no disciple was there to record those prayers. When we hear Jesus again, we hear the last gasps of a dying God/human directed to another person of the Trinity.

From noon to three, the ninth hour, the hour of prayer, Jesus, hanging on a stake, is failing fast. He, too, as all Israel, offers his prayers to God, but these come out in short gasps. He prays a short quotation, a question in Aramaic, the intimate language of the common people, "My God, my God, for what reason have you abandoned me?" (Matt. 27:46) In the hour that Israel seeks God in prayer, is God's own Child abandoned, forsaken in his disgrace and his cruel execution? Neither the Father nor Jesus himself answer. We are left with the question. For what reason, indeed, is Jesus the sinless forsaken? For *our* sins? Then the gasp, "I thirst!" (John 19:28) Does the source of living water, from whose founts those who drink never know thirst again, thirst himself unquenchably? Then a cry, "It is finished!" (John 19:30) The hour has gone. And in his last breath of prayer, a command ripped from Psalm 31:5, screaming, "Father, into your hands I entrust my spirit!" (Luke 23:46). And it is over. He is dead.

Readers who have been following in their Bibles will notice omitted are those wonderful words of comfort in which people for centuries have taken refuge, usually when desiring forgiveness for themselves or for others for sins they are not willing to confess or to repent and desist doing. "Father, forgive them, for they do not know what they do" read the comforting words in Luke 23:34. But these words do not appear in the earliest manuscripts of the gospel of Luke. They cannot be found in the authoritative papyrus p^{75}, nor are they in Vaticanus or in the version of Sinaiticus that was corrected before it was permitted to leave the scriptorium where it was copied. Even the original version of the wildly aberrant codex Bezae, which contains so many traditions that other manuscripts do not have, does not have these words. And they are not in the early translations of the old Latin (the Italic), or the Syriac, or in the primary versions of the Coptic. Instead, they are found earliest only in the uncorrected Sinaiticus from the fourth century, a later version of codex Bezae, which is itself somewhat late, being from the fifth or sixth century, and in some Coptic versions and all throughout the early church fathers from Clement and to the heretic Marcion to Ambrose, Chrysostom, Jerome, and Augustine.

What does this mean? Did Jesus not say these things? Were the words taken from Stephen (Acts 7:60) by some pietistic scribe not wishing that a servant be greater than his master and put into the mouth of Jesus? Was the action of James, Jesus' brother, as Eusebius records, when he knelt in agony praying on behalf of his murderers, attributed back to his holy brother (*History of the Church* 2:23)? Or, are these words true? Are they words out of what we call true tradition? Were they left out of the gospel accounts, as many contend the scene of the woman caught in adultery in John 8 was a true tradition which was simply left out, and later scribes knowing these words were true put them back in? John tells us Jesus did and said many things, and he supposes all the books of the world could not hold them if they were written down (John 21:25). Eusebius, the church historian from the 300's, heard about a healing Jesus sent Thomas to do in the nearby province of Edessa which was not recorded in the book of Acts, and Eusebius himself traveled to Edessa and did indeed find in the court annals the record of the healing of Edessa's monarch by a disciple sent from Jesus (*History of the Church* 1:13:1-22). Are these words' absence, then, a similar omission?

We hesitate to conclude that these words are genuine for two compelling reasons. First, they do not appear in the best and earliest manuscripts of the Bible and when they crept into Sinaiticus they were blotted out before the manuscript was allowed to leave the copying room. This indicates that the earliest scribes who lovingly transmitted the Scriptures did not recognize these words as genuine to Jesus. Second, these gracious words totally contradict the teaching that Jesus has packed into his two model prayers. In these prayers we understand that we must be forgiving others if we expect to be forgiven. Jesus was not being forgiven, he was being murdered -- and cruelly murdered. Further, Jesus' central teaching, repeated over and over throughout the gospels, was "repent for the reign of heaven is at hand." But no repentance is evident here. In each case of a healing, a humbled spirit is demanded of the sufferer (if not, of course, a demoniac) before God's grace will take effect. When arrogance meets Jesus' message, Jesus does not heal body or soul. Why would he forgive these, then, who are not repentant? The words say, "Father, forgive them, for they do not know what they are doing . . . ." Does this mean that God engineered these poor puppet mortals into effecting God's plan and Jesus wants these innocent lackies taken off the hook? What sort of monster is this "Daddy" of Jesus' anyway? Or is pure ignorance at issue, as Paul writes, had they known they would not have crucified the Lord of glory (I Cor. 2:8)? So are these executioners innocent from ignorance? Or is Jesus simply being lightheadly gracious, one last spilling out of mercy from his death throes, the flower scenting the heel that crushes it? That is a lovely image of Jesus and a most appealing one. And yet what does that do to all the teaching he has given earlier? Negate it? In the end can we count on Jesus' mercy, "Aw, shucks, Pop, let 'em all in," no matter how cruelly we butcher one another? We suppose the choice would be left up to each of us what to believe about Jesus, if the manuscript evidence were stronger. But it is not strong. Therefore, it is a most shaky ledge upon which to seek shelter from a life of rebellion against God. Better we should choose the strong rock of repentance and a changing of one's life into a lifestyle of mercy and kindness and communion with God. Jesus may well ultimately forgive some of us gratuitously no matter how we live but the evidence simply does not support this idyllic conclusion and is certainly not a dream to base one's eternity upon. Better we should stumble down the doleful way of repentance, carrying the humbling cross of our Lord to an equally glorious destination as his, the certain hope of resurrected triumph.

And so our Savior dies in prayer. What have we seen revealed in Jesus' last moments? What we have received is an intimate glimpse into the loving communication within the Trinity. We have listened to the voice of God dealing with the pain we humans have caused our Creator in the intimate flow with which concerns are spoken back and forth freely within the God-head. We have glimpsed the only agony known in heaven, where all human tears are wiped away -- the agony of God.

When Jesus rises gloriously three days later and returns to his astounded disciples, he is changed. His work is completed. His hour has been fulfilled. Now he gives the disciples quiet, loving instruction, explaining to them the significance of each of the events that have lead to this glorious conclusion, this eucatastrophe as J.R.R. Tolkien calls it. But while quiet, loving instruction and joyful communion flow between Jesus and his disciples, no more prayers are recorded for us.

10

Summary: What the Lord Taught Us to Pray

The disciples asked Jesus, "Lord, teach us to pray, just as also John taught his disciples" (Luke 11:1). When we explore the answers that Jesus gave, we realize that Jesus included in his replies the information current journalists seek when investigating a subject: what, who, when, where, why, and how. All of these facets are present in Jesus' loving and thorough response.

What Is Prayer?

Jesus both prays and gives models of prayer to tell his followers what prayer is. In Luke 11 privately and in Matthew 6 publicly he provides a sample prayer and then in John 17 he himself employs and adapts that model prayer and builds upon it a perfect intercessory prayer on behalf of others. The two crucial elements that emerge both in the Lord's taught prayers and in the Lord's prayer for his disciples are adoration and supplication. Jesus himself is unique in that he rarely expresses personal need and never confesses personal sin, but he provides by example a rich panorama of prayer types and styles. We see him making forceful requests for his present and future disciples' needs, reverently asking in formal supplication. In addition to requests his prayers express extreme rejoicing, public praise, thanksgiving, sung praises, blessing and calling down blessings. And beyond request and expression of appreciation Jesus uses prayer simply to express emotion. Reverent but expressive prayer for Jesus can be comprised of a look, an inarticulate sigh, silent weeping, loud talking, crying aloud, crying upward, shouting, exclamations of loneliness, pain, despairing, and affirmation. Prayers for Jesus become gifts and sacrifices to God as part of Jesus' living and suffering. Thus, his prayers are characterized by the genuine expression of emotion and the balancing of requests with appreciation. Our prayer lives should maintain a similar balance.

Over and over in Jesus' example and in his teaching comes the message that is finally articulated in prayer in John 17: to know God to whom we pray is to know Jesus who is teaching us how to pray.

To Whom Do We Pray and Who Are We Who Pray?

To Whom Do We Pray?

If we had to summarize our findings after studying this topic in just one sentence, this would be it: We set out to learn about prayer, or vital human communication with God, and we ended up learning about God, the One to whom we communicate. From the moment Jesus begins shaping a model prayer for his disciples to follow, he addresses the One to whom prayer is sent. "Our Father, the One in the heavens," are the very first words implied in every prayer. Jesus himself in prayer gives us a glimpse of the intimate loving communication that flows back and forth in the Godhead, and Jesus' teaching humans prayer is an invitation for us to join in that communication. The Father revealed by Jesus is an impartial and compassionate Judge who has a special concern for the downtrodden and promises swiftly to punish anyone who oppresses widows, orphans, and others whose lives are marked by poverty and powerlessness. As the parables Jesus taught us reveal, if even a selfish Gentile judge without respect or restraint can grant justice, we do not need to struggle with God to get results. The sympathetic God who loves us, feels our pain, and extends mercy to us wants to share our feelings. We simply need to trust God and live faithful lives wherein God's reign has priority. Jesus has assured his followers that those who have seen him have seen his Parent. Therefore, recognizing what Jesus' attitude and action in prayer is like gives us an understanding of the way the Father will approach and act upon prayer.

Jesus' prayers, we see, flow from who he is. He is imbued with a deep concern for the physical and spiritual needs of people, and this concern compels him to pray and to command us to pray for others. His approach is team-oriented, both in regards to his identity in the God-head, the Spirit causing joy in the Son to the Father, and in his identity with people. Leaving us the Holy Spirit as Intercessor, Jesus himself activates fully in heaven the role he fleshed out among us on earth as intermediary, our perfect high priest praying for us. In this heavenly role, working between our earthly counsel, the Holy Spirit, and our heavenly Judge, the Father, he can either be our defense attorney, pleading our case before God, or our prosecutor, challenging our prayer requests. Aligning with him as his disciples assures us his intercession will be on behalf of our requests. Therefore, he wants us to rejoice exceedingly because our salvation is secure in heaven, not because we may have power over evil on earth. The power that we do have we obtain from asking in his name. Jesus, after all, was the one whose thanksgiving for bread multiplied bread. There is power in following his will, and never is this power more clearly revealed than in his praying.

His prayers at times become a testimony to the Father and an education to his listeners. Even as Jesus' preaching and teaching reveal his divinity, so does his prayer show he is God. During prayer he takes on the pre-incarnate glory that is his, and in his last prayers we listen to the voice of God dealing with the only pain known in heaven, the pain we humans have caused our Creator. Therefore, Jesus' prayer teachings and example affirm our discovery that knowing the nature of God and praying in acceptance and in support of God's purposes allows us to intercede for specific events in working out of God's will. This is what Abraham did, what Hannah did, what Joshua did. Though God has pre-ordained purposes, God has not created a fatalistic universe. God invites those who are aligned with God's purposes into the counsel of the outworking of God's plans for the redemption of humanity and of the universe. The great and merciful God through the enabling of the Holy Spirit and the mediation of the Christ is pleased to work in conjunction with humans who pray sincerely, "Your kingdom come, your will be done."

Who Are We Who Pray?

By assessing the teachings and example of Jesus, we see that true prayer is particularly pertinent to persons who are suffering unjustly, who are becoming weary and might lose their faith in God because they have not received justice over an opponent. By continued prayer, that is devout communication with God, these persons express their trust in God. In point of fact, as staggering as such a conclusion is, God identifies with them. God is like these suffering persons because Jesus taught his parables while on his way to Jerusalem where he would suffer unjustly and cry out in anguish. Therefore, we, too, must always be concerned with those suffering and not be one of those making others suffer. Prioritizing Jesus' commandments into the plan of action of our lives aligns us more with the tax-collector than with the Pharisee, for against God's nature we can honestly recognize our failings and we can be freed to rely on God to raise us up.

Thus, when we pray, we need to remember above all to whom we pray. We pray to the just and compassionate Judge who sees in secret, therefore we should not be people who while praying evaluate our piety and the quality of our prayer-life in comparison with other people's. While having the right form of prayer is fine, God looks at the praying heart. Our hearts must be given to God, obedient to Christ's commandments, gentle, merciful, and generous with others. We must be working on being good and faithful servants who need not be ashamed when our house-owner returns and calls us to account.

When and Where Did Jesus Pray?

Prayer, we found, was a frequent and indispensable part of Jesus' life. Jesus regularly prayed at a time and place where distractions were unlikely to occur. He also prayed publicly as well. And he prayed with sympathetic groups. Following his example we should seek intimate prayer in secluded places at times we will be undisturbed. We should also pray in public and join our prayers with those of a sympathetic group, which, when united in prayer, becomes the body of Christ on earth. Although we, too, may find ourselves praying all through the night as Jesus did, we should not simply be out to imitate Jesus' schedule in an artificial manner. Better we should imitate Jesus' fervency in a genuine manner and let that fervency encourage the times and places we pray. Karl Rahner in his book *Spiritual Exercises*, which is a compilation of student notes gathered from retreats he has led on the prayer program of Ignatius of Loyola, wrote, "The Church is not supposed to be a military academy in which everything is uniform, but she is supposed to be the Body of Christ in which He, the one Spirit, exerts His power in all the members. Each one of these members proves that he really is a member of this Body by letting the other members be."[1]

God is interested in why we are praying, for "the why" dictates "what" we pray for and "the how" of our praying becomes the "what's" structured form.

Why Did Jesus Pray?

Jesus prayed in order to help himself make decisions. Prayer was also necessary for Jesus to help him endure the overwhelming demands of his work. In prayer Jesus spoke with his loving Father, who had sent him to do God's will on earth. And prayer was a time when the Father spoke back to the Son showing God's approval and good pleasure. The prospect of Jesus without prayer is inconceivable, as if a child could live a lifetime in a home where there was absolutely no communication with the parents who were taking care of the child, guiding the child's life, helping instill the values that would end in the child's happy and productive maturity -- inconceivable. Prayer for Jesus was the active, extended, and regular communication to God from a loving heart and an obedient life.

In this context Jesus' prayers for his disciples and for us who would follow pleaded with God for unity among us all, a unity that reflects the complete symbiotic love of the one God, that is, plurality in perfect unity. Jesus begged for protection for his disciples while they are in the world and asked that the love of God be given to the disciples. Jesus' prayers were overwhelmingly others-oriented, even while he was facing his own impending death.

Jesus' teaching on why we should pray emphasizes, too, our aligning ourselves completely with God and with each other. The point of answered prayer, he informs us, is the bearing of good fruits. Whatever prayers help us to remain in God, to glorify God, complete our joy, and make us disciples are the prayers God answers potently. A behavioral response is demanded by Jesus' covenant style of prayer, a prayer-life that demands an a-priori agreement between

---

[1] Karl Rahner, S. J., *Spiritual Exercises*, trans. Kenneth Barker, S.J. (New York: Herder and Herder, 1965), p. 255.

God and people: God to answer prayer, people to obey Jesus' commandments. In the behavioral response explicitly highlighted by Jesus, we should be forgiving others and seeking forgiveness and expending our energies in doing good actions, if we expect to get our prayers answered. These are conditions demanded by our part of the covenant. Such behavior shows we are one with God and makes our prayers acceptable to God. Asking not challenging or demanding or doubting or judging is also part of what being at one with Christ in God means. Asking implies remaining at one with God through humility and obedient service to God and one another. If we do these things and fulfill our share of the covenant, then like that of our Lord Jesus the Messiah our calling will become clearer, our work for God will become more powerful, our relationship with God will become more genuine, and possibly we will hear God communicating back to us, commending us as good and faithful servants.

How Did Jesus Pray?

How, then, should we pray? Let us recall how Jesus prayed. Jesus gave simple, short, sincere, God-centered, action-oriented prayers. Jesus taught how to pray by modeling his prayers, which were, nonetheless for being modeled, genuine and sincere prayers. We learn from him humbly to pray simple prayers focused on God, assuring God the behavior God expects of us is being done. Our prayers need not be eloquent and lengthy. But they must be genuine. We are free to express our emotions, if reverently done.

The posture we assume with our body articulates as much as our words do. If we stand, we proclaim God as Judge of judges. If we kneel or fall to our faces, we proclaim God as King of kings. If we lift our hands toward heaven, we proclaim God Priest of priests, blessing others as Jesus did. Prayer postures in the New Testament are used to express grief, fear, petition, thanksgiving, adoration, worship, blessing. Similarly, as we create new positions of prayer, we need to analyze what we are stating in a symbolic way. Our postures tell us about ourselves and our God. Are we sentenced persons before a judge, kneeling for mercy or petition? Are we funnels of God's blessings? Are we priests representing the one pure God?

Practices like fasting, which may be fine practices in themselves, have been none-the-less added to Jesus' words and the church's understanding of what prayer is. But Jesus did not emphasize this kind of asceticism, rather he emphasized remaining in God. Well-fed warriors are sent out into warfare. And we need to be well-fed spiritually through prayer. In the same manner new practices like closing the eyes and sitting, folding the hands, have been added to prayer in the years that have intervened between Jesus' teaching and the church today. Along with these additions, important things have been lost. As John Wesley noted in his Journal on August 15, 1750:

> That the grand reason why the miraculous gifts were so soon withdrawn, was not only that faith and holiness were well nigh lost; but that dry, formal, orthodox men began even then to ridicule whatever gifts they had not themselves, and to decry them all as either madness or imposture.[2]

The God who takes away can also be the God who gives, and renovating our spiritual and physical lives and rejuvenating our prayer lives may elicit God's gracious re-granting of missing gifts to all of us and all our churches.

Key to all aspects of our prayer life, we see, is our attitude. St. Teresa gives us a delightful prescription in her classic, *The Interior Castle*:

> All [the soul's] concern is taken up with how to please Him more and how or where it will show Him the love it bears Him. This is the reason for prayer, my daughters, the purpose of this spiritual marriage: the birth always of good works, good works (7:4:6).

In a contemporary Christianity, plagued with piousness that masks secret lives of adultery, greed, deceit, and selfish ambition, the fulfilling of our end of the covenant with lives of holiness becomes of cardinal importance. St. Teresa knew that prayer is of greater benefit and consequence "when our deeds conform with what we say in prayer." She knew that doing God's will was directly proportional to improving the benefits of prayer, so she counseled, "Let the soul bend its will if it wishes that prayer be beneficial to it. . . ." (7:4:7). So she left us with a message that everyone who would wish to be called by God a Christian should take seriously to heart today, "Fix your eyes on the Crucified. . . . If His Majesty showed us His love by means of such

---

[2] *The Works of John Wesley*, II (Grand Rapids: Zondervan, 1872), p. 204.

works and frightful torments, how is it that you want to please Him only with words?" (7:4:8).[3]

Prayer is part of a life of action. Prayer to the Jesus who walked among us, healed us, was crucified for us, and rose in majesty and power for us can never be merely empty words thrown as a pious bone to placate the deity. Prayer is the emotional expression of a life of active faith that seeks to heal, to reconcile, to raise others up, to fulfill the commandments of Jesus by those joyful people who want to be his true disciples.

In word and deed, praise God.

[3] Teresa of Avila, *The Interior Castle*, trans. Kieran Kavanaugh, O.C.D., and Otilio Rodriguez, O.C.D. (New York: Paulist Press, 1979), p. 190.

APPENDICES

BIBLIOGRAPHY

INDICES

Appendix A

Scripture References to Jesus and Prayer

Organized by Greek Word

[Parallel passage with a different Greek word]

(Passage mentioned in an earlier section)

+ Another Greek word for prayer is included in passage
Synonyms are listed under the more common word

Deomai "Pray for Needs"

Matt. 9:38
Luke 10:2
Luke 21:36 [Mark 13:18 *proseuchomai*; Matt. 24:20 *proseuchomai*]
Luke 22:32
Heb. 5:7 +*deesis, hiketeria, krauge, dakruo*

Erotao "Asking or Challenging Someone"

John 14:16; 16:23, 26; 17:9, 15, 20

Parakaleo "Summon Help"

Matt. 26:53

Anablepo "Look Up"; *Stenazo* "Sigh"

Matt. 14:19; Mark 6:41 +*eulogeo*; Luke 9:16 +*eulogeo*
Mark 7:34
John 11:41 *airo*
John 17:1 ep*airo*

Proseuchomai "Make a Sacred Vow to God"

Matt. 5:44; Luke 6:28
Matt. 6:5-9
Matt. 14:23; Mark 6:46
Matt. 19:13 [Mark 10:13-16 *kateulogeo*; Luke 18:15-17]
Matt. 21:13; Mark 11:17; Luke 19:46 *proseuche*
Matt. 26:36, 39; Mark 14:32, 35; Luke 22:40, 45-46 [John 12:27]
Mark 1:35 [Luke 4:42]
Mark 9:29
Mark 11:25
Luke 3:21 [Matt. 3:16; Mark 1:10; John 1:32]
Luke 5:16 [Mark 1:45]
Luke 6:12
Luke 9:18, 28-29 [Matt. 16:13; 17:1; Mark 8:27; 9:2]
Luke 11:2-13
Luke 18:1-14
(Matt. 24:20; Mark 13:18)

Eucharisteo "Give Thanks"

Matt. 15:36; Mark 8:6-7 +*eulogeo*
Luke 22:17, 19; Matt. 26:26-27 +*eulogeo*; Mark 14:22-23 +*eulogeo*
John 6:11
John 11:41, 43 +*lego, airo, krauge*

Humneo "Sing in Praise"

Heb. 2:12

Eulogeo "Bless"

Luke 24:30, 50
(Matt. 26:26; Mark 8:7; 10:16 *kateulogeo*; 14:22; Luke 9:16)

Agalliao "Rejoice Exceedingly"

Luke 10:21 +*exomologeo, lego*

Phoneo "Speak Loudly," *Boao* "Cry Aloud," *Krazo* "Shout"

Matt. 27:48 *anaboao*, 50; Mark 15:34, 37; Luke 23:46 +*lego*

Lego "Speak"

John 12:27
(John 11:41, 43; Luke 10:21; 11:2; 23:46)

Appendix B

Scripture References to Jesus and Prayer
Organized by Topic

[Parallel references which do not mention prayer]

Jesus' Exhortations and Teachings on Prayer

General Topics

Matt. 5:44; Luke 6:28 *proseuchomai*
Matt. 6:5-15 *proseuchomai*
Matt. 9:37-38 *deomai*
Matt. 21:13; Mark 11:17; Luke 19:46 *proseuchomai*
Mark 12:40; Luke 20:47 *proseuchomai*
Luke 10:2 *deomai*
Luke 18:1-14 *proseuchomai*
Luke 11:2-4 *proseuchomai*
Luke 21:34-36 *deomai*; Mark 13:18; Matt. 24:20 *proseuchomai*

Faith and Asking *aiteo*

Matt. 6:32; 7:7-11
Matt. 17:17-21; Mark 9:19-29 *proseuche*; Luke 9:41-43
Matt. 18:19-20
Matt. 21:20-22; Mark 11:20-25 *proseuchomai*
Luke 11:5-13; 17:6
John 14:13-14, 16: 16:26 +*erotao*; 15:7

Examples of Jesus in Prayer

Jesus Describes his Prayer

Luke 22:32 *deomai*
John 14:16; 16:26 *erotao*

Prayer at Meals

Matt. 14:19; Mark 6:41; Luke 9:16 *anablepo, eulogeo*; John 6:11, 23 *eucharisteo*
Matt. 15:36; Mark 8:6-7 *eucharisteo, eulogeo*
Matt. 26:26-27; Mark 14:22-23; Luke 22:17, 19 *eulogeo, eucharisteo*
Luke 24:30 *eulogeo*

Jesus' Practice of Prayer (other than at Meals)

Luke 3:21 *proseuchomai* [Matt. 3:16; Mark 1:10; John 1:32]
Matt. 14:23; Mark 6:46 *proseuchomai*
Mark 1:35 *proseuchomai* [Luke 4:42]
Luke 5:16 *proseuchomai* [Mark 1:45]
Luke 6:12
Luke 9:18, 28-29 *proseuchomai* [Matt. 16:13; 17:1; Mark 8:27; 9:2]
Luke 11:1 *proseuchomai*
Heb. 5:7 *deesis, hiketeria, krauge, dakruo*

Jesus' Words of Prayer

Matt. 6:9-13

"Therefore, in this way you yourselves pray (*proseuchomai*):

Father of ours, the One in the heavens,
let it be hallowed the name of yours,
let it come the rule (or reign or kingdom) of yours,
let it become the will of yours,
as in heaven also upon earth.
The bread of ours, the daily one, give to us today;
and forgive to us that which is owed by us,
as also we have forgiven (already) the things owed to us;
and do not bear us into temptation,
but rescue us from evil (or the Evil One)."

Luke 11:2-4 *proseuchomai*

And he said to them, "Whenever you pray (*proseuchomai*), say (*lego*),
Father, let it be praised the name of yours;
let it come the rule (or reign or kingdom) of yours;
the bread of ours, the one according to today, give to us today;
and forgive to us our sins, for also we are forgiving
all owing to us; and do not bear us into temptation.

Luke 10:21-22

In that hour he was extremely joyful (*agalliao*) in the Holy Spirit and said:
"I publicly praise you (*exomologeo*), Father, Lord of the heaven and the earth, for having hidden these things from wise and intelligent people and having revealed them to babies; yes, Father, that such a choice was pleasing to thee. Everything has been given to me by my Father, and no one knows who is the Son except the Father, and who is the Father except the Son, and to whomever the Son may wish to reveal."
(Matt. 11:25-26 also).

John 11:41-43

And Jesus raised up (*airo ano*) his eyes and said (*lego*):

"Father, I thank (*eucharisteo*) you that you heard me.
And I myself had known that always you hear me, but on account of the crowd standing around I spoke (*lego*), in order that they may believe that you yourself sent me."

John 12:27-28

"Now my soul is disturbed. And what shall I say (*lego*)? Father, deliver me out of this hour? Rather, on account of this I came into this hour. Father, glorify your name."

John 17:1-26 *erotao, epairo*

"Father, the hour has come; glorify your Son, in order that the Son may glorify you, just as you gave him authority over all flesh, in order that all whom you have given to him he might give to them eternal life. And this is eternal life, that they may know you, the only true God, and the one you sent, Jesus Christ. I myself glorified you upon the earth, the work having finished that you gave me that I might do; and now glorify me, you, Father, with you with the glory which I was having with (in the presence of) you before the world existed. I made known your name to the people whom you gave to me out of the world. Yours they were, and to me you gave them, and your word they kept. Now they know that all which you have given to me is from you; because the words which you gave to me I have given to them, and they themselves received and knew truly that from you I came out, and they believed that you yourself sent me. I myself ask concerning them; not concerning the world do I ask but concerning the ones whom you have given to me, because they are yours, and all that is mine is yours and yours is mine, and I have been glorified in them. And no longer I am in the world, and they themselves are in the world, and I to you am coming. Holy Father, keep them in your name which you have given me, in order that they may be one just as we (are). While I was with them I myself was keeping them in your name which you have given me, and I guarded (or protected), and no one out of them was destroyed except the son of destruction, in order that the Scripture might be fulfilled. And now to you I come, and these things I speak in the world in order that they may have my joy fulfilled in them. I myself have given them your word, and the world hated them, because they are not out of the world just as I myself am not out of the world. I do not ask that you might lift them out of the world but that you might keep them out of evil (or from the Evil One). Out of the world they are not, just as I myself am not out of the world. Sanctify them in the truth; your word is truth. Just as you sent me into the world, I also sent them into the world; and on behalf of them I myself sanctify, in order that also they themselves may be sanctified in truth. But not concerning these only do I ask, but also concerning the ones believing on account of their word in regard to me, in order that all may be one, just as you, Father, (are) in me and I in you, in order that also they may be in us, in order that the world may believe that you sent me. And the glory which you have given to me I have given to them, in order that they may be one just as we are one, I in them and you in me, in order that they may be perfected in unity, in order that the world may know that you sent me and loved them just as you loved me. Father, what you have given to me, I wish that where I am myself those may be with me, in order that they may perceive my glory which you have given me, because you loved me before the creation of the world. Righteous Father, also the world did not know you, but I myself knew you, and they themselves knew that you sent me, and I made known to them your name, and I will make known, in order that the love with which you loved me may be in them and I in them.

Matt. 26:39, 42, 44; Mark 14:36, 39; Luke 22:42

Three times Jesus prayed:

"Daddy, Father, all is possible to you;
bear away this cup from me;
but not what I myself wish but what you (wish)" (Mark 14:36).

"My Father, if it is possible, let this cup pass away from me; however, not as I myself wish but as you (wish)" (Matt. 26:39).

"My Father, if this cannot pass unless I drink it, let your will be done" (Matt. 26:42).

Matt. 27:46; Mark 15:34

At the ninth hour Jesus calls out to God in his despair:

"My God, my God, for what reason have you abandoned me?"
boao, anaboao, phoneo

Matt. 27:50; Mark 15:37; Luke 23:46
"Father, into your hands I entrust my spirit!"
phoneo, phone, megale, krazo

Appendix C

How did Jesus Keep From Praying As the Gentiles Did?
(A Comparison of John 17:1-19 with Matthew 6:1-18
and John 14:9-27)

While introducing his model prayer in Matthew 6:7-8, Jesus warned his disciples not to pray as do the pagans who do not know the true nature of God and therefore must pray with many words. We see how few words he himself used in the last prayers of Jesus recorded in Gethsemane and on the cross and we recall how few words Jesus recommended in his model prayers. The lone exception to the rule might appear to be in John 17. Readers often seem to get tangled up in all the prepositional phrases, in the term "the world" repeated again and again, in the apparent repetition of the plea for "being one," until a reader might wonder if these are not indeed many words.

Simplicity in Jesus' Prayers

Does Jesus vary his language when he prays? He has warned his disciples not to be like the Gentiles and babble (*battalogeo*) many words (*polulogia*), what we might depict as batting words of prayer out at God like so many fungo hits scattered into the outfields of heaven. But when we examine Jesus' own example of a major prayer (John 17), do we not wonder at first sight whether he has indeed employed many words? Again and again we hear prepositional phrases of but slight variation, and these are repeated up to four times in exact phrasing in the case of "not of the world," not to mention his fourteen repetitions of *kosmos* in a mere nineteen verses! Does he violate his own rule, disregard his own advice? Or, does his own language become more simple when he prays? A comparison with two teaching passages may begin to give us insight into what is distinctive about Jesus' style of praying.

To explore the complexity of Jesus' language, let us compare a 334 word sample of Jesus' prayer in John 17:1-19 with his teaching about prayer recorded in Matthew 6:1-18, a 344 word sample which also includes the brief two sentence "Lord's Prayer," a slight pericope unfortunately too brief to serve as a sample but still a provocative inclusion. As a control let us add a third sample from John 14:9-27, a 354 word sample which contains many of the same themes and even some phrases later included in John 17 but in this case as teaching and not as prayer. Thus we examine a teaching in Matthew 6 and a teaching in John 14 contrasted with a prayer in John 17 and a brief prayer taught in Matthew 6.

What we are asking in this study is, does Jesus vary his language when he prays to make it simpler? Does he follow his own advice when he preaches about prayer when giving his model prayer in Matthew 6:9-13 when he himself prays, as evidenced in his long prayer in John 17? Questions of how much the differences between Matthew's and John's presentations of praying differ simply because we have two different gospel writers are addressed by the inclusion of a control passage, John 14:9-27, as an example of John's presentation of Jesus' teaching as contrasted with Matthew's presentation of Jesus' teaching in Matthew 6.

What do we discover when all the data is recorded and analyzed? Figure #1 gives the breakdown of all the statistical data comparing the three passages in regard to the complexity of their language. What do we discover? The least complex is the John 17 passage, Jesus' own prayer, in regard to average clause length (syllables divided by number of clauses) (column I) and average sentence length (total number of syllables divided by sentences) (V). Thus, we see the clauses and sentence of Jesus' praying recorded in John 17 tend to be shorter than the sentence and clause lengths he employs when teaching, even when he is teaching his disciples how to pray in short units. We see that he links together the shorter prayer unit lengths of the Matthew 6 prayer into long sentences when he teaches how to pray, but the shorter sentence length of prayer is maintained in John 17 when Jesus himself prays.

All of the "Lord's Prayer" has been recorded as one or two sentences in Greek. While punctuation normally was not prevalent in the early uncial papryri scroll and codex manuscripts until scribes began to use punctuation marks more liberally in the sixth and seventh centuries,[1] when Sinaiticus, for example, was transcribed in the 300's, we can notice in the text that John 17 was accorded numerous punctuation marks while Matthew 6:9b-13, the "Lord's Prayer," received only one, the colon-appearing mark, the double point, which indicates in Sinaiticus the end of a passage or chapter. When scribes did add punctuation to the "Lord's Prayer," they recognized the organic unity of the ordering of the seven short main clauses with their almost Hebraic poetic matched pair quality, that unity that had kept earlier scribes from assigning punctuation. As a result commas and semicolons rather than periods are found today in the two standard Greek texts, Nestle-Aland and the United Bible Societies' *Greek New Testament*. Such a conclusion, however, was not accorded Jesus' own prayer in John 17. The text of John 17 in Sinaiticus is filled with stigmata separating its clauses, those points above and on the line which indicate stops.[2] Sinaiticus indicates sixteen periods and six semicolons in our sample of Jesus' prayer in John 17 against six commas plus two semicolons and only two periods in Jesus' taught prayer in Matthew 6:9b-13 in the UBSGNT text. The Nestle-Aland text has only recorded one period. The punctuation assigned to Jesus' words shows, then, that the earliest scribes through today's committees recognized that Jesus maintained short sentence units when he prayed but linked these short clauses together into longer didactic sentences when he taught these units as a model of how to pray.

On the other hand, both the John 17 prayer and Matthew 6 teaching passage have almost the exact same ratio of clauses to main clauses (column II).[3] This we derive from dividing the total number of clauses by the total number of main clauses. Therefore, both the

---

[1] See F. G. Kenyon, *The Chester Beatty Biblical Papyri: Descriptions and Texts of Twelve Manuscripts on Papyrus of the Greek Bible. Fasciculus II: The Gospels and Acts* (London: Emery Walker Limited, 1933), p. ix; B. Metzger, *The Text of the New Testament: Its Transmission, Corruption, and Restoration* (New York: Oxford University, 1968), pp. 26-27.

[2] A. T. Robertson, *A Grammar of the Greek New Testament in the Light of Historical Research* (Nashville: Broadman, 1934), pp. 241-243; F. Blass and A. Debrunner, *A Greek Grammar of the New Testament and Other Early Christian Literature*, trans. and ed. R. Funk (Chicago: University of Chicago), 1961, p. 10

[3] The text used for gathering data is the UBSGNT except where otherwise noted.

Matthew 6 teaching passage and the John 17 praying passage contain about the same amount of subordination.

John 14 in contrast has the least amount of ratio of clauses to main clauses. Therefore, the teaching passage in John 14 is the least complex of the three passages in two areas. It has the least subordinate clauses (that is, it has more main clauses to total clauses) and its average main clause length is shorter.

In regard to word size (figure #3), that is, the distribution between monosyllabic and polysyllabic words, the two John passages are more similar to each other than to Matthew. This can be expected since the material in both passages is similar. In regard to sentence changes (figure #4), too, the two John passages are more similar to each other than to Matthew in regard to addition (pleonasms, polysyndeton) and omissions (largely ellipsis). In the case of transpositions, the most dramatic similarity between the two John passages occurs. Both John passages tend to move the verbs to the end of clauses while the Matthew passage seems to move the verbs forward to positions preceding the nouns.

On the other hand, the verbs provide a dramatic proof that Jesus does simplify his language when he prays in the case of verb density (figure #5). According to *Paul's Literary Style*, the stylistic/linguistic study of Paul's manner of communicating, "As the verb density decreases, the language tends to be more structured and clearer to read."[4] That is, the message is more direct, more spelled out. Both the Matthew 6 and John 14 teaching passages contain far more verbals (15 and 11 infinitives and participles respectively) than does the John 17 passage (3). While the John 17 passage contains the most number of finite verbs, it also contains the least number of passive verbs and the fewest adverbs. Therefore, when Jesus teaches as in Matthew 6 or even teaches the same material as in John 14, the verb density increases. When he prays it decreases. Thus, when he prays he is more direct and in that sense simpler.

John 14, suprisingly, has the greatest number of main clauses to sentences. In fact, it has many clauses. Why is this? We will look at a possible reason for this particular difference when we contrast all

---

[4] Aída Besançon Spencer, *Paul's Literary Style: A Stylistic and Historical Comparison of II Corinthians 11:16-12:13, Romans 8:9-39, and Philippians 3:2-4:13, An Evangelical Theological Society Monograph* (Winona Lake: Eisenbrauns, 1984), p. 64.

of our findings about Jesus' style of praying and teaching with a still larger control, Paul's varying of style in his communication with similar recipients to Jesus'. In the meantime, we note John 14 is distinquished by many main clauses, the least number of subordinate clauses, and by the most main clauses per sentence. Yet these main clauses are of the shortest length in our three samples (for example, "I am with you this time and do you not know me, Philip?" "The one having seen me has seen the Father." "But the Father remaining in me does his works." "Otherwise, on account of these works believe.")

Now, when this material in John 14 is prayed in John 17, Jesus becomes shorter in the length of his sentences, but the ratio of clauses to main clauses increases. This appears to be because he is re-establishing relationships between God and Jesus' disciples and explanation is needed. The preponderance of prepositional phrases, many of which are repeated, carefully set the nature and boundaries of these relationships.

Similar in all three passages is Jesus' use of simple/compound versus compound/complex sentences. The totals 2 simple as opposed to 13 compound/complex sentences in John 17 and 1 simple versus 11 compound/complex sentences in Matthew 6 appear nearly identical. Both passages are overwhelmingly compound/complex, suggesting that this is the nature of Jesus' discourse whether he is teaching or praying. On the other hand, the use of personal pronouns increases dramatically in the two John passages when Jesus is speaking with intimates (91 in John 14, 78 in John 17) than when he is publicly preaching (52 in Matthew 6). Thus in John the sense of intimacy is created by the extensive use of pronouns as opposed to Matthew 6 where Jesus creates intimacy by using definite articles (65 or 18.9% in Matthew 6 versus 41 or 12.3% in John 17). Jesus' style in all three passages is markedly a nominal rather than a verbal style (figure #6). He employs 134 nouns and adjectives in Matthew 6, 133 in John 17, and 141 in John 14, while he uses 83 verbals (verbs, participles, infinitives, adverbs) in Matthew 6, 94 in John 14, and 82 in John 17. While these similarities of style draw the passages together, at the same time in contrast in Matthew 6 he uses adverbs to describe a concept, for example, be as this, not as that, not like this, but like that. These are descriptive comparisons, some even extended metaphors. In John 17, however, much meaning is packed into the repeated simple phrases. He builds a chain of identities, creating a kind of name tag out of the prepositional phrases. So, the disciples become "the disciples you gave me out of the world," the prepositional phrases identifying Jesus' and the disciples' relationships to the world, to each other, and to the Father.

What the sampling shows, essentially, is that while Jesus' sentence length may have decreased, the complexity of his thought, shown by the increase of subordinating clauses, has increased. So we see by this that whatever Jesus meant by fewer words, his introduction of subordinate clauses to convey his complexity of thought is not a part of what Jesus means. Coming to the Parent as a little child does not mean doing so in puerility of mind.

The Matthew 6 teaching passage on its side has the most variety in three ways and in one way it is as complex as John 14. In nearly four out of five of its columns (figure #1) it has the highest level of complexity. The greatest difference can be seen in columns I and III in the average clause lengths. The prayer in John 17 has the shortest average clause length, perhaps, because it is communicated to the most intimate audience, the Father. John 14 to Jesus' inner disciples is a little longer in clause length. The Matthew 6 teaching to the disciples and beyond them to the crowds contains the largest clause length of the three. And the same fact is true of the average sentence length. Matthew has the longest, followed by John 14. And John 17 has the shortest.

Therefore, we can observe that when Jesus says to use few words and not pray as do the Gentiles, he seems by his own example to mean in regard to length of clauses and length of sentences. Praying in few words for Jesus is done in short clauses and short sentences. He does not mean in complexity of thought. Jesus' thought in John 17 is complex as he balances off the relationships: the disciples with himself, the disciples with the Father, the Father with Jesus, the watching world with all. But he prays in simple, brief clauses in shorter sentence lengths than the ones he uses in teaching.

Now, we notice that when we examine all the statistical data, the three columns that yield the most relative difference, the most significant for our study are, first, with the greatest difference, the average clause length, second, the average main clause length, and third, the average sentence length. While the first category and the third fit into the pattern we have observed, John 17 standing in contrast to the two teaching passages in regard to its simpler clause and sentence length, category III, the average main clause length, belongs to John 14. Matthew 6, we see, is highest in average main clause length, followed by the prayer of John 17. John 14's teaching passage is lowest. So, while the prayer may have the shortest average clause length and sentence length, it does not have the shortest average main clause length. Why not?

A fascinating comparison can be made if we compare the findings of Paul's communication with his churches in *Paul's Literary Style* (figure #2) with these two columns of most difference in Jesus' communication. As we recall, the Corinthian church was currently hostile to Paul. The Romans were not known directly by him and the Philippians were most open and friendly. Can we compare these examples with Jesus'?

We do not often recognize the undercurrent of anxiety of Jesus in the great teaching passages of which John 14 is a part, but it is certainly there. The passages begin with the souring of the triumphal entry celebration when Jesus is confronted by the Greeks in John 12:20ff. Realizing his hour has come, he finds his soul troubled, hides himself, suffers the calumny of the Pharisees in his absence. The passages peak as Jesus, exasperated with Philip's asking to see the Father, cries in John 14:9, "How can you say, 'Show us the Father?'" Frustrated, he pleads in 14:11, at least believe for the sake of the works themselves. The entire teaching ends in chapter 16 as Jesus queries in John 16:31-32, "Do you now believe? Look, the hour is coming, indeed it has come, when you will be scattered each to his own home and me you will leave alone . . . ." Essentially, Jesus is not certain about his disciples and their loyalty. He is certain about their understanding of him -- they are clearly confused. This must be why he fills the John 14 teaching passage full of promises in the main clauses. And these promises depend on conditions placed in subordinate, or what we call conditional clauses. The emphasis in John 14 finally rests upon the promises available to these vacillating disciples and the kind of behavior required to receive them. What we see in the prayer in John 17, however, is Jesus is certain about his Parent and his Parent's loyalty.

A rough parallel can be drawn for comparison purposes between the findings of Paul's varying of style with the three churches and Jesus' communicating with his three audiences: the uncertain disciples in John 14, the disciples and the crowds beyond them in Matthew 6, and his heavenly Parent in John 17. The hostile Corinthians can be paralleled with the uncertain disciples as the group least understanding of his message. The Romans whom Paul had not met are similar to the crowds Jesus did not know in his formal address in Matthew 6, the Sermon on the Mount. Finally, the open and friendly Philippians are most parallel of Paul's three groups to Jesus' intimate communicating with his Father. What do we find? Striking similarities.

In comparing the ratio of clauses to main clauses (total number of clauses divided by total number of main clauses) in figure #2, we see that both Paul and Jesus employed the least number of subordinate clauses and the most number of main clauses in communicating with the hostile Corinthians and the uncertain disciples. Meanwhile Paul and Jesus employed the medium number of subordinate clauses with the unknown Romans and half-known crowds (disciples plus crowds), and the most with the friendly Philippians and the loving Father (though this final figure and that of the early open disciples and crowds are nearly identical).

We have noted that in the ratio of these main clauses to sentences (total number of main clauses divided by total number of sentences) the greatest number of main clauses to sentences occurs in communication with the hostile Corinthians and with the uncertain disciples, a marked difference here. The other two figures are relatively the same: 1.67 for the Romans, 1.63 for the Philippians as contrasted with 2.3 for the crowds, 2.4 for the Father. Thus we see that hostility and uncertainty, betrayal and desertion, which characterize the Corinthians' dealings with Paul and the disciples' with Jesus, appear to form the reason for the communicating difference, not the consideration of whether Jesus is praying or preaching.

Circumlocution in Pagan Prayers

What, in contrast, did pagans do in their "endless repetitions"? Interestingly, a major portion of pagan repetition in prayer was comprised of evoking the names for the deity. Under the editorship of Hans Dieter Betz a team of scholars translated the Greek magical papyri collected by Preisendanz and the demotic spells. Typically, these pagan prayers consist of an elongated evocation of a deity, followed by a recounting of an incident from that god's legend and a plea for the incident to be reenacted in the life of the one praying, and often the prayer ends with a howling ululation of the god's name.

So one prayer, for example, begins "(IA)RBATH AGRAMME PHIBLO CHOEMEO" (the names of the gods), passes into a divine howl, "(AE) EEE IIII OOOOO YYYYYY OOOOOO (O)," then makes one's request, in this case that the gods see in the sick for whom prayer is being offered Helene who was healed in legend and therefore that the gods condescend to heal. The name of the god(s) is then repeated and howling ends the prayer. Another Egyptian prayer, translated into 269 words, consists of 226 words devoted to the divine names and 57 words asking for aid to be sent "immediately, immediately, quickly, quickly" (PGM XIXa, 1-15). Yet others (like PGM XIXb, Part 2, 16-54 and PGM CXVI 1-17) consist primarily of a magical design made of the god's name preceding the brief request.[5] Nearly endless repetitions and elaborations of the divine name(s) are what are central. The god's name is invoked as magic. The god is flattered into action. The god is pushed by a plea of urgency and often shrieked to as an opening and closing of the prayer. How greatly these elaborate charms contrast with the simple plea of Jesus to the one Father in heaven.

Summary

In summary we see that when Jesus tells us not to pray as do the Gentiles, he exemplifies in his own example a style complex in thought in regard to ratio of main clauses and subordinate clauses to sentences yet simple in regard to directness of speech, using finite verbs to say what he means, not couching his requests in passive verbs, or enhancing them with adverbs, or slipping them into participles and infinitives. He also employs short average clause lengths and short sentence lengths. While not babbling many words (a related noun form *batalos* means stammerer), Jesus still employs many words to pray long prayers and even repeats words in prayer, as his repetition of *kosmos* shows. What he does not do is pray in an indirect, roundabout fashion of long convoluted sentences filled with verbals and passives and divine names and divine flattery. He prays in direct concrete speech in short sentences. He says what he means and then stops.

---

[5] Hans Dieter Betz, ed. *The Greek Magical Papyri in Translation including the Demotic Spells* (Chicago: University of Chicago, 1986), pp. 323, 256, 257, 314.

Figure #1: COMPLEXITY OF WRITING

	I	II	III	IV	V
	AVERAGE CLAUSE LENGTH (Syllables + # of Clauses)	RATIO OF CLAUSES TO MAIN CLAUSES (Total # of clauses + Total # of Main Clauses)	AVERAGE MAIN CLAUSE LENGTH (Total # of Syllables + Total # of Main Clauses)	RATIO OF MAIN CLAUSES TO SENTENCES (Total # of Main Clauses + Total # of Sentences)	AVERAGE SENTENCE LENGTH (Total # of Syllables + Sentences)
John 14:9-27	723 69 10.48 (80.01%)	69 43 1.604 (86.24%)	723 43 16.81 (69.12%)	43 15 2.866 (100%)	723 15 48.2 (84.9%)
John 17:1-19	654 67 9.76 (74.56%)	67 36 1.861 (100%)	654 36 18.166 (74.696%)	36 15 2.4 (83.74%)	654 15 43.6 (76.8%)
Matthew 6:1-18	681 52 13.096 (100%)	52 28 1.857 (99.8%)	681 28 24.32 (81.41%)	28 12 2.33 (100%)	681 12 56.75 (100%)
Matthew 6:1-8, 14-18	556 46 12.636	44 21 2.095	556 21 26.476	44 10 2.1	556 10 55.6
Matthew 6:9-13	125 8 15.625	8 7 1.143	125 7 17.857	7 2 3.5	125 2 62.5

Figure # 2: COLUMNS 2 & 4 COMPARING PAUL'S EPISTLES VS. GOSPELS

II Corinthians 11:16-12:13		108 = 1.5 72		72 = 2.3 31	
Romans 8:9-39		80 = 1.8 45		45 = 1.666 27	
Philippians 3:2-4:13		81 = 2.1 39		39 = 1.625 24	
John 14:9-27		69 = 1.604 43		43 = 2.86 15	
Matthew 6:1-18		52 = 1.857 28		28 = 2.33 12	
John 17:1-19		67 = 1.86 36		36 = 2.4 15	

Figure #3: WORD SIZE

	John 14	Matthew 6	John 17
Total Words	354	344	334
Monosyllable	145 (41%)	158 (46%)	137 (41%)
Polysyllable of 2 or more	59 %	54%	59%
Polysyllable of 3 or more	23%	26.7%	20.7%
2 syllable words	129 (36.4%)	94 (27.3%)	12.8 (38.3%)
3 syllable words	49 (13.8%)	49 (14.2%)	41 (12.3%)
4 syllable words	31 (8.8%)	43 (12.5%)	28 (8.4%)

Figure #4: SENTENCE CHANGES

	John 14	Matthew 6	John 17
Addition	19	15	26
Omission	8	0	5
Substitution	50	35	35
Transposition	23	22	26
Total	100	72	87

Figure #5: VERB DENSITY

	John 14	Matthew 6	John 17
Verbs	62	50	64
Verbals	11	15	3
FINITE VERBS			
Active	57	47	62
Passive	5	3	1
VERBALS			
Infinitives	1	6	1
Participles	10	9	3
Adverbs	21	19+	16
VERB DENSITY	17.74%	30%	4.69%

Figure #6: NOMINAL VERSUS VERBAL STYLE

	John 14	Matthew 6	John 17
Nominal (Noun and Adjective)	141	134	133
Verbal (Verb, Adverb, Verbal)	94	84	82

Figure #7: SENTENCE SIZE AND STRUCTURE

	John 14	Matthew 6	John 17
Main Clauses	40	38	36
Subordinate Clauses	29	24	31
Total	69	52	67

Figure #8: EXPLICIT PRONOUNS

John 14	Matthew 6	John 17
91	52	78

Figure #9: DEFINITE ARTICLE

John 14	Matthew 6	John 17	
49 (13.8%)	65 (18.9%)	41 (12.3%)	% of all words

Bibliography

Abbott, Lyman. *An Illustrated Commentary on the Gospel according to St. John*. New York: A. S. Barnes, 1879.

Aland, Kurt, and others. *The Greek New Testament*. 3d ed. New York: United Bible Societies, 1975.

Anderson, Hugh. *The Gospel of Mark*. New Century Bible. London: Oliphants, 1976.

Augustine, St. *The Lord's Sermon on the Mount,* trans. John J. Jepson. Ancient Christian Writers. Westminster, Maryland: Newman, 1956.

Barth, Karl. *Prayer according to the Catechisms of the Reformation*, trans. Sara F. Terrien. Philadelphia: Westminster, 1952.

Bauer, Walter. *A Greek-English Lexicon of the New Testament and Other Early Christian Literature*, trans. and ed. William F. Arndt and F. Wilbur Gingrich. 4th ed. Chicago: University of Chicago, 1957.

Bernard, J. H. *A Critical and Exegetical Commentary on the Gospel according to St. John*. 2 vols. International Critical Commentary. Edinburgh: T. & T. Clark, 1928.

Berrigan, Daniel. *The Words Our Savior Gave Us*. Springfield, IL: Templegate, 1978.

Betz, Hans Dieter, ed., *The Greek Magical Papyri in Translation, including the Demotic Spells*. Chicago: University of Chicago, 1986.

Blass, F. and A. DeBrunner. *A Greek Grammar of the New Testament and Other Early Christian Literature*, trans. and ed. Robert W. Funk. 9th ed. Chicago: University of Chicago, 1961.

Bloesch, Donald G. *The Struggle of Prayer*. San Francisco: Harper and Row, 1980.

Brown, Francis, S. R. Driver and Charles A. Briggs. *A Hebrew and English Lexicon of the Old Testament*. Oxford: Clarendon, 1907.

Bruce, F. F. *The Gospel of John*. Grand Rapids: Eerdmans, 1983.

Bultmann, Rudolph. *The Gospel of John: A Commentary*, trans. G. R. Beasley-Murray; R. W. N. Hoare, and J. K. Riches. Philadelphia: Westminster, 1971.

Buttrich, George A., and others. *The Interpreter's Dictionary of the Bible*. 5 vols. Nashville: Abingdon, 1962.

Calvin, John. *Calvin's Commentaries: John - Acts*. Wilmington, Delaware: Associated Publishers and Authors, n. d.

_______. *The Gospel according to St. John 11-21 and the First Epistle of John*, trans. T. H. L. Parker. Calvin's Commentaries. Grand Rapids: Eerdmans, 1961.

_______. *A Harmony of the Gospels: Matthew, Mark and Luke, Vol. 3, and the Epistles of James and Jude*, trans. A. W. Morrison. Calvin's Commentaries. Grand Rapids: Eerdmans, 1972.

Cary, M. and others, eds. *The Oxford Classical Dictionary*. Oxford: Clarendon, 1949.

Chase, Frederick Henry. *The Lord's Prayer in the Early Church*, ed. J. Armitage Robinson. Texts and Studies: Contributions to Biblical and Patristic Literature, Vol. 1, No. 3. Cambridge: University, 1891.

Cohoon, J. W. and others, trans. *Dio Chrysostom*. 5 vols. Loeb Classical Library. Cambridge: Harvard University, 1932.

Colson, F. H. and others, trans. *Philo*. 10 vols. Loeb Classical Library. Cambridge: Harvard University, 1929.

Dana, H. E. and Julius R. Mantey. *A Manual Grammar of the Greek New Testament*. New York: Macmillan, 1955.

Danby, Herbert, trans. *The Mishnah*. Oxford: Oxford University, 1933.

Edersheim, Alfred. *The Life and Times of Jesus the Messiah*. 2 vols. 3d ed. Grand Rapids: Eerdmans, 1947.

Ellul, Jacques. *Prayer and Modern Man*. New York: Seabury, 1970.

Epstein, I., ed. *The Babylonian Talmud*. 35 vols. London: Soncino, 1948.

Eusebius. *The History of the Church from Christ to Constantine*, trans. G. A. Williamson. Minneapolis: Augsburg, 1975.

Feldman, L. H. and others, trans. *Josephus*. 10 vols. Loeb Classical Library. Cambridge: Harvard University Press, 1965.

Finney, Charles. *Prevailing Prayer: Sermons on Prayer*. Grand Rapids: Kregel, 1965.

Freese, John Henry, trans. *Aristotle: The "Art" of Rhetoric*. Loeb Classical Library. Cambridge: Harvard University, 1926.

Gaertner, Bertil. *Iscariot*. Philadelphia: Fortress, 1971.

Gardiner, E. Norman. *Athletics of the Ancient World*. Chicago: Ares, 1930.

Godet, F. *Commentary on the Gospel of St. John*, trans. S. Taylor and M. D. Cusin. 3 vols. Edinburgh: T. & T. Clark, 1900.

Grenfell, B. P., and others. *The Tebtunis Papyri*. 2 vols. London: University of California, 1938.

Gruenler, Royce Gordon. *The Trinity in the Gospel of John: A Thematic Commentary on the Fourth Gospel*. Grand Rapids: Baker, 1986.

Gundry, Robert H. *Matthew: A Commentary on His Literary and Theological Art*. Grand Rapids: Eerdmans, 1982.

Harner, Philip B. *Understanding the Lord's Prayer*. Philadelphia: Fortress, 1975.

Heiler, Friedrich. *Prayer: A Study in the History and Psychology of Religion*, trans. and ed. Samuel McComb and J. Edgar Park. New York: Oxford University, 1932.

Hick, John. *Evil and the God of Love*. New York: Harper and Row, 1978.

Higgins, A. J. B. *The Lord's Supper in the New Testament*. London: SCM, 1952.

Hodgson, Leonard. *The Lord's Prayer*. New York: Longmans, Green and Company, 1934.

Horsley, G. H. R. *New Documents Illustrating Early Christianity: A Review of the Greek Inscriptions and Papyri Published in 1978*. Macquarie University: Ancient History Documentary Research Center, 1982.

Hunter, W. Bingham. *The God Who Hears*. Downers Grove: InterVarsity, 1986.

An Inclusive Language Lectionary: Readings for Year A. Philadelphia: Westminster, 1983.

Jeremias, Joachim. *The Eucharistic Words of Jesus*, trans. Norman Perrin. New York: Scribner, 1966.

______. *Jerusalem in the Time of Jesus*, trans. F. H. and C. H. Cave. Philadelphia: Fortress, 1969.

______. *The Lord's Prayer*, trans. John Reumann. Philadelphia: Fortress, 1964.

_______. *The Parables of Jesus*, trans. S.H. Hooke. 2d ed. London: SCM, 1954.

_______. *The Prayers of Jesus*, trans. John Bowden, Christoph Burchard, John Reumann. Studies in Biblical Theology, 6. London: SCM, 1967.

Kemelman, Harry. *Conversations with Rabbi Small*. New York: Morrow, 1981.

Kenyon, Frederic G. *The Chester Beatty Biblical Papyri: Descriptions and Texts of Twelve Manuscripts on Papyrus of the Greek Bible: Fasciculus II: The Gospels and Acts*. London: Emery Walker Limited, 1933.

Kittel, Gerhard, ed. *Theological Dictionary of the New Testament*, trans. Geoffrey W. Bromiley. 10 vols. Grand Rapids: Eerdmans, 1965.

Lake, Kirsopp, trans. *The Apostolic Fathers*. Loeb Classical Library. Cambridge: Harvard University, 1912.

Laubach, Frank C. *Prayer: The Mightiest Force in the World*. 2d ed. New York: Revell, 1946.

Laymon, Charles M. *The Lord's Prayer in Its Biblical Setting*. Nashville: Abingdon, 1968.

Lewis, C. S. *The Lion, the Witch, and the Wardrobe*. New York: Macmillan, 1950.

Liddell, Henry George and Robert Scott. *A Greek-English Lexicon*, ed. Sir Henry Stuart Jones and Roderick McKenzie. 9th ed. Oxford: Clarendon, 1940.

Lohmeyer, Ernst. *"Our Father": An Introduction to the Lord's Prayer*, trans. John Bowden. New York: Harper and Row, 1965.

Lyall, Francis. *Slaves, Citizens, Sons: Legal Metaphors in the Epistles*. Grand Rapids: Zondervan, 1984.

MacMahon, Henry and Jeanie MacPherson. *The King of Kings: A Novel*. New York: Grosset and Dunlop, 1927.

Madsen, Norman P. *Lord, Teach Us to Pray: Jesus and Christian Prayer*. Huntington, Indiana: Our Sunday Visitor, 1983.

Marsh, John. *Saint John*. Westminster Pelican Commentaries. Philadelphia: Westminster, 1968.

Marshall, I. Howard. *The Gospel of Luke: A Commentary on the Greek Text*. The New International Greek Testament Commentary. Grand Rapids: Eerdmans, 1978.

Metzger, Bruce M. "How Many Times Does *'Epiousios'* Occur Outside the Lord's Prayer?" *The Expository Times*, LXIX: 52-54, Nov., 1957.

_______. *The Text of the New Testament: Its Transmission, Corruption, and Restoration*. 2d ed. New York: Oxford University, 1968.

Morris, Leon. *The Gospel according to John: The English Text with Introduction, Exposition and Notes*. The New International Commentary on the New Testament. Grand Rapids: Eerdmans, 1971.

Murray, Andrew: *With Christ in the School of Prayer*. New York: Revell, 1885.

Neusner, Jacob. *Genesis Rabbah: The Judaic Commentary to the Book of Genesis, A New American Translation*. 3 vols. Atlanta: Scholar's Press, 1985.

_______. *The Tosefta*. 6 vols. New York: KTAV, 1986.

New York Graphic Society. *Fine Art Reproductions of Old and Modern Masters: A Comprehensive Illustrated Catalog of Art through the Ages*. New York: New York Graphic Society, 1978.

Newman, Jr., Barclay, M. *A Concise Greek-English Dictionary of the New Testament*. London: United Bible Societies, 1971.

Nickerson, Colin. "Bernadette Devlin McAliskey on War, Peace, and Justice." *The Boston Globe*, November 8, 1982.

Oldfather, W. A., trans. *Epictetus: The Discourses as Reported by Arrian, The Manual, and Fragments*. 2 vols. Loeb Classical Library. Cambridge: Harvard, 1925.

Origen, *An Exhortation to Martyrdom, Prayer and Selected Works*, trans. Rowan A. Greer. The Classics of Western Spirituality. New York: Paulist, 1979.

Parker, William R. and Elaine St. Johns. *Prayer Can Change Your Life: Experiments and Techniques in Prayer Therapy*. Englewood Cliffs: Prentice-Hall, 1957.

Plummer, Alfred. *A Critical and Exegetical Commentary on the Gospel according to S. Luke*. The International Critical Commentary. 5th ed. Edinburgh: T. & T. Clark, 1922.

Rahner, Karl, S. J. *Spiritual Exercises*, trans. Kenneth Baker, S. J. New York: Herder and Herder, 1965.

Rauschenbusch, Walter. *Prayers of the Social Awakening*. Boston: Pilgrim, 1910.

Religious News Service. "TV Executives Differ Sharply from the Public on Moral Beliefs." *Christianity Today*, 27:7:56-58, April 8, 1983.

Richardson, C. C. "Worship in NT Times, Christian." *Interpreter's Dictionary of the Bible*, 1962, IV, 888.

Rimmer, Harry. *The Prayer Perfect*. New York: Fleming H. Revell, 1940.

Ringer, Robert J. *Looking Out for #1*. New York: Funk and Wagnalls, 1977.

Roberts, Alexander & Donaldson, James, eds. *The Writings of Quintus Sept. Flor. Tertullianus*, Vol. I. Ante-Nicene Christian Library, Vol. XI. Edinburgh: T. & T. Clark.

Robertson, A.T. *A Grammar of the Greek New Testament in the Light of Historical Research*. Nashville: Broadman, 1934.

Roth, Cecil and others, eds. *Encyclopedia Judaica*. 18 vols. New York: Macmillan, 1972.

Sanders, J. N., and B. A. Mastin. *A Commentary on the Gospel according to St. John*. New York: Harper and Row, 1968.

Schnackenburg, Rudolph. *The Gospel according to St. John: Commentary on Chapters 13-21*. 3 vols. New York: Crossroad, 1982.

Schuerer, Emil. *The History of the Jewish People in the Age of Jesus Christ (175 B.C. - A.D. 135)*, eds. Geza Vermes, Fergus Millar, Pamela Vermes, and Matthew Black. 3 vols. 2d ed. Edinburgh: T. & T. Clark, 1973.

Schweizer, Eduard. *The Good News according to Mark*, trans. David E. Green. Atlanta: John Knox, 1984.

The Septuagint Version of the Old Testament and Apocrypha. London: Samuel Bagster, n.d.

Sherwin-White, A. N. *Roman Society and Roman Law in the New Testament*. Oxford: Clarendon, 1963.

Slack, Kenneth. *Praying the Lord's Prayer Today*. London: SCM, 1973.

Smith, Charles Merrill. *Reverend Randollph and the Wages of Sin*. New York: G. P. Putnam, 1974.

Spencer, Aída Besançon. *Beyond the Curse: Women Called to Ministry*. Nashville: Thomas Nelson, 1985. Reprinted by Peabody: Hendrickson, 1989.

_______. *Paul's Literary Style: A Stylistic and Historical Comparison of II Corinthians 11:16-12:13, Romans 8:9-39, and Philippians 3:2-4:13*. Evangelical Theological Society Monograph Series. Winona Lake: Eisenbrauns, 1984.

Taylor, Vincent. *The Gospel according to Mark*. 2d ed. London: Macmillan, 1966.

Teresa of Avila. *The Interior Castle*, trans. Kieran Kavanaugh, O.C.D. and Otilio Rodriquez, O.C.D. New York: Paulist, 1979.

Thayer, Joseph Henry. *Thayer's Greek-English Lexicon of the New Testament*. 2d ed. Marshallton: National Foundation for Christian Education, 1889.

Thielicke, Helmut. *The Prayer that Spans the World*, trans. John W. Doberstein. London: James Clarke, 1965.

Thompson, Frank Charles. *The Thompson Chain-Reference Bible*. Indianapolis: Kirkbridge, 1964.

Thompson, James G. S. S. *The Praying Christ: A Study of Jesus' Doctrine and Practice of Prayer*. Grand Rapids: Eerdmans, 1959.

Trench, Richard C. *Synonyms of the New Testament*. Grand Rapids: Eerdmans, 1880.

Vernon, Edward. *The Lord's Prayer in Wartime*. London: James Clarke, 1941.

Vetter, Irene and Judith N. Cooley. *Jesus' Prayer*. Minneapolis: Augsburg, 1983.

Watts, Isaac. *A Guide to Prayer*, ed. Harry Escott. London: Epworth, 1948.

Wesley, John. *The Works of John Wesley*, II. Grand Rapids: Zondervan, 1872.

Wordsworth, Elizabeth. *Thoughts on the Lord's Prayer*. New York: Longmans, Green, 1898.

Young, Brad. *The Jewish Background to the Lord's Prayer*. Austin: Center for Judaic-Christian Studies, 1984.

Thayer, Joseph [illegible]. [illegible] Greek-English Lexicon of the New Testament. [illegible]

Thielicke, Helmut. The [illegible] Faith. Vol. [illegible]

Thompson, Frank Charles. [illegible] Chain [illegible] Bible. Indianapolis: Kirkbride [illegible], 1964.

Thompson, James [illegible]. The [illegible] of [illegible]. Grand Rapids: [illegible], 1960.

Trench, [illegible]. Synonyms of the New Testament. Grand Rapids: Eerdmans, 19[illegible].

[illegible]

[illegible]

[illegible]

[illegible] Zondervan, 1962.

Warfield, [illegible]. [illegible] Lord [illegible]. New York: [illegible]

[illegible]

Scripture Index

Subject Index

AUTHORS

William David Spencer is a writer, pastor of encouragement with the Pilgrim Church of Beverly-Salem, and summer professor of theology at Gordon-Conwell Theological Seminary, South Hamilton, Massachusetts where he teaches courses in prayer, theology and the arts, and the early church.

Holding a Th.D. in theology and literature from Boston University School of Theology, the Masters of Theology and Divinity from Princeton Theological Seminary, and the Bachelor of Arts from Rutgers University, he has authored *Mysterium and Mystery: The Clerical Crime Novel* (UMI Research Press, 1988), and co-authored with his wife the Rev. Dr. Aída Besançon Spencer *2 Corinthians*, Bible Study Commentary (Zondervan, 1989). He has published numerous articles, stories, and poems in various journals and periodicals and contributed chapters to *Conflict and Context: Hermeneutics in the Americas* (Eerdmans, 1986) and *Beyond the Curse: Women Called to Ministry* (Hendrickson, 1985).

He has served as urban and prison evangelist, campus minister, musician, and educator in numerous settings, including Crosscounter, Inc., Rider College, Trenton State Prison, New York Theological Seminary, Newark Central Corps. of The Salvation Army, Alpha-Omega Community Theological School (A.C.T.S.), extension of The King's College, and the Jefferson County (KY) Adult and Continuing Education. He is an ordained Presbyterian Church (USA) minister.

Aída Besançon Spencer is associate professor of New Testament at Gordon-Conwell Theological Seminary, South Hamilton, Massachusetts, and pastor of organization with the Pilgrim Church of Beverly-Salem.

Having been a visiting scholar at Harvard Divinity School, she earned the Doctor of Philosophy degree in New Testament at Southern Baptist Theological Seminary, the Masters of Theology and Divinity at Princeton Theological Seminary, and the Bachelor of Arts in sociology at Douglass College (Rutgers University). She has authored *Paul's Literary Style* in the Evangelical Theological Society Monograph Series (Eisenbrauns, 1984), and *Beyond the Curse: Women Called to Ministry* (Hendrickson, 1985), which made the 1986 *Eternity* Book of the Year list, *2 Corinthians*, Bible Study Commentary (Zondervan, 1989) with her husband the Rev. Dr. William David Spencer. She has also contributed chapters to *Major Cities of the Biblical World* (Thomas Nelson, 1985), *Conflict and Context: Hermeneutics in the Americas* (Eerdmans,1986), *The New Testament and Criticism* (Zondervan) and *Through No Fault of Their Own?* (Baker). She has published numerous articles and book reviews in journals, magazines, and newspapers.

Born and reared in Santo Domingo, Dominican Republic, she has served as a social worker, minister, and educator in a wide variety of settings, including Community Action--Plainfield, Model Cities, Perth Amboy (NJ) Adult and Continuing Education, Trenton State Prison, Trenton State College, The Salvation Army, New York Theological Seminary (formerly Biblical Seminary) and the Alpha-Omega Community Theological School (A.C.T.S.), extension of The King's College. She is an ordained Presbyterian Church (U.S.A.) minister.

The Spencers are the parents of Stephen William Besançon Spencer.